The Blueprint of Your Soul

Discover Yourself and Your Blueprint Destiny

Joseph Ghabi, B.Msc

The Blueprint of Your Soul: Discover Yourself and Your Blueprint Destiny
by Joseph Ghabi, B.Msc

Published by:
Free Spirit Centre Publishing
www.freespiritcentre.info

Copyright © 2009 Joseph Ghabi, B.Msc
Published: January 2010
ISBN: 978-0-9738231-5-8

All rights reserved. No part of this book may be reproduced or transmitted in any form or by any means, electronic or mechanical, including photocopying, recording or by any information storage and retrieval system without written permission from the publisher.

Printed in the United States of America

Table of Contents

Preface vii
Introduction... x

Section I 1
A. The Blueprint of the Soul.. 2
B. What is Blueprint Destiny?.. 11
C. Understanding Numerology.. 29
D. The Blueprint of Your Soul Insight 39

Section II 43
A. The Blueprint of Your Soul Chart... 45
B. Calculation for the Blueprint of Your Soul Chart 47
    Part 1: Based on Your Date of Birth 47
    a. Blueprint Destiny 47
    b. Blueprint Day of Birth.. 48
    c. Blueprint Attainment.. 48
    d. Blueprint Challenges 49
    e. Blueprint Journey's Cycle.. 51
    f. Blueprint Personal Year: '9 Year Cycle' 51
    g. Universal Blueprint... 52

    Part 2: Based on Your Full Name Used Today 53
    a. Blueprint Expression 53
    b. Blueprint Soul Urge.. 54
    c. Blueprint Inner Self 54
    d. Blueprint Maturity 55
    e. Blueprint Growth 55
    f. Blueprint Intensity Table... 55
    g. Blueprint of Your Family Vibration 56
    h. Blueprint Temperament Behavior 56
    i. Blueprint Sub-Conscious... 56

Section III - Primary Component of your Blueprint 57
A. Date of Birth 59
   a- Blueprint Destiny 59
   b. Blueprint Birthday 62
   c. Blueprint Attainment 62
   d. Blueprint Challenges 63
   e. Blueprint Journey's Cycle 63
   f. Universal Blueprint 65
   g. Blueprint Personal Year: 9 Years Cycle 66

B. Full Name as you Use Today 76
   a. Blueprint Expression 79
   b. Blueprint Soul Urge 79
   c. Blueprint Inner-Self 80
   d. Blueprint Maturity 80
   e. Blueprint Growth 80
   f. Blueprint Intensity Table 80
   g. Blueprint of Your Family Vibration 81
   h. Blueprint Temperament Behavior 82
   i. Blueprint Sub-Conscious 83

Section IV- Meaning of Numbers 85
1. General Meaning of Numbers 87
   a. The Meaning Behind Number 'Zero' (0) 88
   b. The Meaning Behind Number 'One' (1) 90
   c. The Meaning Behind Number 'Two' (2) 92
   d. The Meaning Behind Number 'Three' (3) 93
   e. The Meaning Behind Number 'Four' (4) 95
   f. The Meaning Behind Number 'Five' (5) 97
   g. The Meaning Behind Number 'Six' (6) 99
   h. The Meaning Behind Number 'Seven' (7) 101
   i. The Meaning Behind Number 'Eight' (8) 103
   j. The Meaning Behind Number 'Nine' (9) 105
   k. The Meaning Behind Number 'Eleven' (11) 107
   l. The Meaning Behind Number 'Twenty-Two' (22) ... 109
   m. The Meaning Behind Number 'Thirty-Three' (33) ... 111

2. Interpretation of a Chart 114
   a. Blueprint Destiny 114
   b. Blueprint Birthday 137
   c. Blueprint Expression 151
   d. Blueprint Soul Urge 155
   e. Blueprint Inner Self 159
   f. Blueprint Maturity 164
   g. Blueprint Growth 168
   h. Blueprint Journey's Cycle 172
   i. Blueprint Challenge 187
   j. Blueprint Attainment 189
   k. Blueprint Subconscious 202
   l. Blueprint Family Name 205
   m. Blueprint Intensity Table 218
   n. Blueprint 9-Year Cycle 225
   o. Blueprint Temperamental Behavior 236
   p. Universal Blueprint 238

Section V 239
A. Blueprint Karma 241
B. Blueprint Karmic Debt 247
C. Time to Heal and Move Beyond Your Karma 254
D. Conclusion 262

About the Author 270

Dedication

This book is dedicated to my son, Robbie, and my daughter, Tiffany. You are the blessings of my life …

Acknowledgment

Special thanks to Ashleigh Stewart, who edited the first draft of this book

Preface

I was born with natural mediumistic abilities. I have had the ability to see, sense, feel and sometimes hear things in the world of Spirit ever since I was a child. This was normal to me and I never questioned it at all. I never felt the need to mention it to anyone, and so kept it quiet. Fortunately, keeping quiet about what I was able to do helped me to maintain my ability, and I never ever imagined I would be working with it as I do today.

I started my career with a Bachelor of Engineering degree and a Master of Science degree in Computer Science. Only a few short months into it, I decided to completely drop my career as an engineer because I felt I did not belong in the field. I then became involved in Sales & Marketing, then international business development in the high technology sector, where I had the opportunity to travel to 36 countries. I stayed in that career for 10 years, although I always felt there was something missing in my life. I felt I had a huge inner void, although I had no idea why.

Eventually I understood the cause of my inner void and took the risk I needed to take in leaving my career ... and what a journey that was! Transitioning between jobs was a real challenge for me and I thought it would never end. It was extremely tough at times and particularly hard trying to maintain some harmony between working a mainstream job and managing my inner patience. It was difficult to make ends meet financially, and I still felt there was something missing in my life.

I am sure that many people today are living with that void just as I was, yet they perhaps have a hard time taking the risk of trying to find their calling, or what their purpose for being here really is. From my experience, I learned that it is very important to live your life in the ways you have always dreamed of or else you will seldom feel happy, and will always feel a sense of emptiness.

Perhaps you have the same feeling I used to have, yet might not be doing anything about it. Maybe you feel fear, or are unable to embrace change? Perhaps you are not even aware that you can change? Have you ever stopped to ask yourself why you feel the way you do about your life? What is it that is preventing you from trusting your inner self and connecting with your Soul to find out what it is you would really love to do with your life?

As a way of relieving myself from my inner emptiness, I decided to learn meditation. I later developed into working with the 'Spiritual Healing' energy with the help and assistance of one of my Spirit Guides. I have also worked with Numerology for almost 17 years and have integrated my clairvoyant ability with my Numerology skills. I have always preferred to, and enjoyed working with Numerology from a healing perspective, as oppose to using it as a tool for prediction.

Along with the Numerology, I developed a system of healing. This system is a method designed to heal the child within of the residual emotional trauma from our childhood experiences, and to understand how that period influences our lives greatly today. I will not go into detail about this subject here however; I will go into greater depth about the dynamics of this system in my next book.

So, during the time of my career transition, I went to the absolute bottom in my financial life. At the time, people thought I was crazy for walking away from such a good career, and they still think that today! The difference today though, is that I know I am doing things for me, for my own inner contentment and happiness and honestly, I am enjoying every moment of it! I am enjoying the fact that I can work in the field of healing, and that helping a human Soul is more important, worthwhile and fulfilling than selling a technological solution.

With all of the challenges, trials and difficulties I had to go through and overcome in mind, today I feel a deep sense of pleasure and satisfaction for where my journey has taken me. I feel truly blessed to have found the strength and courage within me to take the risk of pursuing what my Soul had planned for me in my life all along.

So there you have it, a very brief overview of the story of my life. I can honestly say that I feel truly happy with where I am in my life, and that I feel blessed to be able to attune with the non-physical aspects of life, and work with that awareness for the benefits of others as it is very empowering and fulfilling for me as an individual.

Introduction

I recall picking up my first Numerology book; it was in 1993. After reading that, I was then guided to read the book Numerology: The Complete Guide by Matthew Oliver Goodwin, then to The Life You Were Born to Live by Dan Millman. One day after reading those books and contemplating the information I received from them, a sudden feeling of awareness flowed through me. It was as if lifetimes of knowledge about Numerology came to me from the Universe. It was such a profound and moving experience that left me feeling so excited, that after that day I decided to begin working the knowledge I had received, both from the books and what was given to me by the Universe. It was amazing!

I practiced, practiced and practiced as if there was no tomorrow, and I did so by writing Numerology charts for friends and many people I didn't know, for example, celebrities and politicians. Over time, my readings became better and better, until I started seeing Numerology from a newer perspective. My awareness seemed to have evolved into something deeper, and far more significant than I ever considered it to be.

I realized through my work that Numerology is the blueprint of our Soul. Our Soul, the essence of our being and who we are, spends many years preparing for a lifetime here on the earth plane. A lifetime has to be fully anticipated and planned out prior to the Souls incarnation and the information pertaining to the Soul's chosen life path, journey and experience here are all written in a blueprint which is encoded within our name and our date of birth, and this can be translated and understood through use of Numerology.

My fascination with this blueprint, and the way it is drawn grew. I studied it hard and considered it to be a work of art! After careful study and examination, I eventually came to realize that the Soul blueprint is the key to helping us deal with and solve the many problems we face in our lives.

Numerology is really a great tool that can help us improve our life by understanding, accepting and working through all the tasks and challenges that our Soul has planned for this lifetime. We owe it to ourselves, and we owe it to our Soul to investigate our blueprint, our purpose for being here and our Soul as the Source of our life.

Whether you are aware of it or not, you are far more than the human being that was born of your parents, into your environment and the lifestyle you inherited from your religion and culture. You are a significant part of life and have a unique place in this great puzzle we are all trying to understand. Each of us as an individual is an important part of this ever evolving process of awareness, understanding and knowledge of life that our Soul has earned throughout the evolutionary progression of many lifetimes of challenge and growth.

Your Soul is the Source of your being in the lifetime today. What I mean by 'Source' in this case is that your Source, and your reason for being here today is your Soul. When your Soul decided to be born into this plane at this time, it sent your Spirit into this plane, integrating both sides of your spiritual and physical being in order for it to understand and master the lessons and the growth it anticipated for this lifetime.

So with the importance of your individual life in mind, please, always believe in yourself and drive yourself to be the best you can be, regardless of what anyone else in your life says or believes about you, because I bet you become a totally different person the moment you connect with your Soul Source and bring out the essence of the many lifetimes of experiences your Soul has accumulated throughout its eternity.

We all have the answers and solutions to everything that happens in our life whether good or bad. We all have the tools we need to walk our path and live our Blueprint Destiny to the maximum in this lifetime. The harder you resist your experiences and lessons in life, the more difficult your life will be. Remember, you are the master of your own Universe, and that is something beyond your family and the values your society or culture made you believe you are.

Today if you are living the life that everyone else dictates to you, admit it, you are unhappy, stagnant and feel a deep sense of inner loneliness, and all just to live up to the values society places upon you. You feel unhappy and are living in agony and are not aware of the source of it. All you have to do is drop everything and tell yourself you're worth it and decide you want to begin living your life for you, and only you.

Now is the time for you to start going inward and connecting with your Soul, the inner essence within you that is waiting to be realized. It is time for you to open up and allow your Spirit to emerge and finally become who you were truly meant to be in this lifetime.

Why on earth do you need your family if you are suffering because of them? Why must you remain in a relationship that makes you feel empty or even dead inside? Why do you want to do anything in your life that doesn't make any real sense to you? Ask yourself that question ... and really think about the answer.

I understand that some people are skeptical, afraid and might not believe in Numerology. Regardless of your belief, Numerology is still available to help you. With an open mind, it can still help you to understand and bypass the hurdles in your life.

I decided to write this book to give a hand to all human Souls who are ready to take a step towards understanding themselves and the Universe we live in. Are you one of those Souls? Are you ready to hear my message? Are you ready to take a step toward healing your life? The Blueprint of Your Soul is here to help do that by bringing you the understanding you need to begin building your life on a better and stronger foundation than ever before. All the Numerology calculations have also been included for those among you who are interested in deepening their knowledge and understanding of Numerology, and wish to work with it.

We are all gifted. We are all spiritual beings. We all have a Soul with intuition which serves as a central focus of our growth in this lifetime. When you die, your Spirit will leave your body and return to your Soul, its place of origin. Your essence is spiritual; you are a spiritual, human being. You have your own unique connection with the Universe, and it is you and you alone who can open the doors to your own inner heaven. Heaven starts with a frame of mind based on peace, understanding and acceptance. Hell is what exists externally, and is all of that which interferes with our frame of mind and our own state of being in our inner heaven, making it seem we are in a living Hell. Are you living in Hell or Heaven at the moment?

You have the choice to live the way you truly desire. Money, status and power over external things or people will not bring you happiness, or even bring you close to reaching your inner heaven. Unless you try to bring change, you will never be able to judge otherwise and will always remain in a dream world, waiting for something to happen. Please realize that nothing new will ever happen in your life unless you decide to make your own leap within your Universe, in the parameter of your inner heaven, the place your Soul originated.

Anyone and everyone can read this book, and everyone will understand this book at their own level. Only you have the power to reverse your direction and change your life, Free Will allows you to do that. Your choices and actions are the factors of change and in the end, you will be the judge of your own life!

Before we get down to it, again I will note that this book may not be for everyone. However, I do believe it is destined to reach the hands of those people who are ready and willing to read it, considering what is expressed here with an open mind. I recommend that if you feel a small sense of resistance to what you are reading and the idea of change, that's fine and is the nature of healing because true healing only ever takes place at the root of our fears. As we know it is neither fun nor comfortable to look our fears in the face. If on the other hand you are filled with anger, rage or resentment toward what you are reading, then I recommend you simply set this book aside for a period of time and perhaps try reading it again when you are more open and willing to embrace the possibility of change and healing to take place in your life. But be warned however; do not make your discomfort with healing an excuse! Be honest with yourself and if you feel you have the ability to go forth with the information you are being given, then do it!

Have a happy life!

Section I

A. The Blueprint of the Soul

During the journey of evolution of a Soul, the Soul has a choice of whether it wishes to further its evolutionary progress by incarnating into life on the earth plane as a human being or not. Souls also have the option of incarnating into life within other dimensional planes in the Universe, and where they go depends on their own individual level of Universal growth.

It is often true that the more advanced a Soul is, the longer it will take for it to decide to come back here to the earth plane, if it ever does. It isn't always necessary for more advanced Souls to have a human life on earth, simply because those Souls have bypassed the level of learning of which life as a human being has to offer.

We are never alone during our human life. We are constantly being watched over and guided, and our growth is being monitored by Souls called 'Spirit guides' who work in the non-physical realms. These Souls are also working toward moving forward and enhancing their own growth and evolution by helping us in our physical life by directing us and watching how we conduct our life. A great deal of reward comes from working as a Spirit guide that helps Souls progress from the other side. So always remember, you are not alone in this life, you have support from your Spirit guides that are trying to guide you toward receiving all the rewards you deserve to have in this lifetime.

It is important to note that at this point in time, an increasing number of advanced Souls are opting to come back and live an earthly life, and for one main reason. The reason is to be of service to humanity. Those Souls help humanity by sharing their high level of knowledge, wisdom and compassion which is gravely needed right now to help support the planetary progression of earth toward becoming a more Universally Conscious plane of existence.

The earth plane is the most challenging plane of all to exist in. This is because the human race is the most disconnected and farthest from understanding its divinity and purpose for being alive. The experiences that life in the earth plane has to offer provide the grounds for learning many of valuable lessons that a Soul is required to learn in order to progress in terms of Universal understanding and awareness of life and creation.

The majority of us here on the earth plane take our life for granted and that is largely because we feel a lack of purpose, direction and we don't know better than that! We human beings have a very limited level of knowledge and understanding of our true life purpose and both ourselves, and the planet itself is suffering because of that. Many of us think we are here for a picnic and believe we are here to just eat, drink, shop and watch sports! Of course, those are some of the elements make our physical life more enjoyable on a material level, but do you really believe that's all life is about?

When a Soul makes the decision to reincarnate into a lifetime as a human being, it takes a period of the equivalent of many earth years to choose the course of life that Soul wishes to follow. The Soul then decides upon the Karmic lessons, challenges, and experiences it wishes to work upon. Such aspects of the Souls incarnation are chosen specifically to complement the life path and the growth the Soul wishes to attain as a result.

Every single experience you encounter in your life as a human being has been carefully planned from the Soul level. Your parents are well chosen, specific to the experiences you are destined to encounter during your life. Your parents are very important parts of your life path as they are major elements that help you develop your identity growing up, and this influences the way you will handle your life experiences later on. The country and the culture you are born into are also major parts of defining who you will grow to become as an individual and are an important part of your Soul's anticipated path of evolution as they help form your perception of the people and the world around you and, of course, of how you see yourself belonging there.

The Soul's planned Blueprint Destiny is called the 'Soul Blueprint.' If the human aspect of that Soul which incarnated into earth life follows the Soul blueprint to the detail, then that human being is sure to lead a very rewarding and fulfilling life. The unfortunate aspect of all this is that, of course, the majority of human beings here on this earth plane are not even remotely aware that the Soul blueprint exists and, as a result, are most likely out of alignment with it. This is the main reason why we feel such a profound sense of dissatisfaction and lack of purpose when it comes to our life and this is where Numerology steps into the equation.

Numerology is an amazing tool which can be considered as a map of your Soul blueprint. If applied correctly, Numerology can help you identify your Soul purpose, why you are here, your karma, lessons and challenges and just what kind of life you were destined to live from the moment you were born. It even helps you identify with your own individual character, strengths and weaknesses, all of which make you who you are. All of this is easily discovered through the careful examination of your name and your date of birth. We will discuss Numerology and the calculation techniques at a later stage.

The return of your Soul to the earth plane is for the purpose of attaining growth from the experiences you encounter as a human being. This growth then promotes the evolutionary progression of that Soul on a Universal scale. Your Soul also returns to the earth plane to end any unfinished business it has left here, therefore completing an almost endless cycle of many human lifetimes here. Sometimes those lifetimes are wasted, as the human being representing the Soul has a difficult time during his life and ends up in stagnation or caught up in the past, making him unable to progress forward in his growth.

There are so many aspects of our human nature that contradict the essence of our true divinity, all of which lead us farther and farther from the truth of who we really are. Some examples are the resistance we so often feel when it comes to change and growth in our lives. Another major contradiction of our divine essence is our inability to forgive each other for the many, and often hurtful deeds we do toward each other in life. Lack of forgiveness is a characteristic that is completely opposite to the nature of the Soul which is non-judgmental and based on unconditional love knowing that any so-called 'wrong' action is always based on the absence of awareness, therefore is forgiven.

As human beings, we also tend to categorize people according to race, religion, place of birth, skin color, and social and financial status. Again, these are not characteristics of the Soul, which is based on non-judgment and unconditional love and acceptance. These are just human biases. The Soul does not judge another for where they come from and their background because the Soul knows that the country, background, race, religion and creed a human being was born into was specifically chosen for a reason, and that reason was part of the Soul's blueprint and life path design, so all is as it should from that angle be as far as the Soul is concerned.

The reason your Soul decided to return for another earth life in the form of you is simply to fulfill karmic debt created by the other human beings your Soul incarnated into being during previous lifetimes. It is through fulfillment of Karmic debt that the Soul is able to evolve to a higher level of being in the Universe because behind each Karmic debt lies a very significant life lesson.

The cycle of lifetimes in the earth plane keeps repeating over and over again. Many lifetimes pass almost wasted as human beings are not understanding their reason for being alive and specifically the existence of their Soul and its purpose of attaining evolutionary progression in the Universe. On a lower level, we human beings are even having difficulty understanding our evolution as a human race, specifically our collective evolution as a diverse society made up of many different creeds, cultures and religions. How can we ever possibly begin to grasp the understanding behind the purpose and existence of our Soul if we are yet unable to understand our existence as one race of human beings coexisting on one planet?

Although we are quite disconnected from the understanding of Soul on the earth plane, the way we experience life here is still influenced by the operation of our Soul on a much higher level of our being. Our Soul can still influence our reactions to events in our lives, the way we act in day to day life and more specifically, the Soul is greatly involved in the evolution of our karma, even if we are unaware of it. This is because it is in the interest of the Soul to keep us as aligned to its original blueprint as much as possible.

Karma is probably one of the most misunderstood and feared aspects of life by those of us who have some awareness of just what karma means. This is a shame because karma is in fact one of many blessings yet to be realized by mankind as a whole. Realistically speaking, the law of Karma is a blessing because if it is understood correctly, the law of Karma can help us fulfill the inner void that most of us are experiencing in life because we are living a life that lacks purpose.

Karma can fulfill the lack of purpose so many of us feel because it brings meaning to the many challenging events we encounter throughout our entire life. So although karma is blessing in disguise, because we do not understand it, we still blame it for our misfortune and use it as an excuse to justify all our 'wrong' actions in life. Karma is supposed to be understood, not abused, and eventually when we do begin realizing and accepting what the law of Karma really entails, I believe we can evolve out of our troubled times in this world, we can evolve beyond sickness and disease, and begin living the life we are supposed to live, a life based on the understanding of Soul combined with the essence of being a human spiritual being having a physical experience on the earth plane.

This is the time in our physical world where we are being called to confront the reality of the condition of our inner and outer life as race of human beings on planet earth. It is time for us to begin asking ourselves deeper questions about the reality of our life, our reason for being and of how the Universe works collectively. Many civilizations, with Atlantis as a common example, which existed long before ours did were far more advanced than we are today but were eradicated due to a lack of Universal understanding, If there is any civilization which is not in accordance with the divine plan of evolutionary progression and is functioning contrary to the Universal Laws, it will be wiped out because it is simply the nature of the Universe to abolish that which is not in accordance with its one divine plan.

Much of the way we are functioning as human beings is contrary to divine law, particularly when it comes to the greed of the human mind which, in reality, is almost driving us down a road that leads to the destruction of all we have ever accomplished in our time on the earth plane.

Humanity is headed in the same direction as those civilizations that faced mass destruction in past times; are we happy to be driving down that road again? Do you feel that as a race, we are ready to learn from our past actions and mistakes? Unfortunately, from what I see so far in the way we are living collectively, I don't think so.

You may be shocked by the nature of what has been written here and my views but take a good honest look and consider the way we function as human beings. We exist as a power-driven race, which seeks to fulfill our inner lack through controlling, dominating and owning people, places and things. Not only do we base our happiness on things that exist outside of us, but we also blame our unhappiness on exterior things too, such as people, our finances, our lack of material possessions or whatever else it is that we believe makes us feel miserable and unfulfilled.

We are functioning in a purely external way to the point that we have totally forgotten we have an inner responsibility for ourselves and the way we choose to adapt and react to the external circumstances that take place in our lives minute by minute. We all have a choice to create our life in exactly the way we would like it to be, but choices come from responsibility and if we constantly base our feelings of happiness or misery on external circumstances, how can we ever take charge of our power of choice and make responsible choices? It is impossible.

Due to our lack of awareness, and the fact that we have forgotten our essence, which is based on unconditional love and compassion, we are very often unable to forgive ourselves and others for creating unfortunate in our lives. We are unable to forgive ourselves and if we have hard time forgiving ourselves, how can we forgive others? That is no longer the blame of our karma, this is our own responsibility.

We were all born into this plane as students and this means we will always have something to learn. When you are born, you started using the name you were given to define your identity and the uniqueness you are bringing with you to this plane. We have all been writing the story of our life from the moment we were born and this story begun with your first cry when you left your mother's womb and entered the physical world, up until the day you take your very last breath. We are all constantly writing our own story, however many of our stories are left unfinished because we became stagnant in life and have been circulating in our patterns over and over again. Our Soul tries to help give us the urge to release ourselves from that pattern, yet we still insist upon pushing our Soul into a dead end.

Many among us consider the story of their family tree to be the source of their existence and they pride themselves on the fact that they were born of it. Have you ever stopped to ask yourself why you were born of that particular family? In many ways, we need to take a closer look at our roots as they will help us identify why our life runs into endless circles and cycles of years that seem to lead us nowhere. We will not get anywhere in life unless we wake up one day and decide that enough is enough, and consciously choose to take the time to close all the issues, patterns, belief systems and whatever else is no longer working for us. It is so important to deal with the issues that lie at the core of our existence today as they can help lead us to understanding the reason for us being here in the first place. These issues can lead us to the wisdom and understanding that in turn will connect us with our own Soul and its purpose.

So where do you stand in your life today? Maybe nowhere, or somewhere but you are not sure where and just where you are going? Regardless, you are here now, so let's take a turn for the better and get to work doing something about it, shall we?

In every lifetime, your Soul draws up a blueprint to plan the path your life is destined to follow. When you are born your society identifies you by your name and your date of birth. In an ideal world, we should also be identified by our Soul blueprint. Governments, companies, schools and society as a whole accepts you as a unique individual, and to go along with your name and your date of birth, the government also provides you with a number that will identify you. So if you are unique enough to hold a social security number or whatever name your country uses, then tell me, what do you really know about your uniqueness and what makes you an individual in your life today?

My experience tells me that over 80% of our problems can be solved immediately the minute we know what it is we really want, as opposed to just experimenting in life, hoping we will eventually find out. What I mean here is that when you are working in a job that you know you love, you want to do and it enriches your life, and you become a different person. When you are with the right person in your life, without any superficiality then you are a different person. When you have the opportunity to deal with your life the proper way, then you become a different person. This, of course, implies that your life becomes happier, richer and more fulfilling as a result. Being a different person simply means: understanding who you are, being who you want to be and being able to deal with your life on a regular basis for you and not just to suit and impress other people around you. Unfortunately, no one ever told us any of that before. We have been raised to follow systems and institutions that substitute an awareness of life with fear of God, guilt and the 'evil' side of life order to keep people living in fear, enough so that they will stay associated with the group, or religion they belong to, so for the rest of their life, and whether they like it or not or believe it or not, they will be controlled by a system.

I believe there was a time when we were all told about the true essence of life; however, much of it became lost in translation throughout the generations. Regardless of what was lost, what have we done with the knowledge and wisdom of all the sages that have come to us before, like Jesus, Mohammed, Buddha and all the others? How many people have really applied that wisdom into their lives properly? This is the problem; no wisdom or knowledge is worth anything unless it is actively applied into your life and only you can do that. Do you think it is worth giving it another shot now?

B. What Is Blueprint Destiny?

Who am I? What am I here to do? Where I am going in my life? Why am I unlucky in my life? What do I need to learn about my life? Why is everything happening to me? Oh my God! The world is falling apart and I cannot cope anymore! What is wrong with me? I am stupid. I am ugly. No one wants to be with me. What's wrong with me and why can't I be like everyone else? I bet one, some or all of these questions have entered your mind at one point or another in your life. So many questions yet where are the answers? Well, I intend to answer those questions in my way and from my understanding throughout the course of this book.

Those questions are just some of the many that fill the minds of people as they go about their daily life. We are all walking through life wondering where we are going and why, at the same structuring our life upon values that do not make any real sense to us as individuals. Does it really matter how we walk through our lifetime? Does it really matter how we think? Does it really matter how we see ourselves? Why not just stop walking around wondering, instead, try having a full stop of your life and try to center and ground yourself for a change.

If any of the above questions are swimming around in your mind then my immediate answer to you is just STOP. What is the point of walking around, and wondering without any direction in your life? There is no point! So far you have probably tried everything yet doors keep slamming in your face over and over again. You are trying to move forward without really being aware of who you are and what your strengths and weaknesses are, or what your challenges are in life? If this situation sounds familiar to you, then what is the point of walking, and where exactly are you walking to? You don't know? You might think you know where you would like to go, but are you looking in the right direction? What makes you think you are walking in the right direction? You make believe that is the right direction for you, you are convinced about that but I invite you to please think again.

On what grounds did you base your assumptions about your life beliefs? Who put the idea in your head? Was it you or other people and the circumstances around you? I believe we have some work to do here. If any of my questions have made you think, then there is definitely something you need to look at. You need to pay attention to your thoughts, the way you think about yourself and the patterns that exist in your life. In order to solve our problems, we need to be able to look closely within ourselves, not somewhere else. Taking courses and workshops are fine but how do these courses and workshops affect or interfere with the way you think about yourself?

Are you ready to change direction in order to make place for some new learning in life? Remember, in order to acquire whatever it is we need to improve in our life, we need to learn to be able to question our values and our way of thinking. Are you ready to make that change? Not sure? Then ask yourself this question? "Who am I?" Can you answer that in a nutshell without thought or hesitation? If your answer is along the lines of, "Well, I am. Hmm, well I think I am. Hmm, oh yeah I am so and so and this is what I do," please stop now and have a closer and deeper look at yourself again.

So, you are having hard time defining yourself, or at least who or what you thought you were. Gee, you keep changing your mind because you define yourself according to the many things you do. Now that is no good either, is it? So to begin with think about what you do have that is common to all human beings. Do you know what I am getting at here? Let me explain!

We all have a name and a date of birth. Have you ever bothered to consider why we have a name and a date of birth? Have you ever wondered why you were born on the date you were? Have you wondered why, whether you like it or not, you have that particular name? Perhaps you have given it a passing though in the past, yet gave up wondering and settled for thinking it is just another coincidence. There are no coincidences in life, many events are predestined to take place, as long as you do not change the course of your life and as a result take a detour from your path of Blueprint Destiny.

What causes a detour in your path of Blueprint Destiny to occur? Let's find out. You have the opportunity to learn a new and simple awareness that will help you move forward available to you now, so what are you waiting for? Let's get on with it!

Let's begin talking about your vibration and learn about how you can define who you are according to that vibration. It is time to set aside your old ways of thinking about yourself and redefine yourself from scratch, as if you were a child wondering about life and all the things going on around you. Are you ready to embark on this experience of a lifetime? You know it can change your life for the better!

So what is vibration? Vibration refers to the energy in and around us. What is energy? Energy is the atoms and molecules that allow manifestation of everything that moves, that breathes and that exists. Everything is made of energy and has energy around it. Do you recall when you were a child and you touched something that was hot? You probably touched a hot surface several times and were burned before you realized that every touch would produce the same discomfort that caused you to feel pain. Of course, then you became conditioned to expect pain as a result of touching a hot surface which prevented you from doing it intentionally again. The same goes for how we are conditioned to act and react to all of the situations we encounter in the world around us as children, and as a result constitutes the way we see and believe the world to be.

All energy around us vibrates at different frequencies depending on its state of matter; this is why we call it 'vibration.' Vibration is the frequency of the energies that we encounter throughout life. The piece of furniture you are sitting or lying on right now has a different vibration than the piece of pie you ate for dessert. The same goes for all animate and inanimate objects in life.

If everything that exists around you is vibrating, then so must you be. You were born according to specific energies that accumulated the moment you were born. These energies were stamped, sealed and defined by your name and the date of birth your Soul chose for you. Your family, your religion and the country you were born were all chosen and planned for you before you were even born. The moment you were born, you began vibrating according to the energies you were born with. So what is your vibration? We will go through simple calculations later that will help you determine your vibration.

Your life on this plane and at this time is not a coincidence. It was an event that was completely planned out for you to learn and grow through certain experiences in order for your Soul to gain the highest and greatest amount of evolution it possibly can in one lifetime. This makes you important, and means you have a purpose, even if you are not aware what that purpose is yet. You have something you need to accomplish in your life; you are not a waste of time. Your life has a great deal of meaning to you and to your Soul.

So what is a Soul? I would like to elaborate more on what I said earlier in order to help you understand what I am talking about. I will explain the concepts as best as I can in accordance with my understanding. Souls are continuously evolving energies that vibrate in our Universe. Souls are constantly working to acquire knowledge, understanding and awareness of the workings of our Universe. The reason and purpose behind the acquisition of that knowledge is to help Souls further advance in their evolution with the goal of reaching the ultimate energy of all energies, which is my God, your God and everyone else's God. You might refer to God as the great light, creator or Source but in the end, regardless of your title, it is still the same great energy.

In order to facilitate growth under the circumstances of learning through experience, there must be different levels available for

Souls of varying degrees of awareness to gather within. It is to my understanding that there are 13 dimensional levels in our Universe. The 13th Dimension is the God level and the Souls who reach that level of understanding and awareness and are conscious of their evolution of Soul, have reached the ultimate attainment that all Souls are striving toward. This has nothing to do with any religion or belief system.

On the other side of life in the non-physical realms, we are all considered equal and deserving of the same amount of love and compassion, and regardless of the dimension your Soul exists in, your Soul still has the same ability to feel and vibrate the level of love and compassion as any other more evolved, or advanced Soul.

On a Soul level, we all have same amount of potential and can accomplish the same things if only we strive toward that. The only difference that exists between Souls is their level of conscious awareness of the workings, and the dynamics of the universe and how it functions. Keep in mind, however, that I said 'conscious' awareness, which means the awareness that the Soul has that it is conscious of. All Souls are equal in potential and have the seed of knowledge within that gives them the drive to move forward in their evolutionary progression. At the seat of all our being, we know who we are in essence, we understand who we are in essence and we understand the work of the universe in essence. So in essence, we are no different from one another, just that some Souls are more conscious of their consciousness than others and that is what defines us as individuals.

Regardless of their level and what has been already attained, Souls will keep striving for more growth and evolution. This does not mean Souls are competing however. It is not about fulfilling the ego's desires; it has nothing to do with that. This is about divine purpose, and we all know and understand this on a Soul level, even if we are not conscious of it. It is also not about one Soul being better than the other. On the Soul level, we understand that although we may vibrate in a different dimensional level according to our level of growth into consciousness, we all still have the same amount of potential. To really grasp this concept, you need to take a moment to consider how you would define what is human, egotistical based ways of thinking and what is universal conscious awareness, and the difference between the two. From what you have learnt so far, on considering the two, you will see they are total opposites and are two states of being that are not in accordance with each other at all.

On the other side in the non-physical realms of life, there exist love, awareness and compassion. There is no Hell in the way we portray it on this plane. In fact, living on this plane is more like Hell! Why do I say that? Well, because Hell can be compared to the darkness of the Soul and when we are disconnected from our divinity. When existing in such darkness, we end up killing, suffering, hating, being angry, lying, stealing, being greedy, looking for power, and looking for fulfillment in only material things. These things are happening, they do exist on this plane and this is one reason why the biggest challenge a Soul can take is coming back for a lifetime here because such a way of being is so different to the natural essence of a Soul.

How can a Soul understand feelings of hate? How can a Soul understand the desire to murder another? How can a Soul understand the need to lie? How can a Soul understand religious divisions? How can a Soul understand anger when anger does not exist in their non-physical dimension? How can they understand all of these things when those characteristics do not exist in the nature of a Soul and its way of being based on love and compassion?

The only way a Soul can understand such things is to learn through feeling and experiencing the range of emotion that exists in the hearts of the human beings who suffer daily in this world. There is duality in life and this experiencing this duality is part of the learning curve that Souls are required to go through in order to reach different stages of enlightenment. Although this may be hard for us to comprehend, or even accept at our human level of awareness, Souls must understand the darker side of life in order to really understand the nature of light, does it make sense?

Conscious Awareness refers to the most aware state of being that Soul can reach. Growth into being Consciously Aware is necessary for the development and evolution of a Soul and this can be attained through understanding of Universal Law, the dynamics of the Universe and creation, and of love, compassion, non-judgment, and unconditional love.

Before incarnating, your Soul studies the theory related to its anticipated life here on this plane. It has calculated all the scenarios that might occur as a result of the many possible choices you could potentially take in this lifetime. Your Soul has also provided you with all the solutions you may need in order to steer you back in alignment with your Souls preferred path should you stray. An example that this can be compared to would be like graduating from university and starting out working in your field. You might feel strange and out of place being at work because so far, all you have are theories in your head; you have never really practiced the many things you have learnt. You quickly realize that in reality, things are not the same as you were taught in school; you learned a few formulas, but the practice is totally different! The same goes with your Soul. For example, your Soul studied the theory to understand the experience of being physically abused, and how a human being might respond and react to that. However, when the experience actually happens to a person, the feeling is totally different and more profound compared to what it could ever be imagined in theory. The same principle applies when it comes to experiences of a person being unloved, unwanted or unrecognized. In the human reality, such experiences will come in different shapes and forms, and with vastly different feelings than what was anticipated in theory at the Soul level.

God is not the judge of what you have or haven't done in your lifetime. God is non-judgmental, accepts you the way you are and respects where you are in your individual journey toward attainment. Your Soul will be the judge of your life when your journey in this world will come to an end.

God gave you Free Will and it is up to you what you do with it. God will never judge you. God will never punish you, and if God did, it would contradict the essence of what God is all about. On a human level, we always use God's name to suit our interests, and often it is to justify our actions, or inactions. We usually use God to gain control or power over people or circumstances in this plane, and God is often used when we need an excuse for things we have said or done, or to keep people frozen in fear or guilt.

When you pass over to the other side when your physical life has ended, your Soul will flash the events of your entire lifetime in front of you so that your Soul can evaluate what has or has not been accomplished during that lifetime, nothing less nothing more! It is not about making you feel guilty or like a failure for not accomplishing certain things. You will not be going to hell for your actions either, so do not worry! The purpose for this 'evaluation' is for the Soul to simply evaluate the accomplishment in terms of its evolutionary progression.

It is important to note here that your Soul is not just in you, but around you and existing outside of you. We all have a piece of our Soul invested in us as our inner essence; this is what we call our Spirit. The Spirit is like a mass of energy from the Soul, created specifically according to, and in alignment with all of the experiences you are destined to encounter in your life as a human being. The Spirit holds all the knowledge, skills and abilities you need to help you handle your life lessons, and fulfill your Soul blueprint in this lifetime. Your Spirit will provide you with your essence, your personality, your gifts and abilities, and even your intellect and all the inner knowledge that comes to you from your Soul. That is what makes us unique as individuals. You will never find two people who are exactly the same, although there are of course people who share similar goals and interests. The similarity that exists among us helps us to understand and assist each other during our journey on this plane.

You are responsible for any decision you make in your life. It is your responsibility to learn how to forgive and let go of things that did not work as planned, even things which took place during your childhood when you felt you had less responsibility over the direction your life took. Although you are responsible, you also have a choice to let go of things and your Free Will gives you that right to choose. The moment you decide upon a particular direction in life, events will begin to manifest according to your choice and you will be directed toward your chosen road. You will always live according to your choices whether they were conscious or unconscious choices, and whether they are positive or negative in nature. The Universe does not filter your experiences according to what things should be or were meant to be, your life is created in exact proportion to the choices you make, it's that simple. How we choose is very important because this is what determines whether we live according to our Soul blueprint, or stray from that path by making a few detours. In the end, regardless of the decisions you make and where you end up as a result, it is always possible to get back on track in your life as long as you are willing to do so.

Your blue print is drawn up with all the possible scenarios that could occur in your life accounted for. A great deal of practice takes place on the other side before you are born, and this is in order to help you through your life experiences. Keep in mind that regardless of how well your Soul has planned your life path, you are likely to encounter obstacles and hurdles influenced by other people and these can cause you to detour from your Soul blue print. Do not worry about that though because in life, your worst experience can become your best asset. You might find this idea strange, but it makes perfect sense if you consider the fact that difficult experiences present us with challenges that can help us grow, and this is exactly what our Soul wants to further its evolution. Keep in mind though that growth comes from working through challenges and moving forward without getting stuck in resistance and stagnating in your issues. It all depends on how you look at things; you can view challenges as an opportunity to grow and expand your awareness in life, or you can choose to see challenges as negative by remaining stuck and feeling victimized. In the end, the choice is yours.

Before you were born, while your Soul was practicing and analyzing your life blueprint on the other side, you were aware of all the Souls destined to cross your path in your physical life. Our encounters with other Souls are really the essence of our learning because it is our interactions with others that provide us with all the experiences and lessons that are necessary to keep us moving toward fulfilling the growth and evolution our Soul is looking for. The way we deal with other people and the relationships we keep really help us to form our identity as individuals.

Depending on how we are treated by others, particularly our parents, we grow up with either a positive self-image or a negative one. This of course determines how your life will unfold, all according to how much you value yourself, how much you believe in your potential, how much happiness you feel you deserve, and as a result the way you make choices in the future. Consider this example; you developed an eating disorder during your youth as a result of an abusive childhood and grew up feeling worthless, and insignificant. Now, while growing up, you decided to become a Nutritionist because you thought it would help you solve your problem. You thought that by studying the eating disorder it might disappear, so instead of actually dealing with it, you tried to cover it with your profession. Unfortunately, it didn't go away, and you are still trying to manage to survive your pain and the scars that were left behind from the abuse you endured as a child.

In reality no-one is ever born with an eating disorder. It is not genetic or a part of your DNA. A situation like an eating disorder occurs like a symptom of the experiences you lived through during childhood and how your self-image was formed as a result. Maybe you were abused, mistreated or lacked attention as an example; do you think it would be possible to grow up with a glowing positive self-image, feeling worthy, confident and deserving of happiness as a result? I don't think so and unfortunately children seem to have this innate ability to blame themselves for what takes place in their environment, so as a result, an eating disorder becomes an outer manifestation of the inner blame and form of self-torture and punishment for where you feel you failed to please others as a child.

In an example such as this one, your experience of having an eating disorder did not support you in choosing the right career for you. On the bright side though, it probably helped you to realize that your problem is not the eating disorder itself, because if it was understanding food, nutrition and health in a positive way would have helped you change your attitudes and habits around food. In a case like this, the lesson is that understanding the effect of your childhood, the way your relationships with others affected you and the emotional impact they had upon the way you see yourself is the key to helping you solve your problem instead of just looking at the symptom, the outer manifestation of a deeper problem within.

The majority of people do not believe that their childhood is relevant, but it really is because it forms the foundation of our life and our identity. Most of us disregard our childhood without understanding how that period affects the way we feel about ourselves and perceive our life. Then as a result, we allow experience after experience to keep piling up miserably, one on top of the other until we reach the point where we realize that our life has no meaning or relevancy anymore. We become depressed and feel worthless, wondering what happened in our life and what we did to deserve being in such a situation. In reality, there is nothing anyone did to deserve to be in a situation like that; it is just that we underestimate the importance and significance of our childhood experiences and the effect they have on our life in the future.

How many of us actually remember our childhood? There are many people who claim to have forgotten large blocks of their childhood. I believe this is because blocking out the memory of difficult times is the only way a child is able to deal with something that is emotionally challenging and that they do not understand. So how many of us have blocked out memories of early experiences for lack of understanding it them? Unfortunately, I do believe there are many!

Parents should pay attention to what they say and how they act in front of their children. Many people think that children are young, and too inexperienced and insignificant to understand anything that is going on around them, but that is not true at all. Young children are far more aware of what is going on in their life than what we give them credit for. Just because a child does not appear to respond or react to our actions right away, it does not mean they are not aware of what is going on. Usually if children appear not to respond, it is mainly because they do not know how to process and express their feelings properly. When feelings are left unexpressed and misunderstood, they begin to manifest in the child as part of his character and his belief of how life is around him. Because we see life according to what we believe, our lives will eventually mirror that which we experienced as children.

If you decided to have children for whatever reason, then please act responsibly and consider that this child is a person and you are completely responsible for how the child shapes his view of life and the world in the beginning stages of his life. First take responsibility for your own life, and then for the life of your child. It is also important to consider that if you are not capable of being a responsible grown up when it comes to your own life, then how can you possibly be responsible for a child? If you feel that this is the case for you, then ask yourself why you brought a child into this life in the first place?

A child is an important lifetime commitment. Even when your child grows up, you are still his parent and his main role model in life. A child is not a toy or a hobby, or something that will help you pass the time away. Nor is a child an asset to help you get more free money and benefits from the government. A child is not a slave who will make your life easier by doing tasks and errands for you. A child is a human being who deserves to be treated with love and respect, the same love and respect you yourself longed for but perhaps never received from your own parents.

In the end, regardless of the way your life is conducted and who you have become as a result of your past, we all have a purpose in life whether we are a child or an adult, and there is no doubt about that. We all have experiences and lessons to go through in this lifetime, and in every other lifetime that our Soul decides to come back for. Because of this, I do believe it would be in our favor to at least try to understand who we are, why we are here and try to get back on the track our Soul had planned for us so we can live life in the happiest and most fulfilling way our Soul wished for us. Happiness is our birthright after all.

Now how are we going to determine your vibration? Before we begin, I would like you to keep in mind that simply learning about your vibration is not enough; you actually have to do something with what you are learning by applying the knowledge in your life before you will ever see changes taking place.

So what is the significance of your date of birth? We all have one so it must mean something surely! Your date of birth can be compared to a set of rules that form the foundation and structure of your life. It is the most important set of rules that your Soul has created, upon which to build the structure of its life blueprint.

Before getting into the fundamentals of this understanding, it is important to note that you must first acknowledge you are largely a spiritual being having a human life experience, and also that you do have a Soul. When you become aware of, and accept the spiritual and Soul aspect of yourself as being ultimate reality, then you begin to put real value on your vibration.

So now that we have reminded ourselves of this simple awareness, let us talk about your Blueprint Destiny. What is Blueprint Destiny? Blueprint destiny, simply put, is the life path we are here to follow and all the goals we are here to accomplish along the way as planned by our Soul. How do we define Blueprint Destiny? Blueprint destiny is a set of events, experiences and occurrences that take place in your life. Blueprint destiny does not only refer to future events that are going to happen. The events that have determined your past also make up part of your Blueprint Destiny. Your course of Blueprint Destiny reveals your purpose in life and what you are here to accomplish. By examining your Blueprint

Destiny through your date of birth, you can identify your Souls intention of being born at a specific time and what it wished to accomplish in its attainment. In short, Blueprint Destiny can then be defined as a set of events that are pre-determined by your Soul in order to fulfill it in the next step in its growth on the path of evolutionary progression in the Universe.

The family you were born into was determined a long time before you were born. The country of choice, the culture and the religion you were born into with has a great deal of significance when it comes to shaping your experiences and lessons in this lifetime. Many people have asked if it is better to be born in one country over another. My answer to that is no, it is not. It all depends on what experiences the Soul is going after to fulfill its learning in this lifetime, so the country of choice must provide the grounds to fulfill certain experiences the Soul wishes to encounter. Unfortunately, on a human level, if someone is born in a third world country, they might envy others who are born in more civilized countries. This is because they lack the knowledge and awareness that makes them understand that they are, in fact, fortunate to be where they are in terms of a growth standpoint because it is fulfilling the Soul's chosen path of growth. Even though life in such a situation may be tough and challenging for people in third world countries, for example, the rewards of such experiences will be felt later on another level.

In reality, wherever we are born and whatever our culture or religion is, we are all the same because we are all here for the same reason. That is for the evolution of our Soul. People who live in the Western world cannot claim to be better off because, in reality, they are not. There is no basis for the belief of being lesser than, or better than another person or place from the perspective of the Soul because we are all here for the same purpose – to learn through experiencing life no matter whom we are or where we live.

Although you may feel that you are worse off in life than other people, don't let appearances fool you. Consider the lifestyle and events that take place in the lives of people who are 'apparently' better off than most, such as Hollywood celebrities, and you will quickly realize that no matter how tough your life seems to be, there are always people who are handling greater challenges than you are, so count your blessings.

We tend to feel envious of people who drive luxury cars, live in big houses full of all the latest technology and can afford to go on exotic holidays every year. We also dream of having the kind of lifestyle that's portrayed in the movies. In essence, that is not reality, at least not your reality, and if some magical powers were able to pluck you out of your life today and transport you directly into the Hollywood lifestyle, you would never be happy anyway. You would feel empty and unfulfilled as that was not the life you were meant to live in the first place. That was not your Soul's intention for this life so it would all seem meaningless and lack purpose to you in the end.

In future, instead of wishing you were something or someone you were not meant to be, gather your energy and project it into making your life worthwhile today, regardless of who you are or where you were born. It is time for you to begin learning how to direct your life to its fullest potential according to the blueprint you were given. By doing this, you will begin to feel happy, fulfilled and content because you will be living the life you were born to live and not an ideal of something else.

You are a unique individual just by being who you are. There is nobody else that exists who is exactly like you and never will be. You should always act and be treated according to your own individual identity, rather than you wish you were or what others would like you to be. You are you and you are the only master of your life. Whether you are the one taking charge of the events that happen in your life, or you let the events take charge of you, you are still the one calling the shots. So now be the master of your Blueprint Destiny consciously and begin understanding your Blueprint Destiny according to the plans drawn for you by your Soul and you will have a happier and easier time in your life.

Another way of defining Blueprint Destiny is as the sum of all the agreements that your Soul has made with other Souls you will meet and interact with in your life. These Souls are in your life to provide you with the lessons and experiences needed for you to grow. This assistance can be either positive or negative in nature, but it is always positive when it comes to giving you an opportunity to grow, no matter how the nature of the experience itself turns out to be.

Is life a planned act? It is to a certain extent, but it is very flexible and we can always make changes in our life by using our Free Will. Free Will gives us the right to choose how we direct our life through choice at any given time. You can choose to move forward in your life or you can choose to remain stagnant, that is your choice and no-one else has the power to make you do anything unless you allow them to influence you.

Stagnation occurs as a result of a choice which has been made, a choice likely to have been influenced by your stubbornness, pride and ego. These are the aspects of our character that make it hard to let go and forgive the people and the events that have shaped your past. Stagnation occurs when you do not accept what has happened to you and you feel like a victim, and then become powerless as a result. In doing so, you are placing your life responsibility in the hands of another person or event and this will leave you feeling powerless to change and move forward because you are unable to recognize your own ability to change things.

Our future is determined by our actions today, and the decisions we made yesterday that still have to run their full cycle. Everything in life runs in cycles, like a rotation of our life experiences. This is what makes our life what it is and if we move forward with the cycle instead of resisting it, it will carry us forward instead of repeating similar experiences over and over again.

The only thing that can ever influence your Free Will is your Soul, because your Free Will is also your Soul's Free Will. You are here because of your Soul, to fulfill its chosen path of evolution; therefore it has the right to influence the course your life will take whenever necessary. If at any time, your Soul does have to intervene in where you are going in your life, it usually means it's time to force you into a position comparable to choosing life or death. Such a circumstance is normally serious and requires a drastic change of direction for you. It would mean either change your life now, or cut this life because, realistically speaking, it is not in the Soul's interest to continue investing energy into a lifetime that is totally unproductive. We do see manifestations of many sudden sicknesses and sudden death happening in the last decade.

An example of a real life situation in which a Soul influences the turn of events would be disease and illness. A life-threatening illness could suddenly manifest, forcing the individual to seriously evaluate who they are, their values, where they are going, and what life really means to them. Many people can get through a situation like this by choosing to be positive and fighting to change their life drastically by recognizing value in being alive. Others choose to fall into the mode of being a victim and allow themselves to fall further into a downward spiral and probably won't survive. The road an individual takes in any case is entirely up to them and will determine the outcome of their life.

At the end of the day, regardless of what happens, your Blueprint Destiny has been designed for you to live a happy life with a terrific ending. When it is time for your physical life to end, you should be able to pass in peace, knowing you have lived a fulfilling life, regardless of what happened. Even those who are living in a less peaceful environment, who are perhaps affected by war, famine or other difficult circumstances, can find a sense of peace within by looking to the richness of life and the experience they are living. I have personally traveled to parts of the world where they are far less fortunate than we in the western hemisphere are, and I found the people living in those places to be some of the most peaceful and grateful people I have ever encountered. Where as in our more 'developed' world as they call it, we have everything in our hand, yet we are still having a hard time coping with life. We do not recognize the value of what we have because we have never really struggled as others have in less developed countries. Life has been so easy for us that all we have has been taken for granted.

There are many possibilities available to help you change your life. You can attend lectures, read books, or perhaps take courses or workshops which have been designed to help you change your life. There are so many possible ways for people to find help and guidance, yet unfortunately most people still enjoy playing the role of victim and insist on staying miserable, feeling sorry for themselves and blaming other people for what happens in their life. Is this the vision of how you see yourself living your own life? Is this what you really want?

C. Understanding Numerology

"Where am I stuck?" "What's preventing me from moving forward in my life?" "What can I do to fulfill my Soul's pathway of evolution?" After being around so many people and hearing the types questions they ask, I decided to begin using Numerology in such a way as to help people better understand their life, their experiences, their challenges, and most of all to understand themselves. After all, if you know yourself very well, then you will never seek any help or advice.

How many of us know who we really are? How many of us know what we want out of life when it comes to relationships, jobs and what is best for us? Remember, a major part of your task in this life is to become aware of your calling, or purpose in this lifetime. That is your responsibility and no-one else can ever tell you what that is. Occasionally you might be given guidance that will help direct you toward discovering and living your own purpose, however, no-one can ever fully reveal what that is to you because that goes against Universal law, the divine order of experience, and your Free Will. If you could find out your life purpose from another person, then you would be stripped of your experience, and all the learning that goes hand in hand with its discovery. If that were to happen, then there would be no point in you being here because the most significant part of our learning comes from self-discovery and why we are here.

In order to become aware of your purpose and get on track with your path of Blueprint Destiny, you need to first become aware of, and understand the essence of the experiences that have already happened in your life. It is important to become aware of, and understand those experiences because the experiences in your life have everything to do with your life purpose. Your experiences will guide you through learning whatever it is you need to learn before you can fulfill your Blueprint Destiny.

This book 'The Blueprint of Your Soul' will emphasize answering the many questions I have been repeatedly asked during my time working with Numerology. This book is geared toward helping you heal yourself using Numerology, as it is an easy tool to help you begin understanding your life and what you have learned from them, regardless of the experiences you went through.

No matter who you are or how you have lived, you still have something to do in your lifetime, and it is time for you to learn how to be responsible for what happens in your life. Responsibility is of major importance here as you are always accountable for your decisions, and whether they are active or passive ones, you are always the one choosing how you shape your life and how you respond to what happens around you. It is important that you understand your experiences and be aware of the choices you made in the past and how they brought you to where you are today. Doing so will help you accept what has happened in your life and become responsible for choosing how you would like to live from now on.

Whatever the problem might be in your life, you still can fix it regardless of how old you are today. All you need is the desire to make your life better. No one, not a medium, psychic, friend, relative or whoever it is that you depend on for guidance will be able to provide you with the answers you need unless you are willing to accept responsibility for your life, recognize the fact you may have made some misinformed decisions and that it is time to fix everything.

Accepting the responsibility for fixing your life goes hand in hand with toning down your ego, pride and stubbornness and allowing the necessary changes to take place. You need to allow yourself to experience some humility instead of pride and stubbornness and accept your experiences, no matter what.

So are you ready to take the challenge of your life, to fix it for your own sake? If not then you need to identify your excuses. We are in this lifetime to grow from our learning, yet the majority of people are just sitting and waiting for things to change while doing nothing at all. They just sit, waiting and waiting for something or someone to enter their life and tell them everything is going to be alright. This is why many people go from one psychic or medium to another, hoping to hear the message that will suddenly make their life better. Well, things like that might happen in a fairy-tale, but let's not forget this is real life!

Your life will begin changing the moment you decide that you want it to. In order to facilitate change you must first be willing to allow it to manifest in your life, your heart, and in your thoughts. Healing can take place in anyone's life, as long as the decision is made to accept it and the changes it brings. In reality you are the only obstacle between you and change; it has nothing to do with anyone else who are, or have been involved in your past. You are the only one who can stop you from changing your life.

Have you allowed your experiences to get the better of you, and as a result are dependent on living in hardship and thriving on other people's sympathy? I have dealt with many people who have fallen into that pattern. Such people are giving their responsibility and power to change the direction of their life away in favor of surviving on other people feeling sorry for them. This fills them with a false sense of importance. These people do eventually end up losing track of where they are going in life and have no idea of how to move forward because they are unaware that they can.

How can you ever move forward if you are dependent on other people's sympathy to define who you are? You cannot! It is impossible to progress in your life living this way. As I said before, though, anyone can change if they really want to. Free will gives you the power to choose your direction at any time and you can make begin making that change right now. Act now because the answer is still 'yes' for change. No matter how or what has happened to you, life will always support you in your decision to change, learn and grow because that is the purpose of your life after all. Know that and trust it.

Throughout your experiences, did you grow to become envious of others, or did you feel jealous of others as they succeeded while you felt like a failure? Did you ask yourself, "Why Me?" Did you always feel that problems always seem to happen to you and no one else? Did you feel victimized by life? If so then the following list probably sounds familiar to you in terms of the way you felt about your life:

- You have lost hope in God.
- You have lost trust in yourself.
- You have lost faith in others.
- You feel everyone around you punishes you.
- You feel victimized by everyone.

Of course, as a result of your experiences, all of your feelings have grown to become real and valid beliefs and emotions within you, simply because this is what you have chosen to invest in by allowing them to stay alive within you. You believe you are worthless and depend upon others' opinions of you to feel worthy as a result, and because of your dependency, everyone treats you like a doormat and takes advantage of you.

This is what I recommend you do now:
- Stop blaming everyone.
- Stop complaining about your life.
- Stop being jealous of other people who are dealing with their life while you are doing nothing.
- Stop believing you are the only one who has problems.
- Stop feeling like a victim and take a long hard look at yourself and identify with the areas of your life that you can begin working upon to bring yourself back to living a happy life up to your full potential.

We tend to get stuck in a vicious circle when dealing with problems. Often it can be difficult to see any way out and, in order to free yourself, you need some help. The help you need is already out there somewhere, but perhaps you have a hard time accepting help and feel you have failed when you need to look outside of yourself for some advice or guidance? In any case, there is nothing wrong with asking for help if you are in need of some clarity. It is time to accept some humility in your life and accept that your experiences are all part of your Soul's journey toward growth and evolution.

Realistically, being dependent on a professional to help you fix your problem for more than a year, in my opinion, is of no help to you either. Either your helper has no real idea of how to help you, or they are keeping you in a place of dependency for their own selfish reasons, be it financially or otherwise. Perhaps, on the other hand, you have been receiving help for so long because in reality you really do not want to let go of your issues, and enjoy the fact that you have someone to listen to you and sympathize with you. If this sounds like a familiar situation to you, then it is time to identify with the reasons why you are not ready to let go of your problems.

Humanity as a whole has many issues to deal with. As individuals, we have many issues to deal with and before we can ever begin to heal our issues collectively, we must begin at the level of self. In order to succeed in our life, we need to really understand and deal with those issues. One way of another, we all have issues that have accumulated from the beginning of our life during childhood. This is the most important period of life that must be revisited, understood and dealt with before you can ever really get a hold of your life and help improve your future.

How can we use Numerology from our name and date of birth to help us understand our life? In order to understand Numerology, it is important to consider your life before you were even born.

Your cycle in this lifetime started at the moment your Soul returned to this plane and you were born. Your Soul has been frequenting life on this plane, as well as many others for time equivalent to many centuries. After such a long span of time and evolution, humanity has advanced technologically, however in terms of human understanding we are still stuck in old patterns and ways of thinking. Because of this, the Souls choosing to integrate into this plane are becoming stuck in their growth due to the stagnation of the human beings that represent them in this lifetime. Souls have to repeat lifetime after lifetime, coming back to this plane for similar experiences because we are crippled by our limitation in the way we look at ourselves and others.

We categorize ourselves and others according to religion, culture, skin color, language and whatever else it is we believe separates us from each other. "If you are not one of us then you are our enemy". Is that a statement of progress in our life? Or does that statement keep us from moving forward in life due to hate and anger toward each other? Perhaps is it just good business to think that way from a political and economic standpoint.

These days it is becoming harder to tell who has the right intention when it comes to what is right for the people and our world as there are so many distinctions. Even within cultural groups themselves, people are categorized. So tell me what the difference is between you and any other human being in the world? We are all human beings. We are all spiritual beings with a Soul that inhabits our body. So what makes you more special than me or anyone else? Nothing in reality!

If you think you are then you have a problem in your life at the moment, then consider some of the bigger issues that are going on in the world and you will see that your problem shrinks to almost nothing. You will start to appreciate your problem, realizing that you are blessed to have only that to deal with in your life and that perhaps you can learn something great from it.

Many people might not like hearing that, but I believe it is time to start hearing things from a new perspective. If you feel that this is not the way for you then just let it go and continue the way you have been going so far if you are truly happy. I feel that without saying the things I say I might not inspire people to anything the way I feel they ought to. On the other hand, I do feel that my ideas will click for certain people who are really stuck in their life and are just waiting to hear that something that will get them moving forward.

So what is Numerology? After drawing up the many charts I have done for so many people in the past, I have always been amazed by the individuality and uniqueness of every single person and their chart. There really are no two people in the world who are the same. I do not use a computer to draw a chart; I like to do it myself because I enjoy exploring and feeling the essence of the chart's creation in the first place.

There are many different ways of doing a chart and you can use any method you feel attracted to. Although some of the methods have slight differences, you will almost always end up with the same results. In some cases, the result will be slightly different from one chart to the next, but this is not critical because you will always get the bigger picture of the chart's meaning in the end.

We will begin our chart by looking at the date of birth to calculate our Blueprint Destiny. Blueprint destiny is our potential in this lifetime, and the goal we are working toward through being on this plane in the first place. Blueprint destiny is the fundamental component of your blueprint and can be found from your date of birth.

Your date of birth is meant to be unchangeable, although some people have tampered with that date. For example, the parents of a child born in December might register their child's birthday as if it occurred in January in order to make them younger. If this is the case for you, then I recommend that you find out your real birthday so you can calculate your true Blueprint Destiny. It may also be interesting for you to compare both your destinies, the true one with the one your parents made for you to see which destiny is best suited for you in your life.

The number of your Blueprint Destiny is usually made up of the sum of two numbers that are reached when you add the day, month and the year of your birth together. For example, January 2, 1980 would be 1+2+1+9+8+0=21/3. You then add 2+1=3, so 3 is the Blueprint Destiny in this case. We will learn about the calculations in more detail later, I just wanted to illustrate what I was talking about at this point of the book.

I personally believe the first number and vibration of your Blueprint Destiny is the foundation of the majority of the problems you will face in your life, which is 2 in 21/3 from my previous example. This vibration is the only vibration you have no control over. It is usually the case that as children we have no proper way of dealing with this vibration when it is predominant during our early life because we are so young.

This vibration is the vibration that was with you from birth right up until you were 18 years old. It makes up the base of all our problems and it is important that we begin to do something about understanding it and dealing with it.

We really need to act on this now before time passes us by because many people are still sitting and waiting for a miracle to happen that will save them. Others have spent sometimes 20 years in therapy and are yet to see any change happen. What does that tell you? Yes, it is time to think about you and your life from a new perspective.

The less you deal with your childhood the more complicated your life is destined to become. On the other hand, the more quickly and efficiently you deal with your childhood experiences the easier your life will become. Some people seem to be luckier than others when it comes to their childhood experiences and may have had an easier time with a pleasant upbringing, for others of course that is simply not the case.

So what happened in your childhood that is reflected in your life today? If you are not sure then why not take a closer look at the way you do things. The way you conduct your relationships is based upon what you learnt from your parents, their experiences with each other and how they dealt with you. The way you handle your money today is the same – a reflection of how you were taught to think about and handle money by your parents and how they dealt with their finances. The way your career goes also has a great deal to do with your upbringing. These things stand even in the case where you might be acting out in rebellion against beliefs that your parents tried to ingrain in you that you did not agree with. Whether you are acting according to their ways or against them, you are still directly influenced by your parents and their way of doing things.

You may be asking where karma comes into all of this and, of course, there is karma in our life that needs to be dealt with. Your karma was well chosen according to the environment and family you were born into. This is in order to help make your experiences and lessons easier to deal with. As an example, maybe you are having problems dealing with other people because you are very shy. When you were a child, you became used to your parents doing everything for you and avoided dealing with other people, however that is affecting your life adversely today. Why do you think that problem still exists today, even though you are all grown up? Of course, it is because, during your childhood, your parents supported your shyness and fear of dealing with other people, making you dependent on others to do things for you. One day, you were then left to deal with your life all by yourself, your parents were no longer there to do things for you and what happens next? You are feeling lost being left by yourself to deal with your issue and don't know what on earth to do because your fear has become your reality.

Facing this type of situation can be devastating for some people in their life, yet in the end, it is their reality and they must deal with it before their life wastes away. We must try to begin learning how to deal with our life properly from an early age so we can grow up being able to handle the responsibility of ourselves and our life.

Many of us, regardless of our age, still act like a child, the child that never dealt with his or her issues. If you want to heal your life then you have to begin by healing your childhood. Often I ask someone if they have dealt with their childhood and they quickly answer "yes" with attitude. If you feel you have dealt with your childhood, then again, I ask you to look closely at your life today and see if there is anything, and I mean anything, that reflects your childhood. Answer this question honestly because in the end you are only kidding yourself.

You are alive and that means you deserve to live the best life possible, so why not try to at least save your own life, regardless what age you are today? In this book, I will not go into the subject of how to heal your childhood experiences as this requires a whole book of its own. My next book will handle that subject so for the time being let's get back to the Numerology.

D. The Blueprint of Your Soul Insight

Numerology is not just a bunch of numbers that have been put together by your Soul. It is not a coincidence that you were born on a particular date of birth and that your parents named you what they did. This book will bring you to a new understanding and awareness, and I don't just mean another new way of calculating your numbers, or a new way of prediction or interpreting of your numbers. This book is about healing. It is about you the human being and the Soul you are representing in this lifetime.

As humans we are always looking for things to happen in our lives, then when they do not happen the way we expected, we complain and ask, "Why me? Why am I always the unlucky one who doesn't have good fortune?" Actually, we all have a mission in this lifetime and that means that life has something in store for us. However, most of us will leave this plane without even knowing that or what Blueprint Destiny had in store because we are so stuck in unresolved issues from the past. We all have a life to live and were meant to enjoy living it, regardless of what happens to us during our life span.

If you were to meet a Numerologist, the first thing you might ask would be, "What does my future hold?" Well, in reality your future will always be a reflection of your past until you deal with it. We mirror the events and keep creating the same type of reality over and over again because that is all we know and understand as being true.

The circumstances that make up your life today are based upon, and reflect your understanding of your old experiences. If the way you feel about your past experiences is mainly anger, hate, frustration, with feelings of betrayal, abuse and having no trust or self-confidence, then that is what you will attract and see in your life experiences today. The same goes for relationships. Why are there more divorces today than ever? We meet people who are a reflection of ourselves, who are able to provide us with a lesson we need, but those relationships are never meant to be and are not an expansion of ourselves. Such relationships provide us with the missing link in our learning and we are meant to move on until we are ready for the real deal. This is the difference between the seasonal quick fix and the everlasting relationship.

We look for a compatible companion to be with according to their Zodiac sign and whether they are a match with ours or not. In reality, whether or not you have compatible signs will never solve your problems in even the best of matches if you do not really want to deal with and heal your old issues in the first place.

Healing works for some people and doesn't for others and the only reason it doesn't is because they choose not to heal. Unfortunately there are so many people among us who do not want to heal and back up their choice with all kinds of excuses. In the end who are they trying to convince? They are the only ones who are losing out on living the best life possible.

Although life can be rough at seem unfair at times, there is a good reason for all things that happen. All experiences are part of our learning and although that doesn't make it right to hurt another Soul, it is still part of our learning and we will feel the effect of being on the other side of experiencing our actions either later in this life time or a future one:

- You are here to feel the lack of justice in this world.
- You are here to witness the anger.
- You are here to see the abuse.
- You are here to feel the pain of the killing.
- You are here to observe and try to understand the conflict of all religions on this plane.
- You are here to experience the jealousy between people.
- You are here to learn and grow and it is time for us all

to begin growing together exploring a new appreciation for life by understanding it from a new perspective. It is also time for you to begin living your life for you and you alone.

- Your family is here because you agreed they would be the vehicle that would help provide your Soul with the experiences it needs to evolve in this lifetime.
- Your religion is here to provide a belief system that gives you a foundation upon which to base your faith.
- Your experiences are here to provide you with the means to obtain the knowledge that is needed to help you grow.

So where do you stand in your life today? Let's take a look.

Section II

A. The Blueprint of Your Soul Chart

From your Date of Birth

Date of Birth: Month ____ Day ____ Year _____
Calculation = _____
Calculation = _____

MAIN CORE NUMBERS:
From your Date of Birth

Blueprint Destiny: ☐☐ = ☐
Blueprint Birthday: ☐☐ = ☐
Blueprint Attainments: 1) ☐ 2) ☐ 3) ☐ 4) ☐
Blueprint Challenges: 1) ☐ 2) ☐ 3) ☐ 4) ☐

Age Timing of Blueprint Attainments & Blueprint Challenges:

1st phase begins at birth and ends at age ☐☐
2nd phase begins from age ☐☐ to age ☐☐
3rd phase begins from age ☐☐ to age ☐☐
4th phase begins at age ☐☐ until the end of life

Blueprint Journey's Cycle:

Blueprint Influential Learning ☐☐ = ☐ (ends around age 27)
Blueprint Personal Experiences ☐☐ = ☐ (ends around age 57)
Blueprint Harvest Results   ☐☐ = ☐ (until the end of life)

Blueprint Personal Year:

Month + Day + Today's Year
☐☐ + ☐☐ + ☐☐☐☐ =
☐☐ + ☐☐ + ☐☐ =
☐ + ☐ + ☐ = ☐☐ = ☐
Universal Blueprint: ☐☐☐☐ = ☐☐ = ☐

From Your Name Used Today

Full Name Used Today: _____
Calculation = _____
Calculation = _____

Blueprint Expression: ☐☐ = ☐ Blueprint Growth: ☐☐=☐
Blueprint Soul Urge: ☐☐=☐ Blueprint Maturity: ☐☐=☐
Blueprint Inner–Self: ☐☐ = ☐
Blueprint Family Vibration: ☐☐ = ☐
Blueprint Intensity:

1	2	3	4	5	6	7	8	9

Blueprint Karmic Lesson(s): ☐☐☐☐☐
Blueprint Modified Karmic Lesson(s): ☐☐☐☐☐
Blueprint Sub-Conscious: ☐☐ = ☐

Blueprint Temperament Behavior:

Mental (1,8) ☐; Physical (4,5) ☐; Emotional (2,3,6) ☐; Intuitive (7,9) ☐

1	2	3	4	5	6	7	8	9
A	B	C	D	E	F	G	H	I
J	K	L	M	N	O	P	Q	R
S	T	U	V	W	X	Y	X	

B. Calculation For The Blueprint of Your Soul Chart

1	2	3	4	5	6	7	8	9
A	B	C	D	E	F	G	H	I
J	K	L	M	N	O	P	Q	R
S	T	U	V	W	X	Y	X	

Letter values for reference in following calculations:

January = 1, February = 2, March = 3, April = 4, May = 5, June = 6, July = 7, August = 8, September = 9, October = 10 = 1, November = 11, December = 12 = 3.

Note: November is 11 a Master Number, so leave it as is.

Part 1: Calculation based on your date of birth:

a. Your Blueprint Destiny is ____ ____ / ____

Write Down your Birthday starting with the month:

_____

Add month of birth + day of birth + year of birth = Blueprint Destiny Number:
Blueprint Birthday in Numbers is:

___+___+___+___+___+___+___+___ = ____

Reduce to One Number: ____
Example: November 26, 1975 = 11+2+6+1+9+7+5 = 41 = 5
Blueprint Destiny is 41 / 5

The numbers 11, 22 and 33 are Master numbers, therefore are not reduced into two single numbers during the calculations. They must remain as is. For example, if you have the numbers 11 or 22 as your day of birth in your Blueprint Birthday, or were born in November, you leave it as it is and add it as 11 or 22, instead of breaking the number down and adding it as 1+1, or 2+2. When you have added each of the numbers of your birth date together, if the total is more than 9, add the two numbers together until a base number of 9 or less is achieved. Exception: do not reduce the numbers 11, 22 or 33, the master numbers.

b. Your Blueprint Day of Birth is: ___ ___ / ___

Add Day of birth: ___+___ = ___
Example from above: 26 = 8
Your Blueprint Day of Birth is 26 / 8

If your Blueprint Day of Birth adds up to or equals 11 or 22, do not reduce the number.

c. Your Blueprint Attainments are:

1) ____; 2) ____; 3) ____; 4) ____

1st Phase Blueprint Attainment is: ____

Day of birth _____ + month of birth _____ = First Phase Attainment _____
Reduce the number to a single digit, with the exception of the master numbers 11, 22: _____

2nd Phase Blueprint Attainment is: ____

Day of birth _____ + year of birth _____ = Second Phase Blueprint Attainment _____
Reduce the number to a single digit, with the exception of the master numbers 11, 22: _____

3rd Phase Blueprint Attainment is: _____

Add the First Phase Blueprint Attainment _____ + the Second Phase Blueprint Attainment _____ = the Third Phase Blueprint Attainment _____
Reduce the number to a single digit, with the exception of the master numbers 11, 22: _____

4th Phase attainment is: _____

The month of birth _____ + the year of birth _____ = Fourth Phase Blueprint Attainment _____
Reduce the number to a single digit, with the exception of the master numbers 11, 22: _____

d. Your Blueprint Challenges are:

1) _____; 2) _____; 3) _____; 4) _____

1st Phase Blueprint Challenge:

The difference between the day of birth ___ and the month of birth ____ = First Phase Blueprint Challenge _____

2nd Phase Blueprint Challenge:

Difference between the day of birth ___ and year of birth ____ = Second Phase Blueprint Challenge ___

3rd Phase Blueprint Challenge

Difference between the first and second phase blueprint challenge = Third Phase Blueprint Challenge _____

4th Phase Blueprint Challenge:

Difference between month of birth ___ and year of birth ____ = Forth Phase Blueprint Challenge _____

Timing Blueprint Attainments and Blueprint Challenges:

The First Stage Blueprint Attainment and Blueprint Challenge begins at birth. To calculate the end of the First Phase Blueprint Attainment / Blueprint Challenge, subtract the Blueprint Destiny number from 36. The result is equal to the end of the first phase Blueprint Attainment / Blueprint Challenge.

First Phase Blueprint Attainment / Blueprint Challenge begins at birth and ends _____

Second Phase Blueprint Attainment / Blueprint Challenge begins the following year. This Blueprint Attainment / Blueprint Challenge ends 9 years after the ending of the First Phase Blueprint Attainment / Blueprint Challenge.

Second Phase Blueprint Attainment / Blueprint Challenge begins _____ and ends _____

Third Phase Blueprint Attainment / Blueprint Challenge begins the following year. This Blueprint Attainment / Blueprint Challenge ends 9 years after the ending of the Second Phase Blueprint Attainment / Blueprint Challenge.

Third Phase Blueprint Attainment / Blueprint Challenge begins _____ and ends _____

Fourth Phase Blueprint Attainment / Blueprint Challenge begins the following year and remains until the end of life.

Fourth Phase Blueprint Attainment / Blueprint Challenge begins at _____

e. Your Blueprint Journey's Cycle:

1. Your Blueprint Influential Learning ____;
2. Your Blueprint Personal Experience ____;
3. Your Blueprint Harvest Result ____

1. Blueprint Influential Learning ____;

Your first Life Cycle, as I like to refer to it, is your 'Blueprint Influential Learning':

Blueprint Influential Learning = __ (birth month) = __+__ = ___
This Cycle ends approximately by your 27th birthday.

2. Blueprint Personal Experience ____;

Your Second Life Cycle, as I like to refer to it, is your Blueprint Personal Experience:
Blueprint Personal Experience = __ (birth date) = ___+___ = ____
This Cycle ends approximately at 57th birthday.

3. Blueprint Harvest Result ____

Your Third Cycle, or your Blueprint Harvest Result:
Blueprint Harvest Result = ____ (birth year) =
____+____+____+____ = ____ = ____+____ = ____

f. Your Blueprint Personal Year: Understand '9-Year Cycle'

The month your birth occurred ____ + the day of birth____ + the year in question (the year we are currently in, e.g. 2010) ____ = the Blueprint Personal Year (reduce number to single digit): _____
If your month and day of birth has not yet arrived in your current year, use the previous year in your calculation. Examples:
November 26 1975. In 2010, before November, use 2009:
= 11 + 2+6+2+0+0+9 = 30 / 3. So Personal Year is 3.
June 18 1964. In 2010, after June:
= 6 + 1 + 8 + 2 + 0 + 1 + 0 = 18 / 9, so Personal Year is 9.

January = 1, February = 2, March = 3, April = 4, May = 5, June = 6, July = 7, August = 8, September = 9, October = 10, November = 11, December = 12.

8. Universal Blueprint Year for 2009 / 2010

Again we are using the year we are currently in to calculate the Universal year:
2009 = 2+0+0+9 = 11 = 2
2010 = 2+0+1+0 = 3

You can download the chart to practice at:
http://theblueprintofyoursoul.com/

Part 2: Calculation Based on Your Name Use Today:

a. Your Blueprint Expression is ____ ____ / ____

Your first name: __ __ __ __ __ __ __ __ __ __ __ __ __ __
Numerical value of each letter: __ __ __ __ __ __ __ __ __ __ __ __

__ __ __ __ __ = _____

Your middle name: __ __ __ __ __ __ __ __ __ __ __ __ __ __
Numerical value of each letter: __ __ __ __ __ __ __ __ __ __ __ __

__ __ __ __ __ = _____

Your 2nd middle name: __ __ __ __ __ __ __ __ __ __ __ __
Numerical value of each letter: __ __ __ __ __ __ __ __ __ __ __ __

__ __ = _____

Your last name: __ __ __ __ __ __ __ __ __ __ __ __ __
Numerical value of each letter: __ __ __ __ __ __ __ __ __ __ __ __

__ __ __ __ __ = _____

The total numerical value of your name (your Blueprint Expression Number) = _____

Example: Nadia Roberts
N A D I A   R O B E R T S
5 1 4 9 1   9 6 2 5 9 2 1
= 30/3   = 34 / 7 = 3+7 = 10 /1
Your Blueprint Expression is 10 /1

When you have added each of the numbers of your name together, if the total is more than 9, add the two numbers together until a base number of 9 or less is achieved. Exception: do not reduce the masters numbers 11, 22 or 33.

b. Your Blueprint Soul Urge is: ___ ___ / ___

Your first name: __ __ __ __ __ __ __ __ __ __ __ __ __
Numerical value of vowels only: __ __ __ __ __ __ __ __ __ __

__ __ __ __ __ __ = _____
Your middle name: __ __ __ __ __ __ __ __ __ __ __ __
Numerical value of vowels only: __ __ __ __ __ __ __ __ __ __

__ __ __ __ __ __ = _____
Your last name: __ __ __ __ __ __ __ __ __ __ __ __ __ __
Numerical value of vowels only: __ __ __ __ __ __ __ __ __ __

__ __ __ __ __ __ = _____

Total numerical value of vowels (Soul Urge number) = _____
- Y is considered a vowel. Its value is 7. Y is a vowel when there is no vowel in a syllable. Example: Yvonne, Sylvia, and Larry.
- Y is also considered a vowel when it is preceded by A, E, I, O, U and sounded as one sound. Example Hayden, Doyle, and Raymond
- W is considered a vowel. Its value is 5. W is a vowel when it is preceded by A, E, I, O U and sounded as one sound. Example: Bradshaw, Matthew, and Lowell.

c. Your Blueprint Inner Self is: ___ ___ / ___

Your first name: __ __ __ __ __ __ __ __ __ __ __ __ __
Numerical value of consonants only: __ __ __ __ __ __ __ __ __

__ __ __ __ __ __ __ = _____
Your middle name: __ __ __ __ __ __ __ __ __ __ __

__ __
Numerical value of consonants only: __ __ __ __ __ __ __ __ __

__ __ __ __ __ __ __ = _____
Your last name: __ __ __ __ __ __ __ __ __ __ __ __ __ __
Numerical value of consonants only: __ __ __ __ __ __ __ __

__ __ __ __ __ __ __ = _____
The total numerical value of consonants (your Soul Urge Number)
= _____

Discover Yourself and Your Blueprint Destiny 55

d. Your Blueprint Maturity is: ____ ____ / ____

Your Blueprint Maturity Number = Blueprint Destiny + Blueprint Expression Number
Your Blueprint Maturity Number = ___+___=____=____+____ =____

e. Your Blueprint Growth is: ____ ____ / ____

Your Blueprint Growth number = the sum of your first name
Your first name: __ __ __ __ __ __ __ __ __ __ __ __ __
Numerical value for each letter: __ __ __ __ __ __ __ __ __ __
__ __ __ __ __ = _____

f. Your Blueprint Intensity Table from Your Name:

List the number of times that each number is used in your name:

　　　_____ 1s in name;
　　　_____ 2s in name;
　　　_____ 3s in name;
　　　_____ 4s in name;
　　　_____ 5s in name;
　　　_____ 6s in name;
　　　_____ 7s in name;
　　　_____ 8s in name;
　　　_____ 9s in name;

1. Blueprint Karmic Lessons

It is the missing number from your name with a zero (0) related to any vibration from 1 to 9. This will be your karma in your life.

2. Blueprint Modified Karmic Lessons

It is the missing number from your name with a zero (0) related to any vibration from 1 to 9 but that number is available somewhere else in your chart. That will be a less intensified lesson of your karma.

g. Your Blueprint Family Vibration: __ __ __ __ __ __ __
__ __ __ __ __

Numerical value of each letter: __ __ __ __ __ __ __ __ __ __ __
__ __ __ __ __ = _____
The total numerical value of your last name (your Blueprint Family Vibration) = _____

Example: Nadia Roberts
R O B E R T S
9 6 2 5 9 2 1 = 34 / 7 =7
Your Blueprint Family Vibration is 34/7

h. Your Blueprint Temperament Behavior:

Blueprint Physical ____; Blueprint Mental ____;

Blueprint Emotional ____; Blueprint Intuitive ____.

Blueprint Physical Element = Count the number of 4s and 5s in your full name = ____
Blueprint Mental Element = Count the number of 1s and 8s in your full name = ____
Blueprint Emotional Element = Count the number of 2s, 3s and 6s in your full name = ____
Blueprint Intuitive Element = Count the number of 7s and 9s in your full name = ____

i. Blueprint Sub-Conscious

Blueprint Sub-Conscious = 9 - Count the number of zeros (0) in your intensity table = ____

Section III

Primary Components of Your Blueprint

A. Date of Birth

This fundamental component of your blueprint is a very important aspect in your life. This component of your life is normally fixed. You are born on a specific date that will determine many facets of your life, including the direction that will lead you to happiness, your freedom and understanding of why you are here on this plane now. We were all born with a 'flavor.' What's yours?

Your Soul has a lot to do with your understanding of things. The extent of your awareness your Soul has is essential in determining how much understanding you have within your inner-self's 'gift basket.' Souls vibrate an awareness that is in accordance with their own individual level of evolution. Regardless of their level, the contents of this book can be understood by anyone who maintains an open mind.

When it comes to the understanding and awareness of Soul, humanity is falling behind. Many people are too rational and do not believe that there is anything beyond this life. On the other hand some people do believe in reincarnation, while others seek the assistance of mediums to communicate with Spirit and prove the survival of life after death. Many people acknowledge the existence of our Spirit guides and guardian angels, while some are aware of the word Soul and understand it in a way that suits them.

a. Your Blueprint Destiny

Have you ever wondered about the significance of your date of birth? The minute you were born, you became entitled to live the Blueprint Destiny that was arranged by your Soul. If you open your mind to this concept that your life has a specific purpose, then many things will start to make sense to you about your life, yourself and the people around you.

As we discovered before, Blueprint Destiny is simply a set of planned experiences that have been arranged for you to live though during this lifetime. Your Blueprint Destiny will be better fulfilled if and when you are able to fully understand the essence of your childhood experiences because these are the foundation upon which you will build your understanding of life and the way you see yourself. Many of us have become stuck in and unable to understand and let go of those experiences and this prevents us from living out our Blueprint Destiny to the full potential. We were all born to live through those events in our early life and they are critical in determining the outcome of our life.

Can you be the leader of your life with low self-confidence? Can you be whatever it is you dream of becoming, yet are still unable to express your deepest desires and emotions? Can you live to be you when you do not even trust yourself? I don't think so! So in order to get back on track in your Blueprint Destiny, you need to go step by step and begin slowly understanding the events which took place in your life while growing up.

When you add the numbers that make up your date of birth, you will end up with 2 numbers that must be added in order to reach your Blueprint Destiny number.

For example:
Born: July 15, 1974
July is the 7th month of the year
7 + 1 + 5 + 1 + 9 + 7 + 4 = 34/7
34/7 is the Blueprint Destiny.

The first two numerical vibrations that are added to reach the final number of your Blueprint Destiny are just as important as your Blueprint Destiny number itself. These two numbers characterize the early stages of your life and unfortunately most people become stuck in those vibrations and as a result stop growing mentally and emotionally.

The first number '3' in the example above is the vibration that will be carried throughout childhood, until the age of 29 in this specific case. Anyone who has the number '3' with them in their childhood should have an easy life growing up, full of joy, fun and happiness. However, many of us will say, "Well I have a '3' and that certainly was not the case in my life!" So what changed for those people; something must have influenced their life otherwise? The answer to that is yes, it did.

As a child and on average, until the age of 18 years, you live under your parent's roof and probably don't have much of a say in what goes on in your life. Your parents are in charge and their influence, your upbringing, your religion, your culture and the environment in which you were raised all have a great deal to do with your life today. When you have not lived a joyful experience, even with the '3' vibration, then it means that somewhere, someone along the way must have interfered with your Blueprint Destiny. As a result you will have a few additional problems to deal with in your experience as a child.

When the first numerical vibration of your Blueprint Destiny has been affected by the actions of other people around you, then it definitely had an influence on your life and how you will progress in your original plan of Blueprint Destiny. All is not lost however; this is the perfect place to begin your healing journey toward creating a new future. View it as a signpost instead of an obstacle and you will be well on the way to redirecting your life before it is too late.

Always remember regardless where your numbers are placed in your chart, you always have to maintain your vibration in a positive way with a positive attitude toward life no matter what has happened in your past. Learning in life often comes from moving from negative experiences into positive ones and the moment we accept that and begin living for the positive, we are well on the way to understanding our lesson in life.

The second number in our example is '4'; this vibration begins at the age of 30 until 39. The 'four vibration' is all about stability and being organized in life. Stability means having a balance between the mental, emotional, physical and spiritual states of being.

The moment you find balance between the positive aspects of the first two vibrations in your Blueprint Destiny, you will better understand the direction you are headed in reaching your final number of Blueprint Destiny, which in the case of this example is '7.' The more positive vibration you work with, easier your life will become. On the other hand, the more negativity you vibrate, the more difficulty you will have in fulfilling your Blueprint Destiny as you will have many additional hurdles to overcome as a result.

Please keep in mind, the first two vibrations of the Blueprint Destiny are those where people tend to become stuck. Those vibrations will determine the amount of growth you achieve from your learning, making them key factors in determining the areas of your life that need to be examined in order for healing to take place. In the end, what you do with the vibrations you are given is up to you. You are the master of your life in the end.

b. Your Blueprint Birthday

The number of your day of birth is there to assist you in reaching your Blueprint Destiny. It is an additional vibration that helps support us toward moving forward in life. Every vibration that makes up your birthday provides an additional edge when it comes to enhancing your strengths and mastering your weaknesses in life.

c. Your Blueprint Attainment

Attainments in my opinion are the blessing from the Universe to us as a gift. They exist in our life to bring a shift in our direction or change in our life. They have a period attached with them and the number will bring you awareness of the tone of that area in your life you are working on. Many times I realize that those vibrations coincide a lot for many of us with the vibration we have been missing in our life. That way, the Universe is doing its job of touching us with clarity for how we feel the effect of that energy in our life.

d. Your Blueprint Challenges

We all have challenges in life. Challenges are the obstacles we encounter. These challenges are in our life to bring the best out of us and are not a punishment. The less resistant we are to the challenges, the easier their effect will be on us. Challenges are the points in our life that identify our weakness and help us grow stronger. Many times they are a blessing to help us focus in on significant problems that need to be faced. We have the possibility of having four main challenges in our lifetime, however on average people seem to have mainly two minor challenges and one major one.

e. Blueprint Journey's Cycle

There are three sub-understandings known to your Blueprint Journey's Cycle which are additional support tools in your Blueprint Destiny. Every understanding in your life has an influence on you, your personality, your strengths and weaknesses in this life. The three cycles are all equally important. Each cycle has its own influence and effects the direction of your life. Regardless of the direction you are in, you can always bring yourself to a better place that makes more sense to you.

1. The Blueprint Influential Learning:

The Blueprint Influential Learning cycle is the most important cycle in your life. It represents the educational years of life and is the foundation of who you will become while growing up. This is a very important cycle that will form and influence your personality. Our childhood is the base and the foundation of all of our understanding about ourselves and life. Our influences from our environment start at the beginning of this cycle from the moment of birth, and its influence will determine a great deal of your growth in this lifetime. During this period, other people are also influencing your life and the direction you will go in. This is not always in your best interest because although everyone may think they are doing you a favor by influencing you, oftentimes what happens is we end up living our life for other people and not ourselves.

2. The Blueprint Personal Experiences:

Childhood is over now and this is the period of your life where you will demonstrate your qualities. The Blueprint Personal Experiences bring a period of work, a period where you will be most productive. This cycle is similar to the first, however here we have more power over our life. At this time, you should be more mature, have more control over your life and be able to deal with people and the events that take place in your life well.

3. The Blueprint Harvest Result

This is the result of your past work in this life. The Blueprint Harvest Result is the time in life to gather, or harvest the rewards of your past hard work and learning. If you handled all of your previous cycle to the best of your capacity and sustained a positive vibration throughout your numbers, this should be a satisfying time for you. Life is based on cause and effect, and any decisions you make on a daily basis determine the direction of your life. I do not personally believe there are wrong decisions. I see life as an unfolding chain of reactions that if followed and understood can lead you to new learning and new circumstances as a result. However, it is important not to resist the flow of the events that take place in your life, regardless of how bad they may seem, because your life and your learning will stagnate as a result.

Even if you had a rough time during the Blueprint Influential Learning Cycle, you still have the power to change and can begin working on that as soon as you move into your Personal Experience

Cycle. In your Blueprint Personal Experience Cycle, you have the power and the free will to completely change your life as long as you are willing to let go of the previous events in your life.

We really have no excuses to justify complaining about our misfortune because it really is a blessing in disguise. We are here to experience some misfortune for the growth and evolution of our Soul, and regardless of the level of difficulty you have encountered, your Soul will always provide you with a way out if you really want it.

There is always a purpose to be fulfilled in everyone's life, and the more you live up to your purpose, the more peace, contentment and satisfaction you will have in your life. Many people may appear to be happy on the outside, but even with all the fame or fortune you can imagine, no one can ever be truly happy and at peace within unless they figure out what their true purpose for being here is. We were all born with a destiny, with something to accomplish in this lifetime, regardless of how small or how big it is. We are not here to just smell the roses or eat, or to even be a doctor or president of a country. Destiny has more to it than that; it is an inner experience as opposed to just defining yourself by what you do.

Everything in nature has a purpose – the trees, the insects and the animals all have a purpose too. Start discovering your purpose now, and live your Blueprint Destiny. Learn about your inner essence, the one you always felt and the things you dreamt of doing before you started listening to what everyone else wanted you to be and your society crushed you. It is time to stop disregarding your own dreams, passion and values, and most of all stop living just to please everyone else. Live your life for you because that is why you are here, to let your essence and your true colors shine through in your life.

f. Universal Blueprint

The Universe changes on the first day of every New Year to bring new insights to our life and a promise of a brighter and more prosperous future if we want it.

In 2008, the Universal Blueprint is 2 + 0 + 0 + 8 = 2 + 8 = 10 = 1, and is a new beginning. 2008 brought a beginning for you if you are ready, so open yourself and be willing to accept the abundance the Universe is ready to lay in front of you. Stop dragging your past with you and turn a new page in the book of your life for a new and brighter future.

g. Your Blueprint Personal Year: '9-Year Cycle'

It is very important to be aware of the cycles that exist in our life. These cycles are significant when it comes to affecting the changes that take place over the years of our lives. In this book, I plan to bring to you an awareness of those cycles. Awareness is important because it brings consciousness, and consciousness brings understanding. Isn't the point of our life to understand our experiences? The moment you understand your experiences, you will begin to glimpse your purpose here. A few Souls come to this plane with an immediate jump into living their purpose; however, the majority have the task of discovering that for themselves along the way.

The moment you become conscious of yourself is the moment you begin to identify the patterns in your life, and begin looking to make a change. Without identifying your patterns and problems, you will always remain stuck in the same kinds of experiences. If, on the other hand, you believe you have no problems at all, then you should be very aware of yourself and your life as it unfolds before you, with full consciousness of where and how you will make your next move on your Blueprint Destiny.

So what is the effect of the Blueprint '9-Year Cycle' on you?

How many of you are always asking, *"How come I always seem to attract the same kind of circumstances into my life?"* We already established that from the moment of your birth, you were born with your Blueprint Destiny number. Your cycle begins with that number and carries on until you reach the end of the Year 9, then it begins all over again with Year 1.

For example, if you were born with a Blueprint Destiny of 7, then your first 9-Year Cycle begins at Year 7 of a 9-Year Cycle, which is the same as your Blueprint Destiny so you have only 3 years to finish your first cycle in life from the above example. That was a short 9-Year Cycle for you. So at age 4, you start in a complete new 9-Year Cycle. So if your Blueprint Destiny is 9 and you are born at the end of the cycle, on your first birthday, you start your first full 9-Year Cycle.

Events come and go in our life. Decisions we make on a daily basis will affect the direction we are heading in by bringing change into our life. Anything we do not deal with in our life in a particular '9-Year Cycle' will be carried on into another '9-Year Cycle.' It's as simple as that!

You have the choice of whether to change or not. In either case, your decisions will affect the circumstances of your life for good or bad. This brings the importance of our Free Will into play, to understand that we always have a choice to change our life and how we choose determines the outcome of events. For example, you have heard about a house that is very haunted because many people are talking about it. You decide for yourself to check the place out and see if the rumors are true. When you arrive there, you experience objects moving on their own and you hear many strange sounds. You feel afraid and uncomfortable with the situation and want to get out. You have a choice of whether to leave that uncomfortable situation or not. It is entirely up to you whether you leave and don't bother the Spirits who are haunting the house or stay and experience the outcome of your decision to remain. Life is either black or white; you cannot have both black and white so you have to choose.

I believe that your most challenging experiences should take place during the first 18 years of your life. Of course, you can have challenges later on; however, the first period of your life is the most important as it creates the foundation of your character and your life to follow.

How many of us have been living the same drama for years and for what seriously? Perhaps you hate one of your parents because of the way they raised you. Or perhaps you are still suffering because of physical or mental abuse you endured as a child. All of those issues in your life today – the hate and pain you still feel – are the result of unresolved childhood issues that need to be dealt with if you want your life to change in the future. This is a very important process and the subject of my next book, which helps one discover a way to resolve those issues. For this moment, however, our main goal is simply to understand these issues and how they affect our life. We cannot heal without understanding, so it is very important for you to first see and understand the patterns in your life before you can remove them.

Here is another common example of a scenario that haunts most people in their life. You have had the same job for most of your working life and you hate it, yet at the same time, you fear losing it. Why have you dragged yourself off to the same lousy job for all those years? Isn't that a contradiction? Can anyone relate to that situation? I have been in that situation myself, and it was awful!

I was an international business development manager in a high tech, telecoms industry. My job enabled me to travel all over the world, and I was really enjoying my life at one point. However, I remember one particular night, sitting on the beach outside my hotel in Dubai. I was hit with insomnia and couldn't stop thinking about life, about the sadness and emptiness I felt inside. I felt a deep emptiness within my solar plexus area, which manifested itself as hunger. I decided to go eat in the hotel restaurant and I kept eating and eating, yet my stomach still felt empty! Walking back to the beach, I still felt that same emptiness in my stomach. I then decided to meditate and to try to make sense out of these feelings. I realized that selling projects and equipment, or developing new business markets, was empty and had no real purpose in my life. I thought about many things – the lows, the highs – and it was all just an empty void. I believe many of you reading this can relate to this experience.

Memories of an vision I saw when I was 8 came back into my mind. I was seeing myself working in healing and helping other people. As I recalled those thoughts, I a smile crept over my face, a smile I was so keen to have! In that moment, I felt a surge of energy from the Universe come over me. It was as if I was being acknowledged and congratulated for recognizing the signals that had been there for some time, signals that were prompting me to change the course of my life. I knew then it was time for me to change my career. That was one of the most challenging times of my life, but I knew I had to do it because what was the point of living and doing a job to please everyone around me, continuing with obligations, while I remained terribly unhappy?

After my decision was made, I came back to Canada and knew it was time to let go of everything in my life, including many people who played prominent parts in my life.

Still today, many people, my family in particular, cannot believe I left a career that many people dream of, only to start again from scratch to do something that I enjoy. I realized quickly that I would never make my family understand what I was getting involved in, and dealt with that by distancing myself from everyone in my life who negated what I was doing. It is not that I did not have a relationship with my family, but I cut the emotional element of the relationship and decided to take advice only from people who are truly happy and living their life to the fullest potential they are capable of. I constantly reminded myself that life is short and, when I observed many older people around me who were always complaining and never happy with anything in their life, it made my decision easier.

Always keep in mind that you always come first in your life, not second. If you are looking to change and improve your life, then ask yourself what the point is in having people around you who don't want to support your change. Those people can easily become a distraction, and will always plant the seed of doubt in your mind that can easily sway you from your path and prevent you from fulfilling your true Blueprint Destiny in this life. Have you ever wondered why it always seems to be you who has to change and adapt your life to suit everyone else, yet no one else seems to bother about changing themselves to support your progress? The answer to that question is simple. The reason not many people are willing to support your change is simple; it is because your progress makes others realize that they themselves are falling behind in life. When they see you moving forward, and they begin to feel inadequate because they are not doing what they are supposed to be doing in their life.

Recognizing and charting how to progress in life is really simple. Life is like a university; Can you graduate from university if you have not completed your first year? Of course you can't, and the same principle applies in our life's course. Since birth, we have been learning day-to-day, moment-to-moment, as we move through our own experiences. Your life is its own unique curriculum, unlike anyone else's, and when you understand the lessons, you will move forward into new experiences in your life. It's as simple as that.

Although life is based on learning how we deal with experience, amazing miracles can happen when we least expect them in order to help move us forward. However, never depend on a miracle to save you from dealing with your life's challenges, because it's the challenges that are also miracles in the end, miracles that will eventually move you forward in a new understanding and awareness of things. Miracles will happen more frequently when you really begin to understand your life. You will see doors opening up for you just when you needed them to and new opportunities arising that will give you the chance to move forward. Trust it because the universe will always support your growth. That is the purpose of your life here after all, and the more you pursue your Blueprint Destiny, the more opportunities you will have to move forward on your Blueprint Destiny.

It is important that you now deal with whatever it is that is holding you back. Please avoid dragging your problems and issues into your next '9-Year Cycle.' In the end, if you keep dragging your past into everything you do, you will stop and realize that so many years have passed yet you are still in the same situation. Isn't that a tragic waste of a lifetime? Compare that to being in a 4-year program in university, yet 8 years of study have passed and you have not graduated. Imagine how frustrating and disempowering it would be in that situation! Well, the same goes for the University of Life and although time will always pass, we can still remain in the same place when it comes to our progression and growth in life.

It is time to move forward now while we still have time on our side. So many of us are wasting our lives, dwelling on the same old issues that have left us miserable for 18, 27, 36 years or more. Doesn't that tell you something? If you are miserable, empty and unfulfilled, then what you are doing with your life is not working. If it has not worked until now, then I am afraid it never will. So why not give it up? If in one 9-Year Cycle, an area of your life – be it emotional, physical, mental or spiritual – does not change, do you really expect it to change in the next 9 years if you are still doing things the same way? Stop being naïve and wake up!

We expect relationships to be our saviors; then they become routine and we fall into the same trap over and over again by attracting the same sort of people and situations. Why is that? It happens when we have not understood our past relationships properly, and so keep repeating the same patterns. It is important to know that our experiences in relationships are a reflection of our childhood experiences with our parents, and similar circumstances in relationships will always arise until we learn to understand and deal with this period of our life.

Every year in the Blueprint '9-Year Cycle' will bring different types of experiences for you to address during a particular year. Also, the energy characteristic of a year will be an indicator of what you and other people go through as a result of your own individual year. A particular year in the cycle will always have an effect on you, as well as the people around you. Of course, the year of your cycle changes at the turn of your birthday, and the same goes for everyone around you.

As you learn to identify and understand the different years in your 9-Year Cycle, you will begin to see how your relationships can often become affected by a clash in your individual goals, or a difference in your outlook to things, all depending on the mix of energies you and your partner are working with at a particular point in your 9-Year Cycle.

It is very important for everyone to do a chart for themselves as an individual. If in a relationship, do a chart as a couple. The numerology chart will help each of you identify both your strengths and weaknesses in life, and understand yourselves better.

Many numerologists would argue that the year of the 9-Year Cycle changes on the New Year on January 1st, not on your birthday. They are right in the fact that the Universal Year changes at this time; however, it is too general to assume everyone shifts their energies at the same time, because every individual is at a different place on their own path. I do not believe we were meant to be robotic, or like clones on this plane because we are so unique in our evolution!

Progression, learning, evolution, enlightenment, learning to love, having compassion and understanding toward others, exploring our feelings, and developing our Soul consciousness are all part of our journey on this plane. We all are here to learn those things, yet our lessons are all very individual, and a numerologist or astrologer would have a difficult time trying to write different combinations of numbers of horoscopes to suit everyone and their uniqueness; this is why individual readings are important. Reading a horoscope prediction in a newspaper gives you a very limited impression because of their generality. And because astrologers are working with very limited space, they are unable to elaborate into specific details. This is why, when you read your regular horoscope, you may feel that it does not reflect what is happening in your life at all. It is not because the astrologer is wrong; it is simply because the information is so general and written in the attempt to suit everyone under a specific sign. I personally believe that information in these types of columns probably makes sense to about 10% or 20% of us.

Have you ever wondered why you were born on one day and not another? Your date of birth is significant when it comes to your evolution on this planet, which is why astrologers need your precise date, time and place of birth. It is required to determine your uniqueness in this vast consciousness, in order for the interpreter to be more precise and able to provide you with the best blueprint presented in your own chart.

I have provided you with my opinion and perspective of the importance of our individuality and will now leave it up to you to decide whether your Yearly Cycle begins in January or on your birthday. After some trial and error, you will eventually figure out which option is best for you. You be the judge here!

To Calculate Your Personal Year:

If your birthday falls between January 1 of last year and today, use this year in your calculation.

Example 1: Birthday = May 7, 1975. In order to establish the yearly cycle, you would put this year added to your day and month of birth in place of the year of your birth.

May is the 5th month.
$2010 + 5 + 7 = 15 = 1 + 5 = 6$

Example 2: Born Dec. 11, 1952. If you were born in December (and we are calculating this in November 2010), because we have not yet arrived at your month of birth (which falls in the same year), you would calculate using 2009:

Born: Dec. 11, 1952. In 2009, $2 + 0 + 0 + 9 + 1 + 2 + 11 = 16 = 7$. This would mean that in November 2009, you are finishing off your year 7, soon to enter into year 8 when your birthday arrives on December 11, 2010.

When January is upon us with the start of a new Universal Year's vibration, we will all feel a change in the air, bringing the start of a new phase. This change, or phase, will become stronger and have a greater effect on us and will fit better within our vibration which started on our date of birth. I have tested and observed the '9-Year

Cycle' a great deal because I feel that understanding it provides us of the most effective tools we can use to improve our life. It is also very simple to apply.

You are the Master of your own Blueprint Destiny and no one else can be a better judge of you and your life than your own self. The numerological explanations are always the same for each year of the cycle, and can be referred to for every '9-Year Cycle' you enter. So what is the blueprint '9-Year Cycle'? The only change is in the Universal Year so if it is 2007, 2007 = 2 + 0 + 0 + 7 = Universal 9 year. 2008 will be 2+ 0 + 0 + 8 = Universal 1 year.

The Blueprint Universal Year has an effect on the larger events that take place in our life, such as conflict between countries, wars and many other events that occur in our life are greatly influenced by the Universal Blueprint Year.

When you feel you are stuck in a rut, stagnating or experiencing lots of repeating patterns in your life, then consider analyzing your previous Blueprint '9-Year Cycle' and what went on during that time. You will find that it will help you greatly in determining where your problems lie. The Blueprint '9-Year Cycle' will bring us a deeper understanding and awareness of things, and marks our progress in life. Pay close attention to it and you will have more harmony in your life when it comes to your relationships, your work, your attitude towards life, and your finances.

So, if it wasn't already obvious, there are 9 years in a '9-Year Cycle,' and when we have completed one '9-Year Cycle,' then we enter into another. Only after we have learned from our experiences during a particular 9 years, then, and only then, can we move into new experiences. Otherwise we will remain stuck in the same types of situations over and over again until we get it. That's the cycle of life!

How to Calculate Your Blueprint '9-Year Cycle':

Write down your Blueprint Birthday.

The numerical equivalents for the months are as follows:

January is 1, February is 2, March is 3, April is 4, May is 5, June is 6, July is 7, August is 8, September is 9, October is 10=1, November is 11=2, December is 12=3.

Examples of calculations:

Example 1: If you were born on August 12, 1975, what would be your '9-Year Cycle' in 2010?

8/12/2009 = 8 + 1 + 2 + 2 + 0 + 0 + 9 = 22 = 2+ 2 = 4, so you are in your 4 Year in a Blueprint '9-Year Cycle,' and you will be in a 5 Year on your birthday in August.

Example 2: You were born December 14, 1959, so what is your Blueprint '9-Year Cycle' in 2010?

December 2010 is not yet here so you are still in 2009.

12/14/2009 = 1+ 2 + 1 + 4 + 2 + 0 + 0 + 9 = 19 = 1 + 9 = 1 + 0 = 1 but when your birthday arrives, you will be in 1 Year in a new Blueprint '9-Year Cycle' started in 2009.

Example 3: You were born November 26, 1975. In 2010, 11 + 2 + 6 + 2 + 0 + 0 + 9 = 30 / 3, so your Personal Year is 3. (We use 2009 in our calculation because we haven't yet reached November, 2010.)

Example 4: You were born June 18, 1964. In 2010, 6 + 1 + 8 + 2 + 0 + 0 + 9 = 26 / 8, so your Personal Year is 8. (We use 2009 in our calculation because we haven't yet reached June, 2010, so in June, you will start Year 9 of a '9-Year Cycle.')

B. Your Full Name as You Use It Today

Your name is a very important aspect of your vibration. It is the essence of who you are in your life. It is the second most important factor of your life and will determine many of your experiences today. Personally, I do believe that the more you tamper with your name by changing it and having too many nicknames, the more confused you will become in terms of who you are and the way others see you.

Many numerologists calculate the vibration of your name based on the name you were given at birth. From the perspective of healing and in terms of who you are and where you stand in life today, you may not be the person you were born to be; you are probably a totally different person! The moment you stop using your middle name, you are a different person, this is because you have changed your energy. Also, women who change their name after marriage will also change and have a different type of experience in their life.

Anytime we alter our name, we either lose or gain some vibrations, and those vibrations that are either lost or gained will determine the course of our life from then on and the way we start experiencing life as a result. How many of you are called a certain nickname when you are with your family? And how many of you call yourself by a totally different name when you leave them? People in this kind of situation are likely to feel that there are a few things in life that they are not quite understanding, or other things they do, yet their family does not see them in that way. This is part of what can be lost or gained on a personal level when you alter your name.

Usually when people play with their names frequently, they will experience some degree of changes when it comes to their life experiences. For example, women who change to their married name will more than likely encounter new experiences that they are not accustomed to, some things that are totally new to them in their life. All of this is a result of playing with your name and your vibration. The less you use different names in your life, the less upheaval you will have in your experiences from a healing perspective.

Sometimes a change in your name can improve your vibration and better your life. The key point for you to know is that you must be aware of the changes that are taking place in your name the moment you made the alteration. Only that way will you then be able to adjust yourself and be prepared for the changes that are on their way before they hit you hard without warning, leaving you feeling lost, confused and unsure of how to deal with the new events taking place in your life.

Consulting a numerologist can help you either avoid the experiences or help you prepare to deal with them, unless of course those experiences are something that you simply must go through as a part of your Soul's evolution. Either way, becoming aware of the changes before they occur can better help you to prepare for dealing with them when the time comes.

The way we name our children is often influenced by factors related to our culture, religion and other personal factors such as family tradition. The majority of the time, we will have an instinctive feeling about what name we should choose for our newborn baby. In many cases, we make our choice based on the name of the baby's grandfather or grandmother to try and please the other family members by keeping up with the tradition. What we end up with then is a newborn baby that has no karmic lessons in his life according to the name he was given at birth. Why is that? This is likely to happen as in most cases I have heard of where babies have inherited family names, they alter their name to a nickname, or use only perhaps their first and last names while disregarding the middle names they were given at birth. In such a case, new karma will begin to occur in their life because they have lost certain vibrations from dropping parts of their name, and now they need to learn how to deal with that loss which was never intended in the first place. Your original vibration from birth is still implanted in you but when that vibration become unused then it becomes part of our unconscious and the new experiences you encounter from dropping part of your name become unfamiliar and thing that you need to experience at that point.

For example:

I have a new baby who was recently born and we decided to call him Robbie Stewart-Ghabi. 'Robbie' is the Scottish nickname for 'Robert.' Robert is Robbie's grandfather's name from his mother's side.

Robert or Robbie adds up to the same number in either case, 33/6, so this is his development number. The energetic value of either name is exactly the same, as each letter in both names has the exact energetic match, without Robbie losing any vibration if we called him Robbie or Robert but not if we call him Bob. We have no middle name for him because I do not believe in middle names, as they are normally not used by people other than on legal documents which will not really affect his daily life. We chose two last names for Robbie, his mother's and my last name hyphenated as 'Stewart-Ghabi.' That way there won't be any energetic changes in his name.

My wife and I did not try to sit down and figure out a name with zero karma to try to make his life easier. Karma is a field of learning that can spice up his life. We agreed on the name first, and then I did the calculation for it. So in his name, he has two blueprint modified karmas to deal with – 3 and 4. Those numbers are the same numbers both myself and my wife are dealing in our life today. Hopefully we can share our findings on dealing with those vibrations with him in the future.

You see, there really are no coincidences! Now if Robbie decides one day to remove one piece of his last name, for example his mother's name 'Stewart,' he won't lose any vibrations. However, if he takes out my last name, then he needs to deal with the vibrations involved in my name 'Ghabi,' which means he will have a 7 and 8 as additional new blueprint karmas for him to deal with, along the 3 and 4 missing vibrations he already has.

A name is very tricky thing to choose when looking at it from this perspective. We really ought to consider that the child will carry the name we choose for life, so try to choose a name guided by your intuition, or one that you perhaps just like for what it is. Do not choose your child's name just because you think is the best name according to tradition, culture, religion, or even Hollywood. It is time to stop playing with our new generation's vibrations by giving them so many names that they probably won't ever use. Also, please try to avoid the use of nicknames from the beginning. You chose a specific name for your child for a reason, so please make his life less confusing by sticking to it.

a. Blueprint Expression

At birth you were given a full name. Your full name is the key to the past experiences that you brought with you from the Universe into this physical plane. The Blueprint Expression is a person's natural talent. The essence of your expression is the vibrations that make up the grand whole of YOU. You can modify your expression the minute you change your name. I usually refer to the name that is used at the present moment in a chart as your expression, as this will describe you as you are today.

b. Your Blueprint Soul Urge

The Blueprint Soul Urge is a person's inner force. It is what you wish to be, to have and do. Your Soul Urge is what you really fancy most out of life. It represents your secret desires, convictions, aspirations, and endeavors. It is the way your Soul desires to express itself for absolute success. Meditation and yoga are excellent tools to help you to understand this vibration.

c. Your Blueprint Inner-Self

The Blueprint Inner-Self is, as I refer to it, the child within. It is hidden until we awaken that part of our individuality when it is required. Even though it may be called the Blueprint Inner-Self, this part of the personality often becomes an outer self, since it is used to accomplish goals. Your intuition and gifts are stored there. The Blueprint Inner-Self can be judged against by the Soul – what a person is in his or her heart. This judgment gives a more truthful assessment of what the person really is. Meditation and yoga are excellent tools to help you to understand this vibration.

d. Your Blueprint Maturity

The Blueprint Maturity number is measured as being one of the most important numerical vibrations in your life. This number will show you what your life is planned for. If you know the plan, and try to live up to its meaning, your life will be noteworthy, handy, and rewarding. This vibration will start to take effect in your life between 40 and 45 years old.

e. Your Blueprint Growth

The Blueprint Growth number illustrates the energy which will shed light on the essence of a person's experiences and help expand their growth. It is all about the development that a person is after in their life. This vibration will start to take effect in your life between 40 and 45 years old.

f. Your Blueprint Intensity Table

The Blueprint Intensity Table is an important chart in numerology. It can tell how you express yourself in life, retain your responsibilities, and apply your abilities because it explains why or how you react to each numbers vibration. The inclusion is a personality chart. It helps you to determine your broad characteristics, inclinations, what your abilities and powers are, what you work best at, and what will be predictable of you. It also tells you where your strengths and limitations are.

1. Blueprint Karmic Lessons:

A Blueprint Karmic Lesson is a representative of likely disadvantages and obstacles because its energy has either not been practiced in past lives, or it has been practiced in a negative way. Karmic lessons will present you with energies that have not been revealed in previous lifetimes. Presence of a karmic lesson indicates the presence of certain types of situations and the responsibility to use truthful energies to deal with these situations. It is important in very rare cases that we go back to view the past life in order to understand the situation. However, this is not always necessary because your task is to deal with karma as it presents itself in this lifetime. Many people use karma as an excuse to avoid dealing with their experiences. Karma can be solved in this lifetime without having to go back into our past lives.

2. Blueprint Modified Karmic Lessons:

When there is missing number in a name, and that number is one of the foundation vibrations of your chart, this will be called a karmic lesson. Both a karmic lesson and a modified karmic lesson indicate a significant damage of the foundation. However, the intensity of the lesson is somewhat lessened with the modified karmic lesson because the energy is still available in your foundation. Again, I would like to mention that a karmic lesson can be dealt with in this lifetime and there is no requirement to go to back to view past lives in order to fix the problem.

8. Blueprint of Your Family Vibration

Your family vibration tells a lot about you and your spiritual link with the closest people in your life which is your family. When many people share a family name, it represents a lesson you have all chosen to learn together. Understanding your family background will assist you in bringing harmony to these relationships, and also help you heal any wounds that have occurred as a result of experiences with your family. Knowledge of the family vibration will help you fulfill your karmic influence, either by enjoying being in your family, or by healing and closing the karma within the family vibrations.

h. Blueprint Temperament Behavior

There are four planes of awareness by which you disclose your personality, individuality, and general character. They are four elements: Blueprint Mental, Blueprint Physical, Blueprint Emotional, and Blueprint Intuitive.

The degree of constancy between them will point out not only what type of individual you really are, but also in which field of activity or expression you will do your best work. The plane to which you bear the most experience and knowledge is your greatest gain in the matter of vocation.

The planes of Temperament show the Spirit or character of an individual, the way we express ourselves, how we will handle responsibility, and how we will represent our nature and skills. In other words, the planes give the true state of mind of an individual:

1. Blueprint Mental Element indicates your mind, thought, or logical power. The mental perspective is troubled with intellectual, commercial and political affairs.
2. Blueprint Physical Element represents your body or material objects which have form and function according to common sense. The physical perspective is troubled with tangible and practical matters.
3. Blueprint Emotional Element is governed by your emotions or feelings. You are more heart than mind. The emotional perspective is troubled with inner feelings, thoughts and inspiration.

4. Blueprint Intuitive Element signifies that you are more on the spiritual level of thinking than on the practical or physical plane. Your actions are supported by appreciation and wisdom rather than rigid facts. The intuitive perspective is troubled with spiritual, religious and metaphysical matters.

i. Blueprint Subconscious

Blueprint Subconscious is calculated from your Intensity Table, in which it is possible to have all nine numbers represented in your name, or fewer than nine; in fact, as few as three or as many as eight. For example, you may be missing a 2 or an 8. This means that when you encounter a situation that requires the characteristics of a 2 or an 8, there will be some feeling of being naive, or insecure as to how to properly deal with the demands of your financial situation.

On the other hand, you still have the other numbers represented in your name, which means your ability to deal with situations that entail any of those numbers is well-developed. You possess a certain degree of self-confidence and assertion that makes you feel familiar with the situation, and able to deal it with effectively. Hence, a person with eight numbers represented in the name will tend to be more confident in many circumstances than a person with only six numbers.

Blueprint Subconscious reflects the confidence you have in your personal authority and capability, as well as in your ability to deal with unexpected events and situations. It shows your competence to correctly weigh up a situation and to take action appropriately. Blueprint Subconscious also reveals the areas of our personality that need to be strengthened.

Section IV

Meaning of Numbers and Interpretation of a Blueprint Chart

1. General Meaning of Numbers

One number does not determine who you really are. You are a mix of many different qualities, where each number or vibration is portrayed in a mix of uniqueness to you, and only you can understand and sense the meaning of it. You are a master of your own universe; you can take your Blueprint Destiny the direction you chose to. It is all up to you to look at all the events in your life. Our number vibrations have a lot of connotations but it is your choice to do with them what you ought in order to direct your life. In life we have a choice and we usually make many choices on a daily basis. We just need to start looking at ourselves more closely. We need to watch our thoughts. We need to be responsible for every decision we make in our life. Life is fair but we are taking it too much for granted, as events should manifest in our life without us doing anything.

That might happen in some rare cases but it is not a general phenomena manifesting to every one of us. Your Soul planned many events, experiences and life challenges in your life. No number is better than any other number. Each number has its unique vibration, much like musical instruments. Each one is its unique vibration, and has both negative and positive qualities. Most of the time in our life, we evolve by understanding our negative qualities and turn them into positive qualities. Each vibration you have has many qualities, and those qualities, when they are in negative form, do not mean you should be in every single one of them. However, believe me that one negative quality can complicate your life when you are not aware of it. For the sake of our understanding, be honest with yourself and be your own judge once you spot one negative quality in you when it comes to a single number. We are here to learn and understand our being here and the reasons we are here in the first place.

Number vibrations are from 1 to 9 as the basic numbers and 11, 22 and 33 as the master number vibrations. If you have lots of '1 to 9' vibration in you, you have normal human experiences and lessons to learn. There is no number better or worse than another. It is all about your experiences, challenges and lessons you need to do. If you are a Master number, do not let that fact go to your head. A Master number is a special person but, at the same time, is not special. They have more responsibility in this lifetime and in many cases, they have harder life experiences than others, especially if that Master number is an Old Soul, too. People with a Master number are those who are here to do something in their life and help advance the awareness and understanding of humanity, and to help to make a difference in humanity. Master number people are the same human beings as any other human beings, and they have a negative and a positive side of them.

You can have one or more numbers that have some negative aspect in them that make you dwell upon some pity events in your life. Do not think your life is over when you see a few negative aspects in your life or even a few missing numbers in your name. In some cases, there is a flow in our vibration that one number will help often offset the other number vibration, or even help in attaining the other vibration.

a. The Meaning Behind Number 'Zero' (0)

A 'zero' in your numbers shows a lot of inner gifts that you need to discover in this lifetime. Those gifts can change your life and put you on your path that you were always looking for. Without discovering those gifts, your life will always stay as it is, and you will always feel there is something missing. Your life can be sometimes boring and stagnant. You feel your life is empty. The answer is for you to get to know your essence and where your Soul is coming from. Many of these gifts are packaged in many of the tools your Soul provided you before you came into this lifetime. Normally people are afraid to find out about themselves for fear of discovering things about themselves that contradict the reality they believe they are. It is a denial of their true reality. Some inherit the problem from their culture or religion. If you have a zero, you need to learn to meditate, use yoga and start to get in touch with yourself. People with '0' as well '7' are very good at creating the excuse, "I tried to meditate one day but I was not able to concentrate, so I gave up. My mind kept taking me left and right. At least I tried." Wow! Nice excuse here. Do you have a degree in engineering the first day you go school or do you have to hit the books for 4 years until you graduate. Right! So what is the difference here with meditation?

People with 'zero' in their numbers are pure and can reach the truth of which they are, the Source, their Soul. They also have lots of love to offer to others. They possess gifts beyond their human imaginations but fear can have a big effect on their lives unless they deal with it. They need to learn to expand their consciousness beyond their imagination and reach for the stars.

The healing aspect of your life where you might get stuck is in your life. You still have to deal with it. It won't go away. But at the same time, the moment you start deleting your old garbage, then you start filling up with your essence, with the new reality of who you are. You will never know until you seriously try it and then you will be your own judge.

Number 0 General meaning

The Critical 0:

Confused about potentials; confused from internal feelings; denial; hypersensitive; nervous; sarcastic.

The Negative 0:

Afraid of your own gifts; afraid of the unknown; confusion; fearful; limited.

The Positive O:

Boundless; channel for pure energy; inner gifts; inner wisdom; insightfulness; make a decision; making a choice; six-sensed; step into the unknown; take action.

b. The Meaning behind Number 'One' (1)

'Number One' vibration means: You are a born leader. A leader needs his or her following to follow. It is big part of the essence that you are on this plane at this point and time in your evolutionary progression. You are the leader that everyone turns to. You are an individualist, independent and determined. Usually you can reach your goal. You have all the ideas but you should keep your plans to yourself, for you work best alone and quietly. You should cut loose from all family ties, and strike out as a pioneer in a new field. You have the courage and knowledge to explore the unknown. You have executive abilities that best suit you as the head of a business. You learn by experience more than any other number. You dislike being told what to do about anything in your life. You are the one who always cheers your parents up. You are proud, resent criticism, and often display your temper, or have emotional upsets. You are type who thinks you are always right. You always want your own way. Number One possesses energy, enthusiasm, creativity, originality, generosity, determination, courage, and independence. Others turn to people who are 'Number One' for support and guidance, expecting solutions to be provided by the power of creativity of the 'One'.

We all enjoy a positive and a negative side in life. Your negative can vary with you whenever you live that side in your life.

Self-confidence is your major lesson for you to understand, to learn and to build. If you are negatively inclined, you should guard against being lazy, cynical, or even a dreamer, for these traits lead to procrastination and insecurity. It is necessary for people who are ' Number One' to avoid the negatives of being egotistical and dictatorial, arrogance, aggressive and uncooperative, intolerant and judgmental. You may be self-centered, for most 'Number Ones' represent the "ME ... ME ... ME" principle. You are well able to stand on your own feet when you bring your SELF-confidence to the surface. You will encounter in your life lots of experiences that put you down to experience low esteem until new people who move into your life and bring you up to rebuild that self-confidence.

There is a beginning to every event. Therefore, within the 'Number One,' we have many qualities that embrace leadership and courage in you. You strive to stay positive and above your potential to bring your supporters to better understanding and to keep your vibration up with your high energy level.

Individuality: Leader, original, independent, courageous achiever, entrepreneur, strength, and creative

Vocation: You can succeed at being a writer, public personality, entrepreneur, director, inventor, president, designer, pioneer, teacher, engineer, salesman, and leader.

Number 1 General Meaning

The Critical 1:

Aggressive; arbitrary; arrogant; authoritarian; boastful; bossy; chauvinist; conceited; conflicting; constraining; contrary; defiant; demanding; dictatorial; dominating; egocentric; egotistic; grasping; greedy; haughty; headstrong; impatient; imperious; impulsive; insatiable; insolent; militant; obsessed; obstinate; opinionated; perverse; pompous; possessive; pretentious; prideful; rigid; self-centered; self-importance; self-indulgent; selfish; stubborn; unyielding; very proud; willful.

The Negative 1:

Changeable; compliant; cowardly; defeatist; defenseless; dependent; fearful; helpless; impotent; indifferent; indolent; insecure; lack of application; lack of energy; lack of initiative; lack of self-respect; lazy; lethargic; passive; powerless; procrastinator; reluctant; resigned; spiritless; submissive; subservient; vulnerable; weak.

The Positive 1:

Achieving; active; adventurous; ambitious; aspiring; assertive; assured; attaining; authoritarian; bold; commanding; compelling; confident; courageous; creative; determined; dynamic; energetic; enterprising; executive ability; forceful; forward looking; full of Spirit; independent; individualistic; influential; initiative; intrepid; inventive; leader; organizer; original; preserving; persistent; powerful; progressive; resolute; secure; self-sufficient; self-reliant; venturesome; vigorous.

c. The Meaning behind Number 'Two' (2)

'Two' vibration means you are dual in nature. You can usually see both sides of any situation. You serve as a balance between opposing ends and would qualify as good arbitrator or peacemaker. Number Two prefers to follow rather than lead, possessing the qualities of versatility, communication, wisdom, sociability, tact, diplomacy, and intuition. Others turn to people who are 'Two' for friendship, sensitivity, and fun. You are timid, sensitive, and often lack self-confidence and can become too sensitive to criticism. You are always sitting in the back seat. You are emotional in nature, and often turn to music. You have a deep sense of rhythm and harmony. You work better with a partner than in an individual capacity. 'Two' is the feminine principle of receptivity. You are cooperative and patient. You could be found carrying a flag of truce.

It is necessary for people who are 'Two' to avoid the negatives of being insecure, oversensitive, gullible, uncooperative, and troublesome. An abundance of 'Two' in a personal numerology chart might indicate some confusion about sexuality.

The vibration of the Number Two is that of 'light bearer.' It has a core intention of PEACEMAKING, creating friendship wherever it goes.

Individuality: diplomat, friend, artist, kindness, cooperation, peacemaker, gentle, insightful, and sensitive.

Vocation: You can succeed as being an artist, technician, psychologist, spouse, healer, bookkeeper, coordinator, statistician, librarian, accountant, peacemaker, painter, politician, clerk and diplomat.

Number 2 General Meaning

(If you have an 11 Vibration / Number also read after reducing 11 to its foundation base of the Number 2)

The Critical 2:

Condescending; cool; devious; disapproving fault-finding; gossipy; inhospitable; interfering; intriguing; meddling; over sensitive; reproachful; scheming; shy; stand-offish; timid; non-supportive.

The Negative 2:

Apathetic; careless; cowardly; discourteous; faint-hearted; fearful; ill mannered; inactive; inconsiderate; indecisive; indifferent; insensitive; lukewarm; negligent; rude; self-depreciating; sluggish; spiritless; stagnant; tactless; uncaring; uncertain; unconcerned; unmoved; unresponsive; vacillating; weak-willed.

The Positive 2:

Adaptable; agreeable; amiable; background contributor; benevolent; cautious; compliant; considerate; cooperative; courteous; devoted; diplomatic; emotional; feeling; flexible; friendly; genial; gentle; gracious; harmonizing; helpful; hospitable; humble; kindly; loving; loyal; modest; patient; prudent; receptive; responsive; sensitivity to music, rhythm; sensitivity to people; sincere; soft-hearted; supportive; tactful; tender; tolerant; trustworthy; understanding; unpretentious.

d. The Meaning behind Number 'Three' (3)

'Three' vibration means you take life as it comes, love, pleasure, and are essentially youthful. You have the talent for expressing yourself well in speaking, writing, or acting. You are gifted in being creative, but you are not noted for being practical. You dream big ventures, for you think on a large scale, but you always want to inject beauty into every situation. Having a quick and keen mind, you learn easily. You can do almost anything you decide you want to accomplish. You have a super-imagination which means you could succeed in the entertainment field. This can lead to many opportunities and financial success. Number Three possesses the qualities of creativity, optimism, adaptability, enthusiasm, and generosity. Others turn to people who are 'Three' for inspiration, fun, and happiness. You have many talents but you need to be careful in scattering your energies everywhere.

It is necessary for people who are 'Three' to avoid the negatives of being impractical, superficial, worrying, and cheating. 'Three' can be a flirt, without malicious intent, actually without even thinking. You must guard against being too talkative, which can strain situations and even result in loss of friends. You rarely worry or are depressed. You enjoy your social life. Expression is your keynote.

'Three' begins to express a great creativity. Behold the joy of living with expression in its many forms.

Individuality: Inspirational, artist, creative, social, easygoing, visionary, humorous, energetic, and spontaneous

Vocation: speaker, entertainer, beautician, comedian, motivator, coach, writer, musician, artist, parent, salesperson, communicator/all media, actor, and lawyer.

Number 3 General Meaning

The Critical 3:

Biased; blatant; boastful; cocky; condescending; dabbling; exaggerating; extravagant; gossipy; immodest; irresponsible; lacks concentration; lacks direction; long-winded; narcissistic; opinionated; ostentatious; over-enthusiastic; patronizing; pompous; prejudiced; pretentious; prideful; quarrelsome; scatters energies;

shallow; silly; snobbish; stuck-up; superficial; temperamental; vain; wasteful.

The Negative 3:

Anxious; apprehensive; bored; callous; cheerless; complaining; critical; curt; defeatist; dejected; depressed; disapproving; disgruntled; downcast; envious; evasive; fretful; fussy; gloomy; grouchy; grumpy; hesitating; indiscreet; insensitive; intolerant; jealous; moody; pessimistic; petty; reserved; self-indulgent; selfish; shy; spiteful; sulky; tactless; temperamental; timid; touchy; unforgiving; unfeeling; unfriendly; unkind; unresponsive; unsympathetic; vacillating; whining; withdrawn; worrying.

The Positive 3:

Aesthetic; affable; amicable; amusing; animated; appreciated; appreciative; artistic; chatty; comical; compatible; considerate; creative; cultivated; discriminating; eager; emotional; enthusiastic; exhilarated; feeling; fertile mind; friendly; full of inspiration; good host, hostess; good taste; gracious; gregarious; happy; hearty; imaginative; instinctive; intuitive; joyous; kind; literate; lively; lovable; loving; merry; natural; optimistic; original; popular; responsive; self-expressive; social; sparkling; spirited; stylish; sympathetic; understanding; verbal; vivacious; welcoming; witty; youthful.

e. The Meaning Behind Number 'Four' (4)

'Four' vibration means: you are dependable, practical, and reliable. You are well-grounded. You share lots of common sense. You may not be a mental wizard, but you are a stable, solid citizen who is a hard worker and conservative both in your viewpoints and in dealing with finances. If you disagree with another's policy or actions, you can be as stubborn as a mule, refusing to budge. Number Four possesses the qualities of endurance, discipline, motivation, reliability, responsibility, and practicality. Others turn to people who are 'Four' for their loyalty, commitment and honesty. You are good at handling routine work. You are not the creative type, for you lack the necessary imagination.

It is necessary for people who are 'Four' to avoid the negatives of being impatient, dominant, and even violent.

With practicality and determination of 'Four,' we can create order and serve.

Individuality: Dedication, management, conservative, efficiency, organization, application, determination, serious builder, doer, manager, traditional.

Vocation: Contractor, farmer, scientist, employee (safety job), business owner, developer, lawyer, administrator, office worker, body worker, labourer, banker, accountant, politician, lawyer, and government employee.

Number 4 General Meaning

(If you have a 22 Expression, also read after reducing 22 to its foundation base of the Number 4).

The Critical 4:

Argumentative; bigoted; blunt; cantankerous; contradictory; crude; dogmatic; dull; headstrong; humorless; ill-mannered; immovable; intolerant; insensitive; limited; lost in detail; narrow-minded; obstinate; obstructive; opinionated; pedantic; perverse; pig-headed; repressive; resistant; rigid; rude; slow; sluggish; stubborn; tenacious; thick-skinned; uncompromising; uncouth; unimaginative; vulgar.

The Negative 4:

Apathetic; careless; detached; disorganized; impractical; indifferent; lacking authority; lax; lazy; lethargic; negligent; plodding; servile; slavish; submissive; tired; unaccountable; non-adaptable; uncertain; uncommitted; unemployable; unfocused; unproductive; weak-kneed; weak-willed.

The Positive 4:

Accurate; attentive; balanced; businesslike; careful; cautious; competent; composed; confident; conscientious; conservative; consistent; constructive; controlled; conventional; cool-headed; dedicated; deliberate; dependable; determined; devoted; dignified; direct; disciplinarian; disciplined; dutiful; earnest; economical; efficient; endurance; exacting; experienced; faithful; factual; firm; incorruptible; industrious; integrity; law-abiding; loyal; manager; methodical; meticulous; moderate; obedient; orderly; patient; persevering; precise; prepared; productive; prudent; reliable; responsible; serious; sensible; stable; steady; straightforward; systematic; thorough; thrifty; trustworthy; well-behaved.

f. The Meaning Behind Number 'Five' (5)

'Five' vibration means: you desire freedom and expansion in all things. You are versatile and changeable. Experience is your keynote. You learn by promoting new ideas, for which you have a great curiosity. Your process will consist of moving forward and onward, having the courage to let go of the old, and being willing to attempt the untried. You often are impulsive, restless and quick to act. You love adventure, and will even tread in quicksand, for you do things on the spur of the moment without thinking things out. Vibration 'Five' possesses the qualities of enthusiasm, clarity of thought, sensitivity, versatility, passion, and friendship. Others are drawn to people who are 'Five' for their vitality, liveliness, and interesting conversation. You like the company of the opposite sex. You have a serious side to your nature. You are willing to try anything new. This courage can develop into something advantageous for the general good of the public.

It is necessary for people who are 'Five' to avoid the negatives of being indecisive, unfocused, and being a 'jack of all trades, master of none'. 'Five's' should also avoid making commitments, while also being 'over-active.'

With the energy behind the Number Five, we promote new ideas and undertakings.

Individuality: Accomplishment, flexibility, expansion, freedom, activity, influences, adventurer, sensualist, promoter, and flair.

Vocation: Salesman, public figure, detective, traveler, explorer, insurance, psychologist, investigator, developer, speculator, designer, news person, performer, and agent.

Number 5 General Meaning

The Critical 5:

Audacious; bizarre; careless; contrary; disobedient; dissatisfied; drinker; eccentric; excitable; forgetful; frenzied; frivolous; gluttonous; hysterical; ill-advised; impatient; impulsive; inconsistent; incontinent; insatiable; irresponsible; loose; negligent; nervous; outlandish; overactive; over-indulgent; over-sexed; peculiar; reckless; regretful; restless; scandalizing; self-indulgent; shallow; skittish; spendthrift; superficial; thoughtless; thrill-seeking; unaccountable; uncontrollable; unconventional; unexpected; unpredictable; unprepared; unreliable; unrestrained; unstable; unusual; wasteful; wayward; wild.

The Negative 5:

Apathetic; behind the times; boring; cautious; colorless; doubtful; dubious; dull; fear of freedom; fear of new; fear of risks; hesitant; inactive; old-fashioned; out of date; passionless; purposeless; stagnant; static; non-adaptable; uncertain; undecided; undemonstrative; unresponsive; unsure; vague.

The Positive 5:

Active; adaptable; adventurous; agreeable; alert; broad-minded; changeable; charming; clever; convivial; creative; curious; daring; delightful; demonstrative; dynamic; eager; energetic; entertaining; enthusiastic; exciting; flair; footloose; free; friendly; fun-loving; gifted; gracious; gregarious; go-getting; imaginative; independent; individual; informal; inquisitive; intuitive; inventive; lively; many-sided; natural; non-conformist; opportunist; original; plain-spoken;

progressive; promoter; questioning; quick; resourceful; sales ability; skilful; sociable; spontaneous; talented; unique; unprejudiced; up-to-date; versatile; venturesome; vigorous; warm; willing; witty.

8. The Meaning Behind Number 'Six' (6)

'Six' vibration means: you crave love, friends, and companionship. You are devoted to your family to the extent that you often smother them with love and protection. Serving in the community gives you great pleasure. You do not like to be alone and prefer to be in a crowd. While you strive for peace and harmony, you do enjoy a stiff argument as long as no one remains angry when the debate is resolved. You like to see a home run smoothly and orderly. You also like beautiful things and surroundings. Being cautious in money matters, you will invest only in what appears to be foolproof. Most people like you, for you are kind and tolerant. At times, you can become stubborn and argumentative if anyone disagrees with you. You are prone to worry, often needlessly. You also delight in decorating your home artistically. While you strive to please others, you require praise, and you need encouragement. Number Six possesses the qualities of benevolence, compassion, creativity, patience, and harmony. Others turn to people who are 'Six' for wisdom and understanding, and are attracted by the 'grace' of the 'Six'. The 'Six' seeks meaningful relationships, is home-loving, and is always concerned about others.

It is necessary for people who are 'Six' to avoid the negatives of being impractical, excessively idealistic, argumentative, and jealous. 'Six' can be arrogant, bigoted, conceited and seek vengeance.

Without others to love, serve, and cherish all is without purpose. Therefore, the 'Six' vibration brings with it the responsibility to restore humanity and remind all of us of the treasures within life.

Individuality: Beauty, universal love, passion, harmony, trust, morality, domestic, responsible, teacher, conventional, provider, healer and creativity.

Vocation: Doctor, nurse, parent, educator, caterer/ restaurant work, decorator, teacher, cook, healer, civil worker, nurse, body worker/health consultant, traditional professional, counsellor, coach and homemaker.

Number 6 General Meaning

The Critical 6:

Anxious; apprehensive; argumentative; bitter; complaining; conventional; critical; defeated; despairing; discontent; discouraged; disheartened; dismayed; dissatisfied; envious; faint-hearted; fault-finding; fearful; hindering; inferior; jittery; loser; martyr-complex; meddlesome; melancholy; negative; obstructing; over-emotional; over-involvement; over-responsible; over-sensate; overwhelmed; panicky; pessimistic; possessive; regretful; resentful; sacrificing; slavish; smothering; suspicious; troubled; uneasy; unforgiving; unhappy; upset; victimized; weak; worried.

The Negative 6:

Biased; cool; cranky; cynical; dishonest; disillusioned; disinterested; disloyal; greedy; harsh; hostile; impersonal; ill-natured; inattentive; insensitive; insipid; intolerant; irresponsible; lax; listless; loveless; lukewarm; nasty; negligent; non-committal; opinionated; petty; prejudiced; selfish; self-seeking; sullen; tactless; unaccountable; uncaring; uncooperative; unfeeling; unforgiving; unfriendly; unimaginative; uninvolved; unorganized; unreasoning; unreliable; unsympathetic.

The Positive 6:

Accommodating; admiring; advising; affectionate; amiable; appreciative; approving; ardent; artistic; balancing; benevolent; careful; charitable; compassionate; complimentary; conscientious; concerned with home, family and children; considerate; constant; content; creative; demonstrative; dependable; devoted; domestic; dutiful; emotional; ethical; faithful; feeling; friendly; generous; genial; happy; healing; helpful; honorable; humanitarian; idealistic; imaginative; indulgent; kind; likable; lovable; loving; loyal; moral;

obliging; passionate; patient; peace-making; philanthropic; protective; romantic; resourceful; responsible; sacrificing; satisfied; sentimental; serving; sharing; sincere; soft-hearted; steady; supportive; sympathetic; tasteful; teaching; tolerant; trustworthy; tranquil; uncomplaining; understanding; unselfish; virtuous; well-intentioned; balance, wise.

h. The Meaning Behind Number 'Seven' (7)

'Seven' vibration means: you are a deep thinker. You will absorb knowledge from practically every source. Being intellectual, scientific, and studious, you never accept a premise unless you have analyzed the situation thoroughly, and reached your own conclusion. You dislike suggestions from others, mainly because you think you are the authority on any subject. You resent injustice, but you should never attempt to get even, for it will act as a boomerang and will hurt you more than the person you are trying to injure. You dislike manual labor. You enjoy working alone. You are domestic or practical. You are spiritually and philosophically inclined. While you may be religious, you often lean towards metaphysics. You want quiet to meditate and live your inner life. You must learn to live alone and not be lonely. You will usually avoid crowds. Number Seven possesses the qualities of sensitivity, perception, introspection, spirituality, modesty, analysis, truth, and wisdom. Others turn to people who are 'Seven' for advice and support of a spiritual and loving kind. 'Seven' is the number of unconditional love. You believe that seeking knowledge is second only to acquiring understanding and wisdom. Your keynote is perfection, not popularity. You may appear to be cold and aloof, but this is because you are satisfied with your full inner life. You are an idealist rather than a down to earth individual.

It is necessary for people who are 'Seven' to avoid the negatives of being introverted, overly modest, arrogant, or developing an inferiority complex. Failure to achieve spiritual enlightenment can lead to excesses of a physical kind for 'Seven.'

The quest for wisdom and knowledge begins.

Individuality: Vision, solitude, gifted, calculating, Intuition, specialist, inventor, loner, eccentric, thoughtful, spiritual and analyst.

Vocation: Scientist, consultant, professor, religious leader, actor, lawyer, inventor, teacher, occultist, psychic, medium, horticulturist, priest, monk, analyst, earth/maritime occupations, individualist, and observer.

Number 7 General Meaning

The Critical 7:

Aloof; anxious; apprehensive; bigoted; caustic; contrary; controlling; cool; crank; cunning; cynical; deceitful; despairing; detached; devious; distant; distrustful; dogmatic; eccentric; evasive; extreme wavelength; extremist; fanatic; fault-finding; fearful; fussy; guarded; hesitant; humorless; hypercritical; impatient; impersonal; impractical; indecisive; indifferent; inferiority complex; inflexible; insecure; insensitive; intimidated; jealous; joyless; melancholy; nervous; non-committal; obsessed; obstructive; odd; opinionated; out of touch; over-analytical; pedantic; perfectionist; pessimistic; powerless; prudish; repressed; reserved; sarcastic; self-conscious; selfish; shy; spineless; stubborn; suppress feelings; suspicious; tactless; thick-skinned; timid; non-adaptable; uncomplimentary; undemonstrative; unrealistic; wary; weak; withdrawn; worried.

The Negative 7:

Amateurish; awkward; backward; dense; dull; empty-headed; foolish; forgetful; incompetent; inexperienced; ignorant; illiterate; immature; lack of depth; lack of faith; lack of poise; muddle-headed; mystified; naïve; overlooked; short-sighted; silly; simple; slow; superficial; uncertain; undeveloped; unenlightened; unqualified; vague.

The Positive 7:

Accurate; analytical; astute; attentive; authoritative; bookish; broad-minded; calm; capable; clairaudient; clairvoyant; competent; conscientious; contemplative; creative; deep; deliberate; dependable; different wavelength; discriminating; dreamer; efficient; exact; enlightened; expert; faithful; fertile mind; gifted; idealistic; individualistic; influential; ingenious; inquisitive; inspired; instinctive; intellectual; introspective; intuitive; inventive; investigator; logical; learned; mature; metaphysical interests; mystical; observant; occult interests; original; patient; peaceful; penetrating thinker; philosophical; poised; probing; psychic; pure; rational; reasoning; reflective; religious; researcher; resourceful; respectable; responsible; scientific; searching; skilful; spiritual; studious; technical; telepathic; theoretical; truth-seeker; unworldly; visionary; well-read; wise.

i. The Meaning Behind Number 'Eight' (8)

'Eight' vibration means you should never rely on luck, for you must work hard to earn what you get. Justice should be your keynote. You may seem to be restricted. This need not be true if you have learned to discipline yourself. You can have outstanding success by moving cautiously and conservatively, relying on your own judgment. You are a mental person and should be well balanced. You can earn a place of authority. Number Eight possesses the qualities of ambition, intelligence, confidence, and determination. Others turn to people who are 'Eight' for their analytical abilities. 'Eight' is a business vibration. You are balanced and organized. You are more interested in financial success than in spiritual enlightenment. You could succeed in business in a broad field, such as being the president or manager of a large company.

It is necessary for people who are 'Eight' to avoid the negatives of pride, obstinacy, materialism, being immoral, ruthless and unforgiving.

A typical eight may say, "Now that I have discovered heaven, how do I bring it to earth? There is power behind any manifestation and I want to do what it takes to attain what I want." The 'Eight' becomes very busy managing and supervising with its sense of judgment. Behind the vibration of the Number Eight is:

Individuality: Recognition, talented, executive, professional, strength, money problem solver, skilful, efficient, organizer, achiever, judgment, authority, capable, and power.

Vocation: president, editor, publisher, actor, expert, government work, business owner, publisher, contractor, engineer, executive banker, financial analyst, judge and industrialist.

Number 8 General Meaning

The Critical 8:

Abuses power; abusive; aggressive; awkward; bad taste; biased; bigoted; blunt; bullying; cantankerous; chauvinistic; clumsy; cold-blooded; contemptible; contrary; cool; crude; demanding; dishonest; egotistical; fanatic; fraudulent; gross; hard; hot-headed; ill-mannered; impatient; inconsiderate; indecent; inflexible; insensitive; lacking trust; lawless; militant; narrow-minded; negligent; one-track mind; opinionated; over-ambitious; pedantic; possessive; prejudiced; quarrelsome; rebellious; restrictive; rigid; selfish; self-indulgent; shameless; sneaky; stiff; strait-laced; stubborn; tactless; tense; thoughtless; threatening; uncaring; uncooperative; undignified; unprincipled; unreliable; vulgar.

The Negative 8:

Careless; cheating; circumscribed; controlling, cowardly; defenseless; dishonest; disorderly; fearful; fear of failure; feeble; inept; illogical; immature; impractical; inattentive; incoherent; indifferent; insecure; lack of confidence; lack of perspective in material matters; lazy; limited; misdirected; narrow; nervous; non-observant; oblivious; poor judgment; procrastinating; restricted; shameless; short-sighted; slovenly; timid; uncaring; undisciplined;

uninterested; unorganized; unprepared; unrealistic; unreliable; vulnerable; weak.

The Positive 8:

Administrator; ambitious; appreciative; assertive; assured; authoritative; businesslike; candid; capable; clear-headed; clever; commanding; compelling; competent; confident; conscientious; consistent; courageous; dedicated; definite; dignified; direct; director; disciplined; discriminating; dynamic; earnest; effective; efficient; energetic; enterprising; enthusiastic; executive ability; far-sighted; financial awareness; forceful; good judgment; high-powered; honest; honorable; industrious; influential; initiating; integrity; leadership; loyal; manager; material freedom; money maker; opportunist; organizer; persuasive; persevering; planner; positive; practical; principled; pragmatic; progressive; prudent; realistic; reliable; resourceful; respected; responsible; self-confident; self-reliant; serious; shrewd; skilful; spirited; stamina; status; strong; successful; supervising; supportive; systematic; upright; vigorous.

j. The Meaning behind Number 'Nine' (9)

'Nine' vibration means you are governed by the symbol of love, representing the highest form of both universal love and love of your neighbor. You crave personal love, but this should not be your aim, for it may prove to be disappointing. You are the big brother or sister of humanity. Being selfless, you will give, even unwisely, when your emotions are aroused. You are compassionate, broad-minded, and idealistic, and can easily sense the difficulties and needs of others to such an extent that you will suffer greatly if another is mistreated or in want. If your name has many nines, you are equipped to cope with all conditions and circumstances on this earth. Number Nine possesses the qualities of creativity, self-control, harmony, wisdom, humanitarianism and duty. Others turn to people who are 'Nine' for their inspiration and relaxed, carefree nature. You have to learn to live impersonally otherwise you experience much heartache.

It is necessary for people who are 'Nine' to avoid the negatives of being selfish, aggressive, destructive, and arrogant. 'Nine' can also present itself as being a 'martyr to the cause.'

'Nine' holds the vibration of universal love. It teaches us how to accept each other.

Individuality: Creativity, compassion, generosity, emotional, generalist, multi-talented, teacher, healer, artist, old-Soul, actor, humanitarian, devotion, philanthropy, and intuition.

Vocation: Doctor, nurse, minister, occultist, humanitarian, health/body worker, counsellor, artist/craftsperson, community work, painter, writer, and world/community leader.

Number 9 General Meaning

The Critical 9:

Biased; bitter; changeable; chauvinist; confusing; cowardly; crank; cross; deceiving; defeatist; dejected; demanding; depressed; disapproving; disloyal; dissatisfied; dogmatic; doubtful; downcast; dreamer; egotistical; elusive; faint-hearted; fearful; fickle; forbidding; foolish; gloomy; grasping; greedy; grouchy; humorless; impractical; indecisive; ineffective; inexperienced; insecure; intolerant; irresponsible; jealous; joyless; meek; moody; naïve; narrow-minded; over-emotional; pedantic; petty; pessimistic; quarrelsome; resentful; selfish; shy; submissive; sullen; superficial; tactless; temperamental; uncertain; unfaithful; unpleasant; unsmiling; unstable; unsympathetic; vacillating; vague; victimized; wavering; weak-kneed.

The Negative 9:

Aloof; apathetic; biased; detached; discouraged; disloyal; distant; half-hearted; harsh; headstrong; ill-disposed; impassive; impersonal; indifferent; inflexible; intolerant; lack of compassion; limited; listless; narrow; obstinate; oppressive; passionless; repressed; restricted; strait-laced; stubborn; tactless; thick-skinned;

unbending; uncaring; unconcerned; unemotional; unenthusiastic; unfeeling; unforgiving; unkind; unresponsive; unsympathetic; unyielding; vindictive; willful.

The Positive 9:

Affectionate; agreeable; artistic; benevolent; broad-minded; capable; charitable; chivalrous; compassionate; compatible; compliant; considerate; cooperative; creative; decent; dedicated; demonstrative; devoted; discriminating; emotional; enlightened; enthusiastic; fair-minded;; faithful; feeling; forgiving; friendly; generous; genial; gracious; helpful; high-minded; humane; humble; idealistic; impassioned; impressionable; indulgent; inspired; intense; intuitive; kindly; liberal; loving; loyal; merciful; missionary; modest; passionate; philanthropic; reasonable; reliable; responsible; selfless; self-sacrificing; sensitive; sentimental; soft-hearted; sympathetic; tactful; tender; tolerant; trustworthy; unprejudiced; understanding; warm; well-intentioned; willing.

k. The Meaning Behind Number 'Eleven' (11)

'Eleven' vibration means you are an idealist, a dreamer, and sometimes a mystic. Having much vision, you should be an inspiration to others. You can open doors and help others to greater achievements. Being psychic, you should follow your hunches. You belong on the platform, giving speeches or sermons, for people like to listen to you. You must learn to be practical and carry out your plans, otherwise, you are apt to live in the clouds and accomplish nothing. You must learn to keep appointments, and be on time for them. Number Eleven possesses the qualities of intuition, patience, honesty, sensitivity, and spirituality, and is idealistic. Others turn to people who are 'Eleven' for teaching and inspiration, and are usually uplifted by the experience. You should think of others first by serving mankind instead of concentrating on affairs that will yield well only for yourself.

It is necessary for people who are 'Eleven' to avoid the negatives of being, inflexible, impractical and temperamental. You should avoid projecting your own faults onto others, or imposing standards on others that are too high for them to realistically attain.

'Eleven' lives in two worlds. On practical days, it vibrates with the 'Two.' On days that it senses its full nature, it is of an energy that translates from a world beyond. 'Eleven' is often a catalyst for inspiration in awakening Souls and bringing hope to people, yet often not taking any credit for their work.

Individuality: Leadership, visionary, inspiring, artist, celebrity, psychological, radical, sensitive, illumination, dreamy, six-sensed, aware and creative.

Vocation: Psychologist, missionary, philosopher, historian, actor, inventor, explorer, media star, poet, inventor, psychologist, minister, designer, society figure, TV & media personality, welfare worker, explorer, evangelist, psychoanalyst, teacher, speaker, writer, beauty queen, astrologer and occultist.

You are frustrated by the short-sighted vision of many of your colleagues. You are deeply passionate for art, music, or of beauty in any form.

Number 11 General meaning

The Critical 11:

Arrogant; Bullying; Devious; Disobedience; Fanatic; Gossipy; Headstrong; Inhospitable; Interfering; Intimidation; Judgmental; Meddling; Misdemeanor; Offensive; Patronizing; Snobbish; Terrorizing; Timid; Transgression; Unapproachable; Unsupportive.

The Negative 11:

Cowardly; Denial; Depression; Discourteous; Drug Abuser; Egoistic; Ill-Mannered; Impractical; Inconsiderate; Indecisive; Indifferent; Insensitive; Intermingled; Lack of Development; Living in A Fantasy; Negligent; Nervous; Only Dreamer; Overly-Sensitive; Pathetic; Rude; Running From Own Reality; Self-

Depreciating; Sluggish; Spiritless; Temperamental; Tension; Unconcerned; Unexcited.

The Positive 11:

Awareness, Communication, Channelling, Cooperation; Creative; Diplomat; Energetic; Enlightened Individual; Enthusiasm; Humanitarianism; Idealistic; Illumination; Inner Growth; Inspired; Intuitive; Inventive; Mystic; Messenger; Natural Coach; Peacemaking; Religious Leader; Romantic, Artistic; Speaker; Special Powers; Spiritual; Strong Medium; Teacher; Team-Player; Visionary; Writer.

1. The Meaning Behind Number 'Twenty-Two' (22)

'Twenty-Two' vibration means you are a practical idealist and not only do you have visions, but you can see things on a large scale and are able to carry out your plans to achieve your goal. You are a master builder, bringing order to the world. You are an internationalist. Your power and influence can be far-reaching. You should launch projects for the benefit of humanity. You are able to deal with groups effectively. Twenty-Two possesses the qualities of imagination, loyalty, secrecy, optimism, and heightened perception. You are hard-working, logical, well-organized and powerful, and can be a very generous benefactor. You aim to leave the world in a better state than in which you found it. Much is expected of you and if you do not live up to your responsibilities, you may revert to living as a 'Four.'

It is necessary for people who are 'Twenty-Two' to avoid the negatives of being pessimistic, cynical, selfish, manipulative, or of developing an inferiority complex. In the extreme, you could become cruel and tyrannical.

If we build upon a foundation of precision and balance, we will have a master plan. On a practical day, the 'Twenty-Two' becomes the 'Four..' When 'Twenty-Two' senses its full capacity, it can achieve what is barely imaginable.

Individuality: Idealistic, high energy, expansive, innovative, idealist, ingenuity, innovative, visionary, master-builder, government, universal transformation, philanthropic, and great achievement.

Vocation: Expert, coach, ambassador, writer, politician, business owner, lawyer, administrator, president, buyer, diplomat, teacher, organizer, and work affair.

Number 22 General meaning

The Critical 22:

Bad-tempered; bankruptcy; bigoted; blunt; contradictory; crude; destructiveness; dogmatic; exploitation; homeless; humorless, ill-mannered; immovable; lack of control; narrow-minded; obscure; obstructive; opinionated; perverse; pig-headed; prejudice; repressive; resistant; short vision; sluggish; stubborn; suicidal; tenacious; thick-skinned; uncivilized; uncompromising; unimaginative; very limited; vulgar.

The Negative 22:

Disconnected; disorganized; hasty; impractical; non-adaptable; lacking authority; lazy; lethargic; negligent; overbearing; poky; submissive; tired; unaccountable; uncommitted; unconventional behavior; unemployable; unfocused; unoriginal; unorthodox method; unproductive; very dominating; weak-willed; weirdness.

The Positive 22:

Accurate; bridge builder; alchemy; business-like; champion for a cause; charisma; competent; complete control; compliant; confident; conservative; consistent; constructive; conventional; dedicated; deep; deliberate; dependable; determined; devoted; dignified; disciplinarian; disciplined; exacting; expansive; experienced; factual; faithful; financial stability; firm; future vision; genius; idealist; incorruptible; industrious; inspired; trouble-shooter; loyal; master builder; material master; meticulous; obedient; orderly; patient; persevering; philanthropic; creativity; power on both planes; practical idealist; precise; prepared; productive; prudent; reliable; responsible; sensible; serious; Soul mission; spiritual revelation; stable; steady; straightforward; systematic; thorough; thrifty; trustworthy; tycoon; universal transformation; visionary.

m. The Meaning Behind Number 'Thirty-Three' (33)

'Thirty-Three' vibration means you are too powerful and advanced a number for many individuals to handle at this time. When 'Thirty-Three' is found as a total of a name or Blueprint Destiny of a person, you are greatly advanced spiritually. 'Thirty-Three' combines the imaginative self-expression of the 'Three' with the ability of the 'Six' to respond and nurture. You would be a master teacher who could guide the inquiring student into all areas of the known and unknown fields of knowledge and human experience. The fully developed 'Thirty-Three' would be a master performer, enchanting an audience while communicating or indoctrinating the listeners into whatever area the 'Thirty-Three' chooses to guide the aspirant. You are the teacher of all teachers. Number Thirty-Three is the most difficult number of all to bear, as it is the number representing martyrdom and unconditional love. The Number Thirty-Three possesses the qualities of healing, spiritual warmth, and caring, fighting for the oppressed, and taking on the worries of the world. Others, particularly children, are drawn to people who are 'Thirty-Three' by their love. Much is expected of you, for a 'Thirty-Three' is one of the highest master numbers possible. There are not too many who hold that number but they are enough to make major changes in our human understandings. If you do not live up to your responsibilities, you may revert to living as a 'Six.' It is necessary for people who are 'Thirty-Three' to avoid the negatives of being interfering and afraid to heal themselves and others. 'Thirty-Threes' can also wallow in self-pity, even when it is unnecessary, always becoming the martyr. This can attract others who would take advantage of the negatives of 'Thirty-Three.'

Within the essence of 'Thirty-Three' lies enormous potential.

On a practical day, 'Thirty-Three' becomes 'Six.' When it senses its full capacity as teacher of all teachers, 'Thirty-Three' plays a role that will make the big changes needed in the world.

Number 33 – MASTER TEACHER

Individuality: Christ-like, Master Teacher, wisdom, perfection, healer, compassionate, blessing, teacher of teachers, martyr, inspiration, honest, monk, compassion, skill & fame and worldly success.

Number 33 General meaning

The Critical 33:

Anxious; apprehensive; argumentative; bitter; complaining; conventional; critical; defeated; despairing; discontent; discouraged; disheartened; dismayed; dissatisfied; envious; faint-hearted; fault-finding; fearful; hindering; inferior; jittery; loser; martyr-complex; meddlesome; melancholy; misuse of power, negative; obstructive; oppression; over-emotional; over-involvement; over-responsible; over-sensate; overwhelmed; panicky; pessimistic; possessive; poverty; regretful; relationship destroyed; resentful; sacrificing; slavish; smothering; suspicious; troubled; uneasy; unforgiving; unhappy; upset; victimized; weak; worried.

The Negative 33:

Biased; corrupt; cranky; cynical; disillusioned; dull; greedy; harsh; hostile; ill-natured; inattentive; insensitive; intolerant; irresponsible; lax; listless; loveless; nasty; negligent; non-committal; opinionated; prejudiced; selfish; self-seeking; sullen; tactless; unaccountable; uncaring; unfeeling; unforgiving; un-imaginative; uninvolved; unorganized; unreasoning; unreliable; unsociable; unsympathetic.

The Positive 33:

Accommodating; admiring; advising; affectionate; appreciative;

artistic; balancing; benevolent; charismatic; charitable; Christ vibration; compassion; compassionate; complimentary; concerned with family; conscientious; considerate; content; creative; demonstrative; devoted; domestic; dutiful; emotional; ethical; faithful; feeling; forgiving; friendly; generous; genial; happy; healer; honest; honorable; humanitarian; idealistic; inspirational; kind; martyr; master teacher; monk; moral; mystical; obliging; passionate; peace-making; perfect relationship; philanthropic; prolific writer; protected; protective; resourceful; responsible; romantic; sacrificing; satisfied; self-sacrificing; sentimental; serving; sharing; skill and fame; soft-hearted; Soul mission; supportive; sympathetic; tasteful; teacher of teachers; tolerant; tranquil; trustworthy; understanding; unselfish; virtuous; well-intentioned; wise; world communication; worldly success.

2. Interpretation of a Chart

a. Blueprint Destiny

We are all wandering through life, asking ourselves many questions. Everyone, at one point or another, wonders what their Blueprint Destiny on this plane is. You are not the only one who has curiosity about your Blueprint Destiny and feels you need to figure your life out; we are all curious, regardless of our religion, culture or color: Here are some of the questions I have been asked during my consultations with clients:

- Do I have a Blueprint Destiny?
- What is my Blueprint Destiny?
- What does it take to reach my Blueprint Destiny?
- What is my purpose in this life?
- What is the meaning of my life?

These are very good questions and we all have the right to answers. Some people tap into their Blueprint Destiny more easily than others, and some understand their purpose and go after it, which then leads them to their Blueprint Destiny. Of course, there are many who will also go through their lifetime without knowing their Blueprint Destiny. Is there any particular reason for this? Do you feel you have missed out on your Blueprint Destiny? Do you wonder if there was a magic wand that successful people had taped to their hand when they were born that you seem to have missed out on? Or maybe you think they are using the Law of Attraction to help them discover their Blueprint Destiny. Whatever it is, I believe there are reasons as to why certain people are able to see their Blueprint Destiny while others remain searching. However, in the end it is a matter of choice and it is always up to you to identify with what your Soul proposes for you and to act upon it. You hold the biggest veto in your own hand – your free will. Are you using your free will wisely? Your religion will never give you the answers you seek. Your culture will never give you a clue either. You are the only one who holds your own answers and a huge part of you being here in this life is to figure your life out. You are struggling amongst the many problems in your life, for example, your family, your religion, your culture and simply your own understanding of yourself, your experiences and the way you have allowed your experiences to shape your life.

Everyone can be lucky. Everyone can be unlucky.

Everyone can be beautiful. Everyone can be ugly.

Everyone can be kind. Everyone can be evil.

Everyone can be compassionate. Everyone can be unsympathetic.

Everyone can be forgiving. Everyone can be unforgiving.

Everyone can express the Universal love they have within themselves.

Everyone can express the hate and anger they feel within themselves.

Since you can be whatever you they want to be, what is holding you back from achieving what you want to? The answer is you and your own perception of who you are and what you can be. A misconception of things is enough to misguide you and make you feel that everything in your life is a mess, piling on top of you. Also certain experiences may have occurred that were chaotic at the time, making you feel hopeless and you lost track of things and where you are going.

Do you believe that when you were born, you had no self-esteem or no self-confidence? Do you believe you were born with an addiction, an eating disorder, or hate and anger, or whatever problem it is that is dictating your life today. We all have problems one way or another and I do believe there are ways out, but are you willing to take a risk and a challenge yourself to get out?

Many of us go from one psychic to another, waiting for yet another message about how our life is going to be. If you became a psychic message junkie, has your life really changed? If you have been on your knees praying for many years, has your life changed? What are you still holding onto that you are resisting letting go of? What you think is the problem in your life today is not your real problem; in reality, it is just a branch of a deeper problem that started somewhere in your past. What is it you are holding onto from your past? Are your decisions today attached to anything from the past, do your choices and actions reflect anything from your past? Are you able to close the past and go beyond it in order to move forward toward living and understanding your Blueprint Destiny? We all have a purpose for being here. If you have lost the feeling of having any purpose in your life, then it will be hard to walk towards your Blueprint Destiny because the inspiration will not be there. Your Blueprint Destiny is not engraved in stone; there is no one way for you to live and that's it or nothing at all. Your Blueprint Destiny is a part of the purpose and the feeling behind your existence and intention of being part of the Universe around you. The moment you find yourself in your Universe, the events in your life will start to make sense. Finding your purpose among the events that take place will lead you to your Blueprint Destiny. It does not matter how far you go on your Blueprint Destiny; what is important is that you are walking its path, fulfilling it one step at a time without allowing yourself to be consumed by your ego because you will eventually lose the essence of what you are doing and lose your focus and concentration on it.

Blueprint Destiny is the result of your action and reactions to the events that take place in your daily life. The feeling behind the actions and reactions you reveal will shape the course of your Blueprint Destiny.

Your Blueprint Destiny works side by side with the Law of Attraction, so long as you have healed your past and understand your past experiences in life.

Do you have a problem with letting go?

Are you still stuck in your past?
Are you still angry from something in your past?
Do you hate yourself or others?
Do you have pride and a strong ego?
Are you stubborn?
Are you prone to self-sabotage?
Are you self-depreciating?
Do you express your feelings and emotions easily?
Do you pay attention to your contradictions?
Are you dependent on others to fulfill your life?
Are you a perfectionist?
Are you self-centered?
Do you look after your own needs as much as you look after the needs of other people?
Are you standing on your own feet or is everyone else directing your life?
Are you stuck in your past?
Are you rigid and narrow-minded?
Do you value your own freedom or are other people controlling your life?
Do you feel any guilt?
Do you have any fear?
Is your family your only security?
Is religion a limitation for you?
Is your culture your only guidance?
Do you blame everyone for the wrong choices you made in your life?
So how limited are you?
You will feel purposeless anytime you are trapped in any of the above questions. Do not blame anyone. Fix your problem no matter what it is and then you will feel that you have a purpose that will lead you to walking your Blueprint Destiny in this life.

Your numerological chart reflects all aspects of your life that you potentially could or should be living. Unfortunately the majority of people are so far away from living the reality of what their chart illustrates because of distractions from life experiences, which cause them to lose touch with their essence and become disconnected from their true inner guidance system which is their Spirit, their Soul and God. God is part of you, which means you do not need to pray to an external God in order to have your life change. All you have to do is decide to change your life and be committed to it … and it will. You won't get any answers to your problems from anyone else when it comes to fixing your life issues; they can give you ideas but they can never provide you with the truth you seek. That comes only from within. You choose to use your free will, either consciously or unconsciously, to stay stuck in the wrong direction in your life and this is why you are where you are. On the bright side, however, I believe the moment you make a conscious decision to change, answers will be revealed because in that moment, you will become ready to hear them.

Your Spirit, your Soul and God are the essence of life that always have and always will exist in you. It is a part of you and that means you will never ever be alone no matter what. However, you are still responsible for choosing change, acting to make a change and taking risks. Most people try to convince themselves that this is who they are, this is the way they were meant to be and that they are not capable, or meant to change, but according to who or what authority? These are all excuses and the only one you are kidding is yourself. Dig deeper within and reach your Soul and you will soon realize just who you really are and what you are capable of. Instead of dreaming, why not start living your dream? You dreamt your dream so that means that somewhere in you, you do believe that things are possible and not out of reach. However, you need to take a risk.

In order to get rid of your problem, you need to act on your desires, take responsibility and take charge of your own life without blaming others, life and complaining about everything. Instead of wasting time complaining, why not try living on the other positive side of what it is you complain about? You know what it is you complain about, so you must know the opposite of the complaint.

If you believe that the things you complain about are the fault of others and that you are a victim, then you must realize and accept that you have an issue that is a problem which needs to be addressed immediately if any kind of change is to take place in your life.

It is very important for you to accept, understand, forgive and clear your past if you ever expect to have the best possible future. It is time for you to be in the moment, living in the present moment enjoying life as if it were your last day.

After doing many numerology consultations for family members, friends and clients over the years, I have come to realize that the areas where people are stuck in their lives are related to the first two numbers of their Blueprint Destiny. Your Blueprint Destiny means nothing to you if you are stuck, that is because you will not be able to move onto pursuing it fully if you can't move forward. Those two numbers are as important as your complete Blueprint Destiny because they are the foundation of your life path and are the difference between walking smoothly and walking a rocky road. If you consider your free will and its influence, you will always have a Blueprint Destiny because life is created according to your choices, actions and reactions to what goes on in your life. However, you may not reach the original Blueprint Destiny that your Soul chose for you, the sole reason you were born. This is a great shame and is often the case for so many people; it is your own responsibility to take charge of this situation and do what is right for you. You are the only one who can fix it.

It is time to stop all the nonsense in your life. It is time to take charge and get back to basics, get grounded and start moving in the right direction.

It is time to allow healing to take place in your life and heal your past. Many people I have dealt with have told me, "I went back over my childhood and dealt with it, yet I am not getting anywhere in my life!" I bet you already know my answer to that. If you had really healed your childhood, you would not be stuck in your life today. Regardless of your age today, you still have the opportunity to get back to the base of your life and get reacquainted with the innocent child that lives within you. I will go deeper into the subject of healing the childhood experiences in my next book. What is important today, and the purpose behind this book is that you realize and become conscious of your actions and reactions on a daily basis and start tackling your issues once and for all.

Your Blueprint Destiny is a process which is ongoing throughout your life. You can't skip the steps required for your growth in order to reach your growth more quickly. It is not possible regardless who you are and what you do. And even if you become a millionaire with all the material freedom that money could buy, you would still be unhappy and feeling empty. There are so many people like that today unfortunately, and this is because they still have to deal with their basic life issues. Material freedom is not the answer to all your problems as it will never fulfill you in the end. You might fool yourself into believing you will be happy because you are able to buy whatever you like when you are rich, yet how much stuff you are going to fill your surroundings in thinking it will make you happy? No matter how much stuff you have, you will always feel as if you are missing something with a sense of having a deep inner void and emptiness within you. You cannot buy the feeling of belonging to a Universe that is flowing harmoniously because you are vibrating in sync with that harmony, even with all of your money! Harmony comes from within and is a part of your connection to your Soul and your Source, or in other words 'God.'

You are here in this life to learn and there no escape from that reality. We are all here to experience life as a part of your Soul's evolution. Going through those experiences can be very devastating for many of us. However, in the end, it is not the experience itself that is important because it will always come to pass; it is your learning that occurs as a result which is important. Although even more important is that you are able to go beyond the actual events that happen and see and understand what the lesson is in the midst of it all in order for you to grow and be able to continue with your journey through life. If you become stuck in your experiences then you will not grow and move forward, and in that case how can you ever expect to carry on to reach your ultimate goal of your Blueprint Destiny?

If you are not moving forward in your life, then you will feel stagnant, depressed and you will always find yourself having a hard time catching up with the life you envisioned for yourself because your past experiences or people from those experiences can still drag you back to the same circumstances that happened even if it was 20 years later. Remember, when you want to move forward, then it will mean you need to let go of the people in particular who hold you emotionally the most ... and that means making a hard decision. Otherwise, you take one step forward and 2 backward, as if it feels you always are at the same place.

How are your emotional, mental and physical states of being after you have finished an experience? The answer to this will determine your vision of your Blueprint Destiny. The way you see and feel about yourself will determine the direction in which you are walking toward your Blueprint Destiny, although that direction can be altered at any time later on depending on how you feel and what you are attracted to do or become in your life.

You have a purpose, we all have purpose and a Blueprint Destiny to fulfill, every single one of us. It takes a great deal of courage to live up to your purpose and be on track with your Blueprint Destiny. Your purpose is to acknowledge and accept your existence as being a part of this Universe, and your Blueprint Destiny is simply the end result of the understanding all of the experiences that make up your life.

So let's explore what each Blueprint Destiny number means to us and what exactly it is we need to understand from a positive and negative perspective. The more negative vibrations you have in your experience, the more you are steering away from your Blueprint Destiny's connection with the Universe. The more you have a positive vibration in your numbers, then, of course, the more you are aligned and in harmony with the Universe, your Soul and your Source. Again, what I mean by 'vibration' is the vibration of the numbers that make up your chart. It should not take you a lifetime to feel that you have a Blueprint Destiny, discover it and live it. It should not take you a lifetime to realize your purpose for living and to enjoy your life completely, feeling fulfilled and that you are part of this Universe. It does not take a lifetime to live up to that if you really want to. On the other hand, it can take a lifetime walking purposeless if you do not consciously choose to find your Blueprint Destiny and live up to it. The choice is yours in the end and no one else's.

When you calculate your Blueprint Destiny, you will come up with a final number, after reducing the sum of adding your day, month and year of your birth. You need to first focus on understanding the first two numbers, and in some cases four numbers, that are added to reveal your Blueprint Destiny number. Those two or four numbers are just as important for you to understand as it is your Blueprint Destiny.

Here are examples of a Blueprint Destiny with 2 numbers and 4 numbers:

June 4, 1974 = 6 + 4 + 1 + 9 + 7 + 4 = 31/4. The Blueprint Destiny is 4, so we need to understand the 3, 1, 4 before we settle well into our Blueprint Destiny.

September, 22 2006 = 9 + 22 + 2 + 0 + 0 + 6 = 39/12/3. Blueprint Destiny here is 3 so we need to understand the 3, 9, 1, 2 before we settle well into our Blueprint Destiny.

So what does every number that makes up your Blueprint Destiny mean to you? Do the calculation following the explanation in this book and then read the meaning of the numbers in your Blueprint Destiny below.

Blueprint Zero (0) meaning:

Although zero (0) is not a Blueprint Destiny or even a 'number' in numerology, it does hold some metaphysical significance to the person who has that number as part of his or her vibration.

If you have zero, you have a wealth of knowledge in your heart and mind that has accumulated as a result of many lifetimes of experience that your Soul went through. The essence of those lifetimes and experiences are stored within your own essence as part of your being and manifest as your gifts.

Positive Aspect of Blueprint Zero:

Inner Gifts; Inner Wisdom; Insightfulness; Boundless knowledge; Stepping into the Unknown; Channel Pure Energies; Make a choice; Take Action; Make a decision; Mystical.

Negative Aspect of Blueprint Zero:

Confusion; Fear of the Unknown; Afraid of Your Own Gifts; Fearful; Self-Sabotage; Self-Depreciating; Not Believing in Own Potential; Limited.

Critical Aspect of Blueprint Zero

Hypersensitive; Nervous; Sarcastic; Overwhelmed by Own Potential; Confused by Internal Feelings; Denial; Running Away from Own Intuition; Hiding behind Excuses.

Blueprint Destiny 1:

Insight: In this Blueprint Destiny, you are here to prove to yourself that you can be independent and able to stand on your own feet. You have a leadership role to fulfill in your life, yet at the same time, it is important for you to build up your own self-confidence in order for that leadership to shine.

You have an artistic side within that can be awakened at a later date.

You are the type of person who doesn't like being told what to do.

You are an entrepreneur at heart and need to have stability between all the elements in life (i.e., physical, emotional, mental and spiritual).

Positive Aspect for Blueprint Destiny 1

Leadership; Always Happy; Independence; Always Positive; Confidence; Individuality; Creativity; Optimistic; Determined; Stability of all Elements; Artistic; Entrepreneur; Original; Self-Sufficient; Self-Reliant; Ventured; Initiative; Full of Life; Inventive; Executive Ability; Dynamic; High energy; Courageous; Takes Action; Imaginative; Resourceful; Self-Assured; Self-Motivated.

Negative Aspect of Blueprint Destiny 1

Feeling Stuck; Stubborn; Stagnation; Feeling Blocked; Lazy; Lack of Energy; Doubtful; Dependent; Changeable; Unreliable; Vulnerable; Lack of Determination; Lack of Self-Respect; Lack of Energy; Helpless; Insecure; Feeling Lost; Infertile; Unstable; Unpredictable.

Critical Aspect of Blueprint Destiny 1

Addiction; Always Me - Me - Me; Self-Centered; Arrogant; Aggressive; Watch Your Ego; Watch Your intense Stubbornness; Watch Your Pride; Rigid; Lacking Vision; No Self-Confidence; No Self-Esteem; Dominating; Authoritarian; Impatient; Headstrong; Dictatorial; Self-Importance; Selfish; Unyielding; Obsessed; Over-Confidence; Controlling; Domineering.

Blueprint Destiny 2:

Insight: You are here at this time to understand relationships. How well have you dealt with your parents, your teachers, your friends, your co-workers and you personal relationships? You are here to learn how to deal with people and as you may well know, people are not always fun to deal with. People are usually a headache to deal with, particularly those who have never dealt with their issues. You need to use your diplomacy and cooperation in order to see the results of using your inner ability to associate with other people, without being hurt as a result of your involvement.

Avoid being overly sensitive because you can and most likely will end up being a victim or doormat to others.

Positive Aspect of Blueprint Destiny 2

Cooperates with Other People; Relationships; Modest; Good Hearted; Receptive; Collaborate; Inner Gifts; Strong Female Energy; Adaptable; Clear Sense of Boundaries; Humble; Clear Sense of Limits; Gentle; Diplomatic; Sincere; Responsive; Supportive; Understanding; Helpful; Friendly; Intuitive; Devotion; Ability to Associate with Other People; Approachable; Caring; Kind.

Negative Aspect of Blueprint Destiny 2

Being Naïve; Shy; Ashamed; Gossipy; Careless; Spiritless; Ill-Mannered; Inconsiderate; Indecisive; Self-Depreciating; Rude; Fearful; Unconcerned; Uncertain; Hesitant; Vulgar; Insensitive; Embarrassed; Sad; Stagnant; Uncaring; Vague.

Critical Aspect of Blueprint Destiny 2

Suddenly Withdrawn; Resisting Change; Paranoid; Lack of Patience; Aggressive; Overly Sensitive; Enjoys Being a Victim; Enjoys Staying a Victim; A doormat for Others; Depression; Inhospitable; Timid; Unsupportive; Self-Pity; Rude; Sluggish; Introverted; Interfering; Suspicious; Mistrustful; Harsh; Uncooperative; Intrusive; Nosy; Nervous.

Blueprint Destiny 3

Insight: This is one of the simplest destinies to have on this plane! However, if you complicate it, it can be hard to deal with. If you are here to live a '3' Blueprint Destiny, your Soul has probably had one or more difficult past lifetimes involving a great deal of work or stress and is here now to have a more relaxing and fun time. Saying that, it does not mean that your life should be wasted by fooling around either because it is not a joke. You still have plenty to accomplish in this life, yet you will accomplish it by being happy and having a joyous time while doing so.

When you yourself are not happy, you can never make anyone else around you happy.

Everything has to begin with you. You need to express your own emotions because storing emotions inside you will complicate your life later on by holding you back from reaching the happy Blueprint Destiny you deserve, and were born to live in the first place.

You enjoy talking. You enjoy hearing yourself talk. You are popular and enjoy living life to the full. You enjoy being entertained and entertaining others. You are inspirational, sociable and always love having fun.

Positive Aspect of Blueprint Destiny 3

Joy of Life; Expressive; Sociable; Magical; Inspirational; Creative; Uplifting; Encouraging Others; Express Emotion and Feeling Easily; Friendly; Open-Minded; Companionable; Amusing; Fun to be around; Intuitive; Talker; Popular; Sympathetic; Instinctive; Welcoming; Considerate; Enthusiastic; Charming; Joyous; Kind; Chatty.

Negative Aspect of Blueprint Destiny 3

Self-Doubt; Scattered Energies; Moody; Complain; Never Finishes Projects; Always Bored; Evasive; Unkind; Worrying; Withdrawn; Unforgiving; Jealousy; Grumpy; Anxious; Whining; Unresponsive; Evasive; Indiscreet; Cheerless; Critical; Irritable; Envy; Discourage; Whine; Worried; Restless; Intolerant; Disapprove of.

Critical Aspect of Blueprint Destiny 3

Depressed; Criticizes others; Lack of Direction; Self-Centered; Exaggerate; Pessimist; No Expression of Feelings and Emotions; Secretive; Disappointed; Biased; Lack of Concentration; Shallow; Silly; Superficial; Temperamental; Wasteful; Snobbish; Opinionated; Miserable; Cautious; Phony; Childish; Stuck-Up; Saddened.

Blueprint Destiny 4

Insight: You are here to enjoy life here on earth; you have to enjoy what this plane has to offer you. You enjoy having a family, a car, a house and all the goodies you are interested in having and adding to your collection.

You are here to bring yourself to have mental, physical, emotional and spiritual stability.

You should be neat and tidy, and well organized with a solid structure for the direction of your life.

You are a well-disciplined type of person. You are an asset for any employer to have on their staff because of your devotion and dedication.

Positive Aspect of Blueprint Destiny 4

Organized; Structured; Steady Growth; Mental Stability; Emotional; Stability; Physical Stability; Spiritual Stability; Very Disciplined; Highly Practical; Ability to Concentrate; Do not Mind Routine; Pay Attention to Details; Uses Common Sense; Attentive; Accurate; Balanced; Careful; Cautious; Consistent; Confident; Sensible; Efficient; Precise; Devoted; Prepared; Punctual; Neat and Tidy; Honest; Guarded; Kind; Dedicated; Punctual.

Negative Aspect of Blueprint Destiny 4

Careless; Detached; Lazy; Negligent; Uncertain; Lost in Detail; Limited; Opinionated; Obstructive; Gossipy; Slow; Insensitive; Dogmatic; Tired; Disorganized; Inattentive; Drained; Inflexible.

Critical Aspect of Blueprint Destiny 4

Jealousy; Envy; Procrastination; Impatient; Trying to Skip Steps of Growth; Confused; Filled with Doubt; Rigid; Rude; Resistant; Repressive; Narrow-Minded; Headstrong; Selfish; Greedy; Intolerant; Uncompromising; Contradictory; Impolite; Egotistic; Prejudice; Authoritarian.

Blueprint Destiny 5

Insight: You are here to get pleasure out of your freedom. You need freedom from your family, freedom from your religion, freedom from your culture, freedom from your own way of thinking that no longer supports your growth, freedom from your thoughts that do not support what you would like to be and have in your life. Freedom is the single most important aspect of your journey.

Vibration 5 will bring traveling and adventure into your life. You are here for your own expansion and the expansion of your own Soul.

You need to avoid being 'Jack of all trades, master of none.' It is required of you to learn and accept discipline, structure and focus as a part of your vocabulary in order further your learning and advancement through your life without becoming stagnant and lazy.

Positive Aspect of Blueprint Destiny 5

Freedom; Quick thinker; Travel; Spontaneous; Sociable; Skillful; Imaginative; Expansion; Adventurous; Resourceful; Versatile; Fast to Quit; Multifaceted Talents; Seeks independence; Enjoy Change; Enjoy Attention; Adaptable; Free Spirited; Curious; Daring; Charming; Energetic; Broad-Minded; Creative; Exciting; Venturesome; Gifted; Warm; Inventive; Inspired; Courageous; Artistic.

Negative Aspect of Blueprint Destiny 5

Moody; Unpredictable; Always Bored; Restless; Feeling Struck; Pretends; Bluff; Boring; Doubtful; Passionless; Purposeless; Undecided; Fear of Taking Risks; Stagnant; Free of Freedom; Dependent; Vague; Unsure; Uncertain; Cautious; Unstable; Cynical; Impulsive; Insecure; Impatient; Temperamental.

Critical Aspect of Blueprint Destiny 5

Impulsive; Inconsistent; Completely Lost; Wasteful; Wild; Superficial; Careless; Drinker; Extensive Use of Drugs; Irresponsible; Self-Indulgent; Unusual; Negligent; Nervous; Over-Sexed; Shallow; Reckless; Regretful; Restless; Intolerant; Anxious; Agitated.

Blueprint Destiny 6

Insight: You are here to learn about responsibility. Your learning experiment will force you to evaluate the way you handle responsibility in your life by disregarding your own needs.

You are a very responsible person and are here to show others how to be responsible. Keep in mind, however, it is not up to you to be responsible for everyone in your life. If you do take on others' responsibilities, of course, you will be the one who is blamed if anything goes wrong and at the same time they have learnt nothing.

Family is a big part of your life. You are surrounded with family, culture and having your own family will be an important part of your life at one point in your life.

Avoid driving yourself nuts by always trying to be perfect. The moment you release yourself from this, the Universe will show that you still have a long way to go in your life and that making mistakes is a normal and healthy part of learning and growth. Always remember that the moment you stop judging yourself about being perfect is the time you become perfect. Please let go of that stress once and for all!

Positive Aspect of Blueprint Destiny 6

Responsibility; Family; Good Health; Good Listener; Acceptance; Universal Love; Fair; Care Taker; Balance Male & Female Energy; Generous; Intuitive; Healer; Enjoy Community Service; Accommodating; Advising; Friendly; Idealistic; Helpful; Loyal; Supportive; Lovable; kind; Sacrificing; Sympathetic; Satisfied; Romantic; Protective; Patient; Wise; Happy; Content; Creative; Benevolent; Artistic; Affectionate; Helpful; Ethical; Faithful; Religious; Emotional; Careful; Comfortable.

Negative Aspect of Blueprint Destiny 6

Judges Self; Judges Others; Lost in Petty Details; Biased; Over-Protective; Unorganized; Unreliable; Selfish; Unsympathetic; Childish; Non-Committal; Self-Seeking; Negligent; Unfriendly; Prejudiced; Insensitive; Impersonal; Inattentive; Harsh; Greedy.

Critical Aspect of Blueprint Destiny 6

Hypercritical; Irresponsible; Lost in Life Direction; Chaos; Confused; Argumentative; Bitter; Complaining; Unhappy; Victimized; Weak; Worried; Uneasy; Suspicious; Negative; Unforgiving; Fault-Finding; Dissatisfied; Despair; Too Perfectionist; Drive Others Nuts; Mistrustful.

Blueprint Destiny 7

Insight: You are here to learn to trust yourself and believe in the higher Universal power around you. You need to begin accepting your gifts.

You are gifted, resourceful and enjoy your solitude. You are here to understand yourself. You often have a hard time expressing yourself and letting people get to know and understand you because you are still trying to figure that out for yourself.

You are a special person with many gifts; however, many people around you might classify you as being weird, but weird in comparison to whom or what?

You might not understand your gifts and it is possible that you are afraid of them and unknown; however, one day you will find yourself cornered by them and will be left with no choice but to deal with them.

You are a dreamer and have strong psychic and mediumistic power within you that you need to start tapping into. Meditation with communication with your higher self, your Soul and your Spirit guides will help you better understand your purpose.

Positive Aspect of Blueprint Destiny 7

Trust Yourself; Clever; Believe in Higher Universe; Usually Lucky; Intuitive; Spiritual; Enjoys Solitude; Seeker of Knowledge; Inner Wisdom; Analytical; Intellect; Calm; Capable; Strong Medium; Efficient; Psychic; Religious; Dreamer; Inventive; Patient; Truth-Seeker; Resourceful; Wise; Skilled.

Negative Aspect of Blueprint Destiny 7

Undeveloped; Uncertain; Superficial; Incompetent; Naïve; Lack of Depth; Forgetful; Foolish; Dull; Skeptical; Pessimist; Ignorance; Paranoid; Phony.

Critical Aspect of Blueprint Destiny 7

Fear of Your Own Gifts; Abuse of Your Own Gifts; Ignorance; Impersonal; Inflexible; Joyless; Weak; Worried; Withdrawn; Over-Analyzer; Insecure; Hesitant; Detached; Despair; Controlling; Aloof; Apprehensive; Fanatic; Nervous; Selfish; Non-Committal; Inferiority; Impatient; Fear of Success; Fear of failure; Unfriendly.

Blueprint Destiny 8

Insight: You are here to experience power, money and achieve recognition in whatever field you are involved in.

Finances are important part of your life. Material freedom is always what your concern is.

You have a very clear idea in your mind of what you want and just how you intend going after it. You are a leader with executive abilities and power. You enjoy controlling other people and also get pleasure out of managing, controlling and using other people's money.

You show authority and command your vision in a direct way, such that people tend to listen to you and admire your determination.

You always need to be careful about being too controlling in your own pattern and self-sabotage.

Positive Aspect of Blueprint Destiny 8

Ambitious; Capable; Commanding; Material Freedom; Responsible; Skillful; Clear Headed; Assured; Positive; Leadership; Inner Abundance; Direct; Clever; Authoritative; Consistent; Achieving Recognition; Successful; Supportive; Money Maker; Practical; Persuasive; Resourceful; Respected; Wise; Manage Money; Decisive; Shares Blessings Generously; Executive Power.

Negative Aspect of Blueprint Destiny 8

Careless; Issues with Money; Nervous; Restricted; Weak; Vulnerable; Unorganized; Uncaring; Unprepared; Fear of Failure; Dishonest; Cowardly; Lack of Confidence; Timid; Unreliable; Undisciplined; Lack of Management; Stressed; Mismanaging Money; Karmic Learning; Watch Pattern of Money; Run into Pattern; Issue with Money; Untrustworthy; Unpredictable; Helpless.

Critical Aspect of Blueprint Destiny 8

Impatient with People; Afraid of Taking Risks; No Belief of Own Capability; Abuse of Power; Greedy; Self-Sabotage; Workaholic; Power Control; Lack of Humanitarianism; Materialistic; Abusive; Bad Taste; Shameless; Tense; Fear of Being Recognize; Dishonest; Demanding; Uncaring; Threatening; Lack of Trust; Ill-Mannered; Bullying; Chauvinistic; Clumsy; Fraudulent; Sexist.

Blueprint Destiny 9

Insight: You are here for two important tasks in your life.

Nine marks the end of a situation with a new beginning round the corner.

The first task for you and your Soul is to finish up and close all karma and unfinished issues you have been dealing with in this lifetime. This is so your Soul does not have to come back to this plane again and repeat similar experiences in future lifetimes. Your role in this life is to bless those experiences, heal yourself and allow yourself to let go of what is passed in order that you will be able to continue forward in your life journey without looking back or being haunted by the past.

The second of your tasks is service. You are here to be of service, to help and assist others. You are a humanitarian with a great deal of compassion inside you that needs to be awakened in order for you to make a difference in your life and to live the Blueprint Destiny you were meant to by servicing humanity and helping other people in need.

Positive Aspect of Blueprint Destiny 9

Missionary; Humanitarian; Integrity; Benevolent; Broad-minded; Capable; Artistic; Affectionate; Loyal; Generous; Warm; Understanding; Humble; Humane; Friendly; Sympathetic; Emotional; Dedicated; Loving; Inspired; Intuitive; Compassionate; Genial; Enthusiastic; Enlightened; Missionary; Passionate; Forgiving; Modest; Concerned.

Negative Aspect of Blueprint Destiny 9

Detached; Biased; Difficulty of letting go; Stubborn; Unconcerned; Unkind; Unyielding; Impersonal; Vindictive; Narrow-Minded; Harsh; Disloyal; Distant; Withdrawn; Aloof; Biased; Prejudice; Lack of Compassion; Unresponsive; Unbending; Lost; Confused of Direction.

Critical Aspect of Blueprint Destiny 9

Doubtful; Chauvinistic; Cowardly; Defeated; Deceiving; Resentful; Selfish; Submissive; Superficial; Headstrong; Foolish; Self-Centered; Unpleasant; Uncertain; Temperamental; Shy; Joyless; Jealousy; Dogmatic; Dissatisfied; Disloyal; Disappointing; Unstable; Indecisive; Disapproving; Moody; Ineffective; Inexperienced.

Blueprint Destiny 11

Insight: You need to balance your material world with your spiritual world. Both worlds are part of who you are. You are a special person whose Soul came here with a vision in order to make a difference to you and the world around you. Have you realized your vision yet? The world is your playground and it does not matter how small or how big your vision is, as long you strive toward making a difference in the world and in other people's lives.

You need to develop your own intuition and communicate with the other side to attune yourself to the purpose you were born to fulfill. You must trust yourself and your own capability of making a difference and that must begin with you in order to bring forth a stronger result.

You have strong mediumistic potentials and can be a psychic or religious leader. You have an old Soul outlook that will assist you in bringing forth all the knowledge you need to use on your path in this lifetime, so you can spread wisdom and awareness for the benefit of others.

People might be scared of you because of the way you carry yourself and because you are able to see things from a much broader and higher level than they do with their limitation. Some people might not understand you, your way of thinking or your messages, yet don't take it personally.

You have a Master Number 11 vibration and people with that number are special Souls, although it doesn't mean that anyone is below you and not special. We all are special in our own way, yet the only difference is that you have something important to accomplish in your life and more responsibility in your hands. What makes you really special in the end is being able to really accomplish your Blueprint Destiny here, fulfilling it and handling your tasks and experiences in a good positive way.

This vibration can take you worldwide, but if you feel you cannot handle that at the present moment, then you can always fall into the lower case of 11 which is the 2 vibration. This will allow you to do things in your own community, state and country and alleviate any pressure or tension you have. Please refer to Blueprint Destiny 2.

Positive Aspect of Blueprint Destiny 11

Impractical; Idealist; Dreamer; Inventor; Worldly Vision; Master Number; Inspirational; Extremely Capable; Illumination; Visionary; Deep Awareness; Deep Understanding; Caring.

Negative Aspect of Blueprint Destiny 11

Abuse use of Power; Dissatisfied; Fearful; Deep depression; Lost in detail; Dreamer; Unconcerned; Insensitive; Stubborn; Egoistic; Too strong pride; Abuse of substances.

Critical Aspect of Blueprint Destiny 11

Snobbish; Gossipy; Patronizing; Interfering; Terrorizing; Arrogant; Unapproachable; Unsupportive.

Blueprint Destiny 22

Insight: With this vibration, you have the power and the ability of achieving great material freedom. You have the wisdom of your old Soul; however, utilizing this wisdom without giving up can be a tough task for you to master.

You are a Master builder who can take a vision of either yours or someone else's and spread it worldwide in order to help bring you the material and spiritual goals you are here to accomplish.

This is a strong vibration and for many 22s, it can be tough having to cope with its vibration at the same time as dealing with your everyday life issues. You must work for the benefit of humanity in order for you to attain your ultimate goal in this life. You need to discover what vision your vision is, capitalize on it and work it.

You are here to make major changes on a large scale and this can be achieved through your work, perhaps in a commercial vocation, as a politician or someone who is able to make decisions that inspire change.

Positive Aspect of Blueprint Destiny 22

Determined; Inspired; Stability; Organized; Financial freedom; Stability; Devoted; Charismatic; Confident; Faithful; Financial stability; Visionary; Fair player; Deep; Master builder; Genius; Practical idealist; Soul mission; Responsible; Philanthropic; Universal transformation; Spiritual; Balance; Diplomatic.

Negative Aspect of Blueprint Destiny 22

Lazy; Very domineering; Uncommitted; Uncaring; Unconventional; Unfocused; Substance abuse; Unaccountable; Cowardly; Unorthodox.

Critical Aspect of Blueprint Destiny 22

Narrow-Minded; Short Vision; Bankrupt; Suicidal; Homeless; Loneliness; Prejudice; Resisting change; Exploitation; Destructive; Unimaginative; Slow.

Blueprint Destiny 33

Insight: With this Master number vibration, you are here to bring mastery to humanity. You are the Master of all teachers once you master your talents, wisdom and insights. You have the ability to have the Universal awareness and be a fair, wise judge of what brings enlightenment into humanity. You see humanity in general and people in particular from an angle that people themselves have difficulties seeing. You possess compassion to all humanity and you are here to bring a solution to what other people got stuck with in their life. You carry Christ vibration and you vibrate in such a profound and deep compassion that few can relate to you or understand you. People see you as unfriendly because you are cut off from everyone around you but at the same time, people are attracted to you for your clear vision and depth into reaching the human Soul. You have great tasks in front of you but you need yourself to be prepared and cleared about your past experiences.

Positive Aspect of Blueprint Destiny 33

Charismatic; Affectionate; Sacrificing; Concern; Compassionate; Universal Love; Peaceful; Devoted; Charitable; Healer; Honest; Direct; Humanitarian; Forgiven; Peace-Making; Prolific Writer; Satisfied; Content; Skill and fame; Mystical; Worldwide Recognition; Good relationship.

Negative Aspect of Blueprint Destiny 33

Hostile; Insensitive; Uncaring; Unreliable; Hostile; Unsociable; Unforgiving; Non-committal; Cynical; Biased.

Critical Aspect of Blueprint Destiny 33

Oppression; Over-emotional; Fault-finding; Over-involvement;

Fearful; Disheartened; Obstructive; Dissatisfied; Critical; Resentful; Suspicious; Pessimistic; Unhappy; Poverty; Misuse of Power; Pessimistic.

b. Blueprint Birthday

Blueprint Birthday 1:

You vibrate as a leader in this lifetime. Your determination and strong will are very obvious in your actions and reactions to things that matter to you. You have the drive to succeed. You are inspirational and a strong motivator of others. People look up to you and believe in you to always do the right thing. You are independent and it is part of your character that you hate being told what to do.

You enjoy making decisions and you like to work independently, which is why you can succeed as an entrepreneur. You are a pioneer, creator, and an initiator. You are a gambler when it comes to your ideas and many times this is what makes you successful. You have a clever mind and you know what you want and go after it. You have strong business instincts and your knowledge will help you achieve your goals.

You possess a broad vision and a great capacity to enhance other people and inspire them to achieve their potentials. Your will power will be tested, especially during the years 28 to 56. But your opportunity for accomplishment is unlimited.

In general, you're open to other people's ideas, but you can be extremely stubborn and hard-headed once you become attached to your plans and ideas.

When things are not going your way, you can often become angry and frustrated; however, with determination and will power, you can bring personal and financial rewards.

You can be very stubborn and rigid once you have devoted yourself to an idea, something you do more than you realize!

You always need to watch and have a handle on your ego and your pride because they can be in your way in many situations.

You are very curious and dedicated. When you are interested in something, everything else has to wait. This is your quality. Your problem is that you have no patience and you want things yesterday! Chill out a little! Learn to be patient and complete what you have started and you will be successful in life. In matters of the heart, you believe in love at first sight. You won't wait to learn more about the person. Vice versa, people who fail to astound you will hardly get a chance to be your friend. Your emotion is on the extreme side. You can only love or hate, nothing in between and this often shows in your expression.

Blueprint Birthday 2:

You are very cooperative, diplomatic and intuitive. You are also extremely sensitive and this can affect you a great deal when you take things too much to heart. You are very easily influenced by your upbringing. You always see yourself as sitting in a backseat and your lesson in life is to get up from being in the back seat and get into the front seat. You will struggle to do that at times, yet without any resistance, you will eventually do it and are bound to succeed. You love beauty, looking beautiful and love to have attention for being so. On the other hand, your over-sensitivity makes you highly emotional and vulnerable to being hurt or becoming a doormat for others.

You have an artistic and musical side which may serve you as an escape, giving you refuge into a world all your own to help you get by during any situations you are living in at the moment. You enjoy feeling safe and secure in your life. You are very emotional and have lots of feelings to offer but you will always enjoy when you have your close friends and loved ones reciprocate what you give them.

You can easily fall into depression and need to be careful of that, especially when it comes to your lack of confidence. You are aware of what other people think and what's on their mind, and you can easily adjust to that, creating peace and harmony. This is due to the cooperative and diplomatic skills that you possess.

Your high sensitivity to others makes you compassionate, kind, and tender. You have an opportunity to have fame and success, so long as you do actively pursue that goal without just living in a dream world.

Despite your sensitivity, you possess leadership abilities. You are modest, diplomatic and respectful. You have the ability to convince and can be quite powerful.

Your intuition allows you to recognize what people want, even before you are approached by them. You can continue a project better than starting it. You are very attentive to details. You need harmonious and peaceful environments and without them, you can easily become stressed and suddenly withdrawn.

In life in general, you have great common sense but usually fail to follow through. This might happen because you are too busy with your mission and shut yourself from the outside world. You are clever and profound so there's a slight chance you may have a problem with self-control. In matters of love, your love progresses slowly and quietly. You seem to be content with your non-reciprocated love. You are a romantic and loyal lover.

Blueprint Birthday 3:

You are very clever, witty and quick to adjust to any situation. You enjoy flirting and are highly imaginative, communicate well and enjoy talking. You have great enthusiasm. Others find you inspiring, charming and get pleasure from your company.

You possess a strong creative side and you are an artist at heart. You could excel in writing, visual, or performing arts. If you are not professionally involved in one of these areas, you should consider taking up art or something that allows you to express your creativity as a hobby.

You are affectionate, friendly and loving, and you enjoy socializing, entertaining others and being entertained. You possess a great deal of charisma. You can also be moody and your vibration can rapidly go up and down.

You have a fine logic of harmony and art in everything that you do, from the way you dress up to the way you decorate your home and environment. You have a way with plants and, and it is almost as if you are connected to them and can communicate with them.

Be careful not to waste time and energy on trivial matters. Keep your long-term priorities in perspective. You need to take care to avoid getting bored to quickly with the events in your life.

Although you are innocent and romantic, your expression often misleads others into thinking you are an active, fun-loving kid who does not want to grow up. Because of your double personality, it's hard for others to really know the real you. Many consider you as a joker and find it difficult to take you seriously. You are careful and patient. Your love is the greatest trait which often surprises others. Your confidence might lead you to paths in life to which you parents disagree.

Blueprint Birthday 4:

You are a hard worker and are conscious of everything that goes on around you. You are precise and take great care in what you do. You are motivated and accept routine work. You enjoy being committed to someone instead of just casual dating. You are highly disciplined and responsible. You take your obligations very seriously. You are extremely ethical. You usually think before acting, which makes your life quite easy. You often give yourself a hard time by being overly paranoid.

Living on this plane is important to you and whatever material things you enjoy collecting and have in your life are significant to you. You enjoy the good things that life has to offer. You are a straightforward type of person. You care about people and also care of what people say about you. You are proud. You tend to persevere in the face of any obstacle or problem. You enjoy nature.

You love your family and make a wonderful friend. You are an asset for any boss to have as an employee because of your dedication and devotion to your work. You are neat and tidy. Yet, you are not excessively emotional, nor are you very expressive when it comes to your love.

The foundations of your life are your constant focal point and persistence. Whether it is in business, career, or family matters, you take care of the basics. You are highly rational.

You manage people well and are a very fair and sincere person. People like to work under you because you use the slow, patient approach and are sound and secure. You are very centered and focussed.

You must work at being more flexible. Sometimes you only see a situation from a one-sided perspective. You can be stubborn and rigid. You often experience irritation and repression.

You can sometimes be rather insensitive at times. Be careful to avoid working to excess and missing out at what is important to you, which is your quality of life.

People sometimes misunderstand you. You always surprise others with a new side to your character when you are in love. Your love life is full of surprises!

Blueprint Birthday 5:

You have a great deal of curiosity and desire to see far-off places and meet exotic people. Your arena is the world itself, and it is just a matter of time before you are off once again on another excursion. Your biggest learning in life comes from your travelling. You love change, travel and adventure. Just pay attention though that your need to get away is not just an excuse for you to escape and hide from dealing with your reality.

You are highly adaptable and need excitement. You get bored easily. You enjoy attention and always search for independence. You always search for your freedom and get away from your limited life. You relate well to others and have an easy way with words. In fact, like a 3, you have a talent for promotion, public relations and for some writing.

You have difficulty with being bound to a desk and feel trapped working within an office. You easily feel bored and trapped unless there is much variety and change in your life. You become bored and restless easily. You may be a little irresponsible at times and need to bring discipline into your life.

You have a quick and analytical mind. You have multifaceted talents. You may be overly confident and headstrong. You are highly creative and can usually come up with a surprisingly workable solution to most problems using your own or someone else's ideas.

Your social skills are highly developed and your ability to communicate and promote a product or event makes you a natural salesperson. You work well with others as long as there are not too many limitations placed upon you.

You can be impatient and impulsive. You can also overindulge your senses in food, alcohol, sex, and drugs. You must be cautious to protect your health from the excess of your tastes.

Routine is something you cannot stand. Because of your extreme confidence, you hardly ask others for their opinion. You believe in leading your own life, and you have the gift to do so. In your love life, nothing can stop you from making progress. The moment you are in love, you feel ownership of your lover. When a third person gets involved with your loved one, your jealousy becomes fierce.

Blueprint Birthday 6:

You are very good listener and that is what attracts people to you. You care for people and their well being. You are family-oriented and have a talent for settling disputes between people to the satisfaction of both sides.

Your lesson in life is to work to attain your balance. You need to balance your own needs with the needs of others, learning where to draw the line. Whether it is in the realm of the emotions, finances, work, and play or caring for others, you must learn what you do best, where you can be of service, and determine your limits and boundaries. You are a strong healer and have a very strong sense of intuition that needs to be developed. Study and the development of your healing skills bring you great rewards in life later on.

You have a significant amount of artistic talent. You have a deep appreciation of beauty and art. You are highly responsible and that can sometimes drive others nuts. You are generous with people in need, sometimes to an extreme where people feel you are interfering. You have a unique imagination.

Your focus is on relationships. You need to know you are appreciated. Criticism leaves a very harmful impression on you as you take it to heart in a profound way. You will sacrifice your own comfort to support and help others. You are generous, kind, and understanding in nature. You are protective, affectionate and supportive.

Your hidden courage and dedication often surprise others. Your love life is on a smooth path because it grows from friendship. Although you may not make a sweet lover, your authenticity brings happiness to your relationship.

Blueprint Birthday 7:

You possess inner wisdom and many gifts. Going inward is your path of life and is necessary to help you answer the many questions that are always popping into your head. You have a highly developed mind. You have a philosophical and spiritual orientation in life. It is important for you to meditate and do some yoga in your spare time.

You tend to be analytical and rational in your approach to relationships. Emotions are a cloudy and uncertain territory for you, which, very often, you do not trust. You sometimes view emotional people as a bit immature or unpredictable. You try to avoid being in a relationship because you enjoy the space for yourself. You are a loner and enjoy your solitude.

You have an outstanding sense of intuition. You should meditate and do some type of spiritual exercises in order to develop your intuitive talents. You should shun taking anything at face value. Nor should you take disproportionate chances or gamble.

You are not the type who should be given to irresponsible living. It tends to backfire quickly for you. You prefer to work alone and set your own pace. You tend to finish projects once they are started. Your interest leans to the scientific, technical, and metaphysical areas. You can develop into a strong medium, psychic or religious leader due to your vast interest in that arena.

Under your quiet personality, you can be opinionated and stubborn. You must guard against becoming too analytical, ruthless, and distrustful. You can be highly critical and self-centered, traits that can lead to much unhappiness, especially in marriage, if you are not careful. Once married, you tend to be loyal and faithful. Share your emotions with those you trust, and maintain close relationships. This will balance your mental life and will be a source of great comfort.

You are sensitive to changes around you but your feelings are hardly expressed. You hate exaggerations. These qualities are the force behind your extreme persistence. You have enormous desires to please your lover, because of which your relationships often progress quickly.

Your Blueprint Birthday 8:

You see $ signs in anything you look at. You have a capacity to do well in business, and a good sense of money-making. Your approach to business is original, creative and daring. It is wise to avoid partnerships wherever possible. You are highly competitive and close partnerships – especially when power is divided equally – can lead you to indulge in manoeuvring and manipulation.

You have a pleasant and friendly personality. People look up to your wit and imagination. You are unpredictable but respected. Falling in love becomes your routine. Most of the time, you are lucky. You fascinate people with good taste but you never have enough with one. Although your love progresses very fast, it never lasts. Sometimes material attachment to things might come between you and your loved ones for a fear of losing what you have or being distracted, but you always want to be seen with someone under your arm for prestige and security.

You drive yourself to achieve your recognition and a big part of you being here at this time is to do that. You are successful, resourceful and have a practical way of looking at things such that others envy the way your mind is clear and your ambition that keeps driving your success.

You are efficient and can handle large projects. If you do not already run your department or own business, you are destined for such a position. Leadership is your gift. In the same way, you have a great talent for organization. You can manage large groups of people and guide them along the lines of your vision. You enjoy playing with other people's money and controlling other people and this is where you can be very successful in attaining a high level position in your career.

You are a practical person, self-confident and goal-oriented. Others respect you and your opinion. They know that you can be depended upon for your ability to always come through.

You must develop the qualities of persistence and endurance. You will meet many obstacles, which must be viewed as challenges that, in fact, make you stronger. Others will run from the challenge, while your ambition to succeed will support you to face any challenge at hand. Your attitude toward the difficulties in life will be the difference between success and failure.

You enjoy a challenge. The expectations of others stimulate you, especially if they doubt you can pull it off. You tend to be impressive with money. You have a need for status and may show off your hard work with an impressive car or house. You are proud of your family and like to be complemented. You have strong character, but may be domineering and bossy. You have little patience with weakness either yours or someone else's. You have a hard time expressing your emotions.

Blueprint Birthday 9:

You are broad-minded, romantic and compassionate. You should obtain a wide education. You are very artistic, and hold lots of integrity.

You must come to truly understand life to be of greater service to humanity. You have a greater social role to play that will require a blend of the practical and the humanitarian. You have an idea what might work and for the benefit of all.

The more you can be of service to humanity, the greater will be your personal reward on all levels – from the material to the spiritual. You are socially oriented and have a gift of charm. You are affectionate and care about others. You are well-liked and even admired by others. You can relate to people in all walks of life. People to you are people regardless to their color, religion and culture. You have a broad vision of the world and can see the grand plan of things, including international politics and social activities.

You express your feelings well, but sometimes can be quick to remark. You have a strong interest in philosophy and metaphysics. Nines tend to attract money from other sources, such as inheritance or luck but you never express interest in money in the first place. The Universe is always supporting the effort you are trying to do for humanity.

There is an aspect of sacrifice in you that stresses that you learn about forgiveness and unconditional love. You must avoid negative attachments.

You don't really care what everyone else thinks of you. This is why people misunderstand you until they really get a chance to learn about your lovely personality. The opposite sex finds you mysterious and worth searching for. Your wit is remarkable but sometimes you are too fast to follow. You won't make your feelings public even after dreaming about the same person over and over. Your first love lasts forever. You are sensitive to the feelings of your lover, and absolutely loyal. Children enjoy your company.

'Zero' 0 is part of your Blueprint Birthday:

People with a 0 in their vibration will emphasise the wisdom they bring into this life and the knowledge and insight that makes some qualities in them that differ from other people. They need to get inward within themselves and channel all the energies they have that distinguish them from the crowd. They usually are strong in making a decision, make the right choice for them and the situation they are in, and have good judgement.

Blueprint Birthday 10:

See the interpretation for 1 and 0.

Blueprint Birthday 11:

You are very idealistic and possess a great deal of intuition. You would make a fine counsellor or healer. People are attracted to your charisma. You are confident and independent and very intuitive.

You understand people before they expose their inner being themselves. In general, you have an appreciation for what encourages people.

You are highly sensitive, emotional, and reactive. You take the criticism of others personally, and can take some time recovering.

You are a visionary and possess the inspiration that excites others with your ideas for a better world. Your intuition and sensitivity lead you predictably toward philosophical and idealistic quest.

Your leadership ability shines and there is no secret about it, but your life stands more as an example for others, rather than for constant or disciplined leadership. You prefer to let people take up their own struggles once you have helped point the way, rather than be directly involved in the day to day activities of leadership.

You must work hard to keep up focus in the emotional storms you encounter. You work well with others, often inspiring them by your example and your optimism.

The world can be your stage to play and show your vision. Many Souls are waiting to hear from and connect with you. You bring the spiritual aspect and the material freedom on your side. You do well in the business world but it is not things you are after. You explore and solve problems mainly through intuition. You are more a dreamer than a doer. You are concerned with the well being of mankind and seek to make the world a better place.

You are genial, graceful and cautious. People admire your qualities and some even become jealous of you. You are practical, flexible and adaptable to any situation that comes your way. You have based your life upon strong morals, and you are very kind. In love, you are willing to sacrifice yourself for the one you love. Your lover will always have your gentleness, care and loyalty.

Also, look for 1 and 2 interpretations.

Blueprint Birthday 12:

See interpretation for 1, 2 and 3. You have a good mix of vibration in your day of birth.

Blueprint Birthday 13:

See interpretation for 1, 3, 4 and 13/4 Blueprint Karmic debt in Chapter X. You have a good mix of vibration in your day of birth.

Blueprint Birthday 14:

See interpretation for 1, 4, 5 and 14/5 Blueprint Karmic debt in Chapter X. You have a good mix of vibration in your day of birth.

Blueprint Birthday 15:

See interpretation for 1, 5 and 6. You have a good mix of vibration in your day of birth.

Blueprint Birthday 16:

See interpretation for 1, 6, 7 and 16/7 Blueprint Karmic debt in Chapter X. You have a good mix of vibration in your day of birth.

Blueprint Birthday 17:

See interpretation for 1, 7 and 8. You have a good mix of vibration in your day of birth.

Blueprint Birthday 18:

See interpretation for 1, 8 and 9. You have a good mix of vibration in your day of birth.

Blueprint Birthday 19:

See interpretation for 1, 9, 0 and 19/1 Blueprint Karmic debt in Chapter X. You have a good mix of vibration in your day of birth.

Blueprint Birthday 20:

See interpretation for 2 and 0. You have a good mix of vibration in your day of birth.

Blueprint Birthday 21:

See interpretation for 2, 1 and 3. You have a good mix of vibration in your day of birth.

Blueprint Birthday 22:

You act being the boss character, you feel being the boss, and you are the boss but not a leader. Most people look up to you for your ability and assurance although might find you relatively stubborn. Listening should be part of your daily task. You are a unique, special and charming individual. You see things as black or white. You either love or hate someone. Whom you call friends are the selected ones. When you are betrayed, you won't let anyone get away without having hard time. People tend to draw back at first from your energy because you are an old, wise, and mysterious energy, and people are often afraid of how you might respond to any particular situation. Sometimes, you seem withdrawn and disconnected from the people around you. In the early stages of your life, you will have difficulties in understanding yourself and might run into major experiences and lessons in order for you to open up yourself and start bringing in the wisdom you are destined with into this lifetime. With the Master number 22 in your vibration, you are here to bring order to your life and life of others regardless what you do in life.

Blueprint Birthday 23:

See interpretation for 2, 3 and 5. You have a good mix of vibration in your day of birth.

Blueprint Birthday 24:

See interpretation for 2, 4 and 6. You have a good mix of vibration in your day of birth.

Blueprint Birthday 25:

See interpretation for 2, 5 and 7. You have a good mix of vibration in your day of birth.

Blueprint Birthday 26:

See interpretation for 2, 6 and 8. You have a good mix of vibration in your day of birth.

Blueprint Birthday 27:

See interpretation for 2, 7 and 9. You have a good mix of vibration in your day of birth.

Blueprint Birthday 28:

See interpretation for 2, 8, 1 and 0. You have a good mix of vibration in your day of birth.

Blueprint Birthday 29:

See interpretation for 2, 9, 1 and 11. You have a good mix of vibration in your day of birth.

Blueprint Birthday 30:

See interpretation for 3 and 0. You have a good mix of vibration in your day of birth.

Blueprint Birthday 31:

See interpretation for 3, 1 and 4. You have a good mix of vibration in your day of birth.

c. Blueprint Expression

Blueprint Expression 1:

You are a very determined person. You can handle executive and administrative tasks. You prefer leading than following. You are very positive, happy and have strong will power. You have a very good mind and see things very clearly in your mind.

On your negative side, you need to watch your ego, pride and stubbornness. Avoid being lazy or dependent on other people directing your life. Watch not to be aggressive and arrogant.

Blueprint Expression 2:

You are very diplomatic, sincere and care for the feelings of others. You express yourself as being courteous, considerate and very adaptable person. You enjoy resolving conflict between people. You always look for harmony.

On the negative side, you need to watch your over-sensitivity because it always gets you into trouble. You have a delicate ego you need to maintain because that ego can complicate your life if not watched closely. You need to get rid of your shyness.

Blueprint Expression 3:

You are very talented with your words, and are smart and clever. You do that in your writing, speaking, singing or dancing as far you are expressing yourself. You are a good salesman and can sell anything. Basically, you have strong communication skills. You express joy of life, and are very sociable and happy in nature. You inspire through your words and deeds.

On the negative side, you need to watch not to scatter your energies or be gossipy or superficial.

Blueprint Expression 4:

You are good organizer, practical and down to earth. You easily manage the task at hand. People see you as serious, honest and truthful. You are very patient and enjoy the quality of life.

In your negative side, you need to avoid being rigid, stubborn and bossy.

Blueprint Expression 5:

You are adaptable, talented and versatile. You are very clever and quick to respond to circumstances. You do things extremely well. You love changes, enjoy traveling and love having an adventurous life. You have a good analytical ability, and are a quick thinker. You are always enthusiastic.

In your negative side, you need more discipline in your life. You can be lazy and impatient. You can keep changing relationships and jobs without learning what you want and need from your life.

You always have your energies all over the place. You may gorge in eating, drinking, drugs, gambling and sex.

Blueprint Expression 6:

You are very responsible, helpful and friendly. You are a very good listener, loyal and very generous. You put the concerns of other people before your own. You give comfort and help to those in need. People will sense in you universal love and sympathy.

You sacrifice yourself for others. You may express anxiety and worry. You judge yourself and others. Stop being a perfectionist because it does not support your way of life. Watch contradiction.

Blueprint Expression 7:

You have a good mind and a very strong intuition. You always search for answers in your life and the universe around you. You are into the occult. Many see you as weird as you live in your own world, as you see others with no substance in their life. You enjoy your space and being on your own. You are a perfectionist in your own way and enjoy working alone. You are very logical and rational. You show little emotion and work hard just to understand the depth of life. You use philosophical terms to express your awareness. Avoid analyzing, judging and discriminating at times.

Blueprint Expression 8:

You are ambitious, smart and very alert to opportunities. You are organized and enjoy making money. You have a strong sense of self-confidence; you are energetic and love independence. You have good judgment of character. You are here to enjoy your material freedom and you express that freedom very well. You seek material comfort and if overdone, this becomes a negative trait.

Avoid being rigid and stubborn. You may misuse power. You are too materialistic and can be a 'scrooge.'

Blueprint Expression 9:

You are a humanitarian and express that very well. You live, breathe and work hard for your cause. You are caring, daring and feel for others suffering. You give a lot to others and are aware of your own feelings as well as other people.

Avoid being self-centered and selfish. Also it is important for you to stay away from being too needy or, on the other hand, showing a lack of involvement in relationships.

Blueprint Expression 11:

You are inspirational and strive toward making others understand your vision through your idealistic approaches. You are a very good spiritual adviser, you are sincere and a good teacher. You often rely on your psychic, mediumistic and intuitive sides to get you through life. You express your vision of a better world in all that you do. You have a great mind and analytical abilities. You are deeply connected with art, music and beauty.

Nervous tension is always present with you. You were more of a dreamer than a doer in your early life. You may impose your ideas upon others in a forceful and insensitive way.

Avoid becoming inconsiderate, and self-centered, judgmental and temperamental.

It is important that you also understand the lower aspect of your vibration which is Blueprint Expression 2.

Blueprint Expression 22:

You are capable of managing large tasks with ease. You also enjoy solving problems and have a very practical and unorthodox approach to problem solving. You see problems from a different perspective that many others may not even be aware of. You work for the good of all. You have great inner strength, charisma and a clear mind that many people may be intimidated by, even afraid of.

You need to watch nervous tension and depression. Avoid being domineering and selfish.

It is important that you also understand the lower aspect of your vibration which is Blueprint Expression 4.

Blueprint Expression 33:

This is the path of self-sacrifice. Others see in you universal compassion and caring to assist and help others. You have been blessed with the ability to see people for their issues with an intuitive approach and ability to determine what it is they really need. Along with your sympathetic and considerate nature, you strive to fulfill those needs. It is difficult for you to stay behind detached from any suffering; however, you will have a lot more energy to relieve the suffering of those you can help if you work at maintaining an objective point of view. Your path with this Master number will bring you the understanding of universal matters, combined with the earthly financial freedom you need to fulfill the task you are here for in the first place.

It is important that you also understand the lower aspect of your vibration which is Blueprint Expression 6.

d. Blueprint Soul Urge

Blueprint Soul Urge 1:

You are an independent person and are driven toward being the leader or pioneer of any venture you are handling. You are determined, honest and take action. You are very loyal.

On the negative side, you need to watch your ego, your impatience and your impulsiveness.

Blueprint Soul Urge 2:

You enjoy friendship, love, intimacy and companionship. You are a very sympathetic, devoted and an emotional type of person. You prefer marriage to staying single. You give love and affection and you are a person who is devoted to your relationship.

On the negative side, you need to watch being a victim and being naïve. You need to work on your shyness.

Blueprint Soul Urge 3:

You are rarely discouraged, and always fun to be around. You are very easy-going and you can express your fun-loving nature very well. You participate in a lot of activities and anything to do with communication and talking is your territory and pleases you most. You are intuitive, inspirational and people enjoy being in your company.

On the negative side, you are prone to being too sensitive when you are criticized. You also have a tendency to scatter your energy all over the place.

Blueprint Soul Urge 4:

You are very good at establishing routine and order in your life. You also accept your choices well and are able to live with them no matter what. You always look at things from your own perspective, failing to look at the whole picture. You are responsible and disciplined. You do not mind routine work. You lead a stable life and enjoy your security in life. You are disturbed by sudden changes. You are practical and analytical. You have self-discipline and determination.

On the negative side, you can be narrow-minded and headstrong at times. You hide your feelings and are afraid to take risks. Avoid being too domineering and bossy.

Blueprint Soul Urge 5:

You have a good mind and imagination. You always look for freedom, excitement and adventure. You love traveling. You use a progressive approach in your life. You are very resourceful, with a good mind and imagination.

On the negative side, you may have difficulty with being disciplined and handling responsibility. You are impatient and dislike routine work. You keep jumping from idea to another.

Blueprint Soul Urge 6:

You are an open-minded type of person with a lot of universal love to offer. You are very generous, affectionate and express deeply on an emotional level. You are artistic and romantic. You enjoy imposing responsibility on others and see it as your duty to do so. You enjoy family and being in family-oriented surroundings. You are very sincere, love children and enjoy being around them. You can be overly emotional at times and this needs to be avoided. You also need to avoid being over-protective.

Blueprint Soul Urge 7:

You have a technical, scientific mind. You are also interested in the Occult, philosophy and religion. You value spending a lot of time alone. You are a dreamer; you enjoy studying and analyzing facts to gain knowledge and wisdom. You are reserved and always seek perfection.

Avoid being an over-analyzer, withdrawn and repressing your emotions. Take care to avoid living in your dreams and fantasies.

Blueprint Soul Urge 8:

You want wealth, recognition and power. You have a lot of abundance. You enjoy success and status. You have executive abilities. You are confident and have a strong analytical mind. You function well in times of need and under pressure. You possess good judgment skills.

Avoid being domineering. You have the tendency to be self-centered, stubborn and repress your feelings.

Blueprint Soul Urge 9:

You are sympathetic, friendly and generous. You have a sensitive nature and care about other people's well-being. You care about others and are willing to sacrifice yourself to suit the needs of others. You possess a deep understanding of life and a strong intuition. You have artistic abilities

Avoid being overly sensitive and piling up your unexpressed emotions. You may have inner conflict with your spiritual, material and personal ambitions. You need to avoid being critical, moody and judgmental.

Blueprint Soul Urge 11:

You are idealistic and a dreamer with strong psychic abilities. You have a clear vision and mind. You want to give of yourself to humanity. You have great inner strength and inspiring ways that draw people to listen to you.

You need to avoid nervous tension and trying to do more than you are able to deliver. You have to get out of your dreamy state and start materializing your dreams.

You need to understand your lower vibration of Blueprint Soul urge 2.

Blueprint Soul Urge 22:

You have a universal approach to many events in your life. You command respect with a high vision to succeed. You are well attuned to the universe. Some people might be afraid of your strong energy and presence. You want to contribute to the world in a major way. You have strong leadership capabilities. You also have high intelligence and see things from a different perspective.

Avoid being domineering. Watch your nervous tension that results from having a very high level of awareness.

You need to understand your lower vibration of Blueprint Soul urge 4.

Blueprint Soul Urge 33:

You are ready to sacrifice your own desires for the good of others. The highest love is what you desire to give, and you may attract situations where you will feel crucified for what you believe in. You have the courage and strength to endure whatever it takes to promote your ideals and be a bringer of peace.

You need to understand your lower vibration of Blueprint Soul Urge 6.

e. Blueprint Inner Self

Blueprint Inner Self 1:

You are dynamic and resourceful. You appear to be in control, capable and confident. You are courageous and take quick action during difficult times. Others can sense that you will not be pushed around. Your appearance is important to you; you are fashionable, but have your own style. You are known as a pioneer; you have your own ideas of how to do things. You hate to be told what to do. You take risks, but only well-planned risks. You are original and highly creative. People often see you as being stubborn, as if you think only your way will work out. You can intimidate people if you don't soften your exterior somewhat. You have a very strong will power. You are focused and have a creative mind that does not stop.

Blueprint Inner Self 2:

You are aware of details; you are harmonious and appear thoughtful. You have a soft, warm exterior and make a very good companion. People are drawn to you because, among other things, you have a good heart, and are warm and modest. You dress neat and clean. The opposite sex is attracted to your gentle and attentive nature, yet senses the passion beneath your surface. You have sex appeal. Exercise is important in your daily routine. You are very patient and understanding, and a wonderful listener. You have lots of inner gifts you do not credit yourself enough for. You like to play it safe so as to avoid disappointment. You make others feel important and loved. You are sensitive, a peacemaker and diplomatic. People sense your desire for harmony. You must avoid being around negative and avoid arguments because you can be drained easily.

Blueprint Inner Self 3:

You are full of life, with a flair for good things in life and at the same time you are charismatic. You are uplifting, inspiring, and charming in any situation you are involved in. You are a fun person to be around, and people enjoy your company. You are highly attractive. You appreciate fine clothing and jewellry, and enjoy dressing up. You are a romantic and can fall in and out of love rather quickly. Commitment is a difficult hard word for you, however, you are still affectionate and giving. You adapt easily with your environment. Work at developing deep and lasting relationships. Your humor can cause you to rely too much on superficial, humorous conversation and having a good time. You are very lucky and attract many positive opportunities throughout your life. Hard work and self-discipline are the qualities that will almost ensure your success.

Blueprint Inner Self 4

You are very dependable and trustworthy. You radiate loyalty and devotion. People trust you and feel secure with your judgment. You are a good manager. You are a firm but fair person. You are relied upon to do your work efficiently and expertly. You present yourself as someone who values efficiency, being well prepared, and precise. You are careful and have learned to respect just one dollar because you work hard for your money. You are concerned about the security of your future and those you love. Sometimes people in your life see you as strict and headstrong. You enjoy your life here on earth and enjoy the material things you collect. You love intimacy, privacy, and the security a family provides. You are a good provider and protector. You love your country and are an integral part of your community. You are a highly practical person and always use common sense.

Blueprint Inner Self 5:

You are creative, and visualize events in your head before putting them into practice. You are a good marketer. You are a stimulating person. You brighten social gatherings with your fresh and original ideas. You are an articulate, sensual and exciting person. You love your freedom and you see this life as an ongoing adventure. Commitment is hard for you as you always like to explore and have your adventures. Sometimes it is hard for you to grow up and concentrate on one thing at a time. Your weakness is that you love to indulge your senses with food and drink, and can easily gain weight. You have an appetite for anything that stimulates the senses, such as sex, food, alcohol, and drugs. Discipline is a necessity for you. You have an addictive personality. Your versatility and adaptability make you gifted at getting the most out of practically every opportunity in life. You decide quickly on a course of action and your timing is usually good. You are a quick thinker, broad-minded and free-spirited type of personality. You radiate the potential for success, and this attracts others who can further you along your path. You have multifaceted talents.

Blueprint Inner Self 6:

Your nature is warm and cozy. You are very protective and nurturing of people in your surroundings. You create stability, yet at the same time, you drive everyone crazy with the way you handle responsibility. You radiate understanding and compassion. For this reason, you attract many people who require comfort, including the disadvantaged. People tend to come to you to discharge their burdens. You have a fine sense of justice. You do everything in your power to maintain the harmony, and are even willing to sacrifice your personal desires for the good of others. You are not always a very good judge of character. You tend to see the best in others. You also can become too involved in the lives of others. You love children and are a good parent. You are romantic, faithful and affectionate. You are artistic. You are a very good listener.

Blueprint Inner Self 7:

You are sensitive and truthful, and a good teacher. You have a deep level trust in yourself. You are aware of the Universe around you from a deep sub-conscious level. You are very lucky, even during the harder times in your life. You have technical abilities and are interested in science, metaphysics, the afterlife or anything that can stimulate your mind and curiosity. You seem mysterious and different, and people often find you weird and withdrawn. You are highly independent and self-sufficient. You are hard to get to know and do not open up to anyone in your life easily. You are always suspicious of other people's motives, so you prefer to work alone and live in your own world. You are renowned for being spiritual and religious, with your very own ideas regarding the purpose of life and the Creator. Your love of knowledge and wisdom shows well in your life.

Blueprint Inner Self 8:

You value your life, your accomplishments and your material freedom. You appear capable, decisive and powerful. Your leadership and eagerness attract people with resources. People enjoy being around you because you radiate confidence. People sense that you are generous, although only after being convinced of the worthiness of the cause. Your wardrobe is important to you and you know how to make a first impression. You are always after quality and that reflects in your choice of clothing. You radiate your inner abundance. You are assured and ambitious, and can appear domineering and selfish at times. You share blessings generously. You know choices and recognize the value of things you have.

Blueprint Inner Self 9:

You are a compassionate Soul and have a deep empathy for other people's well-being. You have a Universal outlook to life and you see the unfairness and injustice that exists in life. You are not attached to things in your life. You are sympathetic and have integrity. You are a humanitarian, enthusiastic, enlightened and passionate. You care for the well-being of others and at times, you are even willing to sacrifice your personal desires for the good of others. You are generous, dedicated and intuitive.

Blueprint Inner Self 11:

You are aware of everything that goes around you. You are an enlightened individual. You are a fair person and compute every detail in your life. Others may detect radiance around you and feel drawn to you by Blueprint Destiny. Your radiance is a manifestation of the distinguished and inspirational energy that goes through you, seemingly from other worlds. You are a great communicator with other people as well with the other side. You are an old Soul back here again in order to explore other levels of your Soul evolution. You may be an artistic mastermind but one thing's for sure – you have an influential effect on anyone who crosses your path. You are not afraid to recreate yourself as necessary at your accelerated speed, and other people follow your example by becoming more of who they really are.

It is important that you also understand the lower aspect of your vibration Blueprint Inner Self 2.

Blueprint Inner Self 22:

You are stable, determined and devoted to your cause. You carry a charismatic flair that people immediately notice. You have all the qualities of a great leader or a president. Power and authority are freely given to you because you seem like you know what to do with them. People enjoy listening to the passionate way you express yourself. Your humanitarian concerns and generosity give you the reputation of a benevolent patriarch. You are an old Soul, back here again in order to explore other levels of your Soul evolution.

It is important that you also understand the lower aspect of your vibration Blueprint Inner Self 4.

Blueprint Inner Self 33:

You appear to be on point and superior, a modest, self-sacrificing philanthropist. You appear when you are the most needed and then disappear without a thought of receiving anything in return. You attain worldly recognition easily. You attract animals and children of all ages to your loving kindness. You are a good listener and teacher of all teachers and very resourceful individual.

You are an old Soul, back here again in order to explore other levels of your Soul's evolution, probably through your communication with people and also your deep caring for others.

It is important that you also understand the lower aspect of your vibration Blueprint Inner Self 6.

f. Blueprint Maturity

Blueprint Maturity 1:

At maturity, you will have to reassess your independence in life and how you are able to stand on your own two feet. You will need to take some action during this period in your life when it comes to your independence.

Blueprint Maturity 2:

At maturity, you might need to look at your sensitivity. You need to be able to say or do whatever is needed, without conciliating your sensitivity, without guilt and without being too shy to say it.

You need to take action when it comes to accepting and being fulfilled with your attitude towards over-sensitivity, especially when it comes to working through being over-sensitive.

Blueprint Maturity 3:

At maturity, your focus will be on how well you express yourself in front of others. Also how openly you can allow letting the boundaries go that prevent you from enjoying yourself fully. You will have artistic expression during this time. You need to live life fully and enjoy the zest for life without just living to entertain everyone else first.

Blueprint Maturity 4:

At maturity, you need to re-evaluate the limitation you have built around yourself, especially the rules and regulation that are not working for you in your life. You have to switch things around in your life in order to make changes with all that restricts you in your surrounding.

What did not work in the past will never work in your life. You have already tested that, so stop doing the same things over and over and learn to reinvent yourself. A change is badly needed in order to bring passion into your life so you can start living your life to the fullest.

Blueprint Maturity 5:

At maturity, you have to reconsider the element of freedom in your life. You need to learn to be stable, and to focus in order for you to be able to grow in your personal life or career.

It is time to stop jumping from place to place in events or the relationships in your life, and begin focusing on being more disciplined and centering your attention on what you would like to accomplish in your life.

Blueprint Maturity 6:

At maturity, you need to review and reconsider what the word responsibility means to you. Looking into your past will be your guide in terms of being able to see how effectively you deal with responsibility. A change of course might be required at this point of your life, and making drastic changes may also be necessary at this period.

You need to be able to receive and accept love, advice or any other forms of help offered to you to help you fulfill your needs.

This period will be more about the things you do for yourself than about what you do for others.

Blueprint Maturity 7:

At maturity, you will be forced to start going within to learn more about yourself on a deeper level than ever before. You will trust your intuition more and begin to recognize the Universal guidance taking place around you. You will discover your own truths and many of your own inner gifts will be revealed to you. At this time you will feel ready to accept those gifts and begin working with them, as oppose to being afraid or doubting them as you did in the past.

Blueprint Maturity 8:

At maturity, you will be re-evaluating your material freedom and the achievements you have already accomplished in your life. You will re-assess your vocation, your personal needs and the financial situation of your family. You will want, and expect to have, material freedom manifesting in your life, and this will make you feel happy and satisfied. It is very good to have this vibration as your maturity, so long as you have dealt with your past and allowed it to go with love, understanding and forgiveness, and at the same time, letting go of any outworn habits or patterns that do not serve you in your life.

Blueprint Maturity 9:

At maturity, you are pushed to open up your compassionate side and allow yourself to be of service of others, seeing the beauty that exists in doing so, and drawing that feeling of satisfaction closer to your heart. During this period, you will bring the whole picture of the Universe into your life, recognizing your role as a human being on this planet to assist, give and be of service to uplift humanity.

By becoming involved with other humanitarian people or groups, your eyes will open up to see broader horizons, and your mind will widen to see the potential of bringing understanding, compassion and love to this plane, and you will feel a depth of satisfaction out of this.

Blueprint Maturity 11:

At maturity, you will experience newer energies in your life that will start awakening your spiritual side, and your vision toward helping, assisting and changing the way humanity is driving things in our world. You may have experiences that will allow you glimpses into the spiritual world, giving you the urge and the force you need to push you toward pursuing your goals.

Also understand your lower vibration Blueprint Maturity 2.

Blueprint Maturity 22:

At maturity, evaluating your life and all that is important to you bears great importance in your life at this time. Where you are going in your life and on your spiritual path is something you will be forced to reconsider. You are supposed to live with the awareness of a Master builder who is capable of balancing the material world with the spiritual world. You will be urged toward walking in that direction in your life, so be careful not to resist your calling due to fear.

Also understand your lower vibration Blueprint Maturity 4.

Blueprint Maturity 33:

People follow you because you live by example. You are a charismatic energy that people are drawn to and always need more of. You speak with wisdom, and people pay attention because you have the capacity to touch people through their Soul. You are a unique individual and you are here on a mission to serve and improve humanity.

Also understand your lower vibration Blueprint Maturity 6.

8. Blueprint Growth

Blueprint Growth 1:

This vibration is here to bring forward your individuality and support your independence, although without being too bossy or domineering toward others. This vibration will support you in bringing forward your ideas, originality and style. Express yourself! You have the ability to bring your leadership to the forefront and change lives with your vision. You need to shine, express your individuality and start living your life for you by pleasing yourself first before trying to please everyone else.

Blueprint Growth 2:

You need to avoid being shy and a doormat for other people. Put your two feet on the ground and start shining your own personality. You have the quality of cooperation and the ability to assist people with their needs, although please make sure you do not become a victim or disregard your own needs and independence. This is a time for harmony and balance in your life. At this point in your life, you need to learn to start sitting in the front seat, instead of being in the background just doing what everyone else wants you to do.

You should try to express your feelings of friendship and affection in an honest and straightforward way. Your fear of rejection may be the reason behind you having a hard time expressing your feelings and emotions.

Blueprint Growth 3:

This vibration will help you bring your creative side to the surface. You will find yourself beginning to express yourself more than you used to, particularly when it comes to your emotions. Great achievements can take place in your career during this period, and also in your life in general. You need to stop fearing rejection, feeling let down and disregarded. You should express your feelings and emotions easily.

Blueprint Growth 4:

You must learn to work with whatever limitations you have at the moment without allowing yourself to feel victimized by them. You need to learn how to achieve stability, paying attention to any contradiction in your life that will result in procrastination and laziness. You need to be patient and begin working to serve others as well as yourself, as this will help bring a feeling of satisfaction, regardless of how difficult the work actually is.

Blueprint Growth 5:

You are here for the purpose of self-expansion, and need to learn how to use the traits of adaptability and versatility to help you, without getting too excited, or running ahead of yourself and accomplishing nothing.

You need to stop jumping from one thing into another. You need to explore the experience of physical and sensual pleasures to help bring balance into your life with this vibration, although please take care not to abuse those pleasures as a means of trying to escape from your life reality.

Blueprint Growth 6:

You love responsibility and are always ready to open your hand and heart to help and assist others. Keep in mind, however, it is important for you to have balance in your life when it comes to helping others and fulfilling your own personal needs.

Your home is like your own royal castle and you feel at home when it is beautiful, comfortable, safe and stable.

You should be able to receive as much as you are able to give, for life is about give and take, after all! You need to begin listening to the advice you give to others and start living it for yourself instead of always giving it away.

Blueprint Growth 7:

Until now, you have been running and hiding from your own reality. It is time now to bring peace to yourself and truly believe that life can be peaceful, and that peace is within yourself. Earthly materials and money are little compared to your sense of inner peace and satisfaction. You need to spend time alone in meditation, searching for your inner wisdom and the insight to bring forward the essence of your reality and purpose in life at this time.

You need to stop over-analyzing every little thing that crosses your path, and learn to trust and believe in a higher Universe that exists beyond all logic and analysis.

Blueprint Growth 8:

Money and material freedom are your focus and the basis of what you are here to achieve in this plane. Achieving recognition, status and power are part of your accomplishment at this time.

You need to learn about and understand money, while letting go of the need to have more and more without knowing where stop wanting. It is also important that you learn to share your awareness about money, and share it generously. You should know and trust that there is an abundance of money in the Universe and anyone can tap into that whenever they like.

Blueprint Growth 9:

You need to learn about giving without expecting anything in return. Giving of yourself comes in many forms, for example, your time, your expertise, money, friendship, love, affection, sympathy and, of course, lots of compassion! You need to bring your feelings of optimism and inspiration forward and help encourage others to do the same. This will then help them look at life from a positive perspective, being able to overcome their life hurdles and move forward.

Blueprint Growth 11:

You need to develop your intuition more in order to bring your spiritual awareness forward, and then balance it with your awareness of the material world. You need to learn to understand your visions and what they stand for on a deeper level, and then express that vision, with the goal of helping to inspire for others to live their life in a more meaningful and fulfilling way. You have to live by example and by what you preach to others. You need to speak up about the 'spiritual world in the material world' although, it can be somewhat discouraging at times due to some people's limitation, although do not let it stop you.

Also, you need to understand your lower vibration Blueprint Growth 2.

Blueprint Growth 22:

You need to bring either your own vision or someone else's vision forward and into fruition in order to help and assist humanity. You need to balance your physical and material aspects of life with your spiritual side. You have important goals to achieve in this lifetime, and that will begin to manifest and surface the moment you have the desire to assist others.

Also, you need to understand your lower vibration Blueprint Growth 4.

Blueprint Growth 33:

You need to accomplish worldly recognition and bring out the teacher of all teachers that is within you. You sacrifice for other people as part of who you are, but you always need to keep including yourself in what you do, especially doing things for only yourself. You seek perfection in your relationship because that is the way you are. You see things in harmony and alignment with the Universe. You are here to accomplish your Soul mission.

Also, you need to understand your lower vibration Blueprint Growth 6.

h. Blueprint Journey's Cycle

1. Blueprint Influential Learning Interpretation

This period begins from birth until age 27.

Blueprint Influential Learning 1:

During this period, you are here to bring your individuality forward from a young age. You need to learn to express your confidence and ambition, at the same time discover your place in the Universe around you.

You will learn to distinguish yourself from the crowd. You have original ways of thinking, yet when it comes to other people, they will always try to put you down because of their own lack of own self-conviction. Also, the fact that you are capable of expressing your thoughts and feelings may make other people feel intimidated by you because they themselves are not capable of doing those things themselves. Remember, when it comes to relationships with others, it is not always about you but more about other people's issues that manifest into different types of situations so please don't take things personally.

You need to learn to be independent during this time. You

need to always strive to accomplish what you have dreamt of and intended to do from a young age. You have the courage to walk beyond any limitation.

This will be a very strong learning period for you unless you become stuck behind nonsense in your life that will eventually be detrimental to your growth, slow you down and prevent you from fulfilling your ambitions in life.

Blueprint Influential Learning 2:

During this time, you will be learning about relationships and how to juggle things between different people. People can be a headache at times, and you need to learn about cooperation and diplomacy without you getting hurt. You need to learn how to listen and have patience in your life. During this period, you will be forced to learn about your shyness, being naïve and dependent on other people to tell you what to do. Your learning is about being more independent. For some 2s, the learning during this period will be about discovering your psychic abilities. When it comes to this, though, keep in mind that you need to watch out for being ridiculed by others because of your abilities. Sometimes, it's better to keep quiet about what you can do, at least until you have a better grip of working with and understanding your abilities. It is better to talk with people who are open-minded about such things, and who have your interests and well-being at heart. You have a kind and gentle nature but do not allow people to take advantage of it.

Many experiences could possibly happen to you during this period that will have an effect on your life for many years to come. You need to create a place within yourself that is both balanced and at peace.

Blueprint Influential Learning 3:

During this time, you will learn about self-expression and expressing yourself creatively. You will be good with words from a very young age. You can become a great comedian. You are a joker, to the point that many of your friends can misunderstand you when you are trying to be serious, as they are used to you always joking. You need to learn to express your own emotions. People will enjoy your company from a young age. Pay attention to avoid becoming a gossip from an early age. You enjoy communication, sales and even Spirit communication. Any of those things you enjoy can become a great asset in your life in years to come.

You are charismatic and people enjoy being in your presence.

Blueprint Influential Learning 4:

During that time, you must have some discipline in your life and keep your environment neat and tidy. This may be something that will be difficult for you to do and maintain from a young age. People can depend on you easily, as you are reliable. You do not mind routine and you are a loyal friend. You try to understand and distinguish the differences between the needs of your relationships, particularly with your family and your need for time to yourself to either relax or have fun. This way, your life will be more balanced and structured. You will be the type of person who follows structure from a young age and you will stick to that for a very long time.

Blueprint Influential Learning 5:

During that time, you are always all over the place. You get bored very easily. You must learn about discipline, which is hard to maintain at that age. You always need to keep doing wilder, more adventurous and sometimes dangerous things. You keep changing your hobbies. You are curious, energetic and are quick in your own thought. You are charismatic and always shine in situations that build up your character and recognition of your personality.

Blueprint Influential Learning 6:

During this time, your interest in family life will be prominent.

You enjoy being surrounded by family and being part of a family. You are also able to handle responsibility from young age. You care about other people's feelings and well being. You are a good listener and pay attention to details. You can remember everything to the very last detail.

Blueprint Influential Learning 7:

During this time, people may find you withdrawn, difficult to understand and even slightly weird! This is because you are at a period on your life where you are trying to figure yourself out, so how can you explain yourself to others when you are unsure what to even explain? You are quick to learn from a very young age and are very gifted; however, you are filled with much doubt due to the lack of trust you have for yourself. You have many questions you would like to have answered, especially when it comes to the deeper meaning of life and spirituality. This period is a time of strong learning, especially when it comes to figuring out yourself, the Universe you live in, and where you belong, and to accepting the fact you are a little different from most other people.

Blueprint Influential Learning 8:

During this time, you will analyze your family a great deal, especially when it comes to money. You have had an active interest in money from a young age. You always look for ways of making extra cash and you always calculate your expenses and your earnings to the last penny. The way your family influences you when it comes to money will have an effect on you for years to come. You have an inner abundance and you have a prosperous mind and attitude about money.

Blueprint Influential Learning 9:

During this time, you will learn a great deal about your sensibility and your artistic side. You care about people and feel especially attracted toward the elderly. You were quick to learn the importance of forgiveness and detachment from a young age. You might have an interest in religion; however, it may not last forever. You care and like to help but keep in mind that you come first and you should never allow yourself to be hurt or taken advantage of for being kind and caring.

Your Blueprint Influential Learning 11:

During this time and from an early stage in your life, your actions will display your independence and that you have the vision of making a change in the world. At a young age, this vision will be a little hazy and may not make any sense to you at all, but hold onto it because one day it will!

You will learn about your lower vibration at that time which is 11 = 1 + 1 = 2. Refer to the interpretation of 2 earlier.

Blueprint Influential Learning 12:

Refer to the interpretation of 1, 2 and 3 influences from earlier.

2. Blueprint Personal Experiences Interpretation

The age starts at age 18 to 57 years old.

Blueprint Personal Experience Learning 1:

During this period, you need to stop being dependent on others and become able to support yourself and stand on your own two feet.

You need to build your self-confidence, regardless of the experiences you went through in your childhood. This will enable you to explore and nourish your leadership abilities and move forward with your life. You have to bring out your individuality and your originality and become the leader whom many are waiting to hear about. You have the courage to face the unknown and fulfill your Blueprint Destiny.

Blueprint Personal Experience Learning 2:

During this period, you need to learn about and enhance your skills in diplomacy in order to bring peace, and balance to yourself and successful partnerships with other people around you. You need to control your over-sensitivity during this period and stop allowing people to take advantage of you. You have a responsibility toward yourself.

Your adaptability will allow you to adjust to many situations because you see both sides of a situation and you evaluate things accordingly.

You need to find and maintain the peace and balance within yourself in order to allow these qualities to manifest into your relationships.

You need to stop living in the back seat and move forward into the front seat for a change.

Blueprint Personal Experience Learning 3:

During this period, you need to learn to have fun and apply an attitude of joy into all areas of your life. You need to be happy with yourself and your environment. Being in that state will bring happiness to the other people around you. You enjoy being entertained and entertaining others. Relationships can be a little bit tough for some 3s because few people will take you seriously and will not see you as relationship material. In many cases, it is hard for others to make out if you are serious or joking. You need to express yourself and allow your creativity to surface in your life.

Blueprint Personal Experience Learning 4:

During this period, you will learn the value of organization and structure in your life. You will become accustomed to routine work and discipline in your life. You will become neat and tidy, as will everything around you that you're in touch with. Family, money and stability are becoming more important to you at this point in your life. Settling down is a big part of where you see yourself in the future.

Blueprint Personal Experience Learning 5:

During this period, you need to bring discipline into your life instead of being all over the place. Stop being 'Jack of all trades, master of none.' It is time for you to begin focusing on yourself because you are growing up. You cannot remain a kid all your life. You have a lot of charisma, as long as you use it the right way. Your senses are open to receive the beauty and truth of your environment.

Blueprint Personal Experience Learning 6:

During this period, responsibility plays a big role in your life. Sacrificing of yourself for the need of others is part of your learning, but keep in mind that you also cannot neglect yourself and must see to your own needs first before you can be of any help to others. A 'you' that's satisfied can create satisfaction in everyone else around you; on the other hand, if you feel deprived and frustrated with life, that frustration will affect everyone else in your life. In such a case, an immediate change will be required.

Health issues can manifest when your needs are not met; this happens in order to slow you down and start looking after yourself.

You have a generous heart and a need to serve your community.

Blueprint Personal Experience Learning 7:

During this period, you need to be fully honest and true to yourself. The Universe will provide you with many answers to your questions; however pay attention, because those answers can come from anywhere, and may be answered in ways you would not have imagined. It is important to bring moderation into your life. Avoid being rigid; it got you nowhere until now so it won't get you anywhere in the future, so it's time for you to lighten up and try accepting new alternative ideas, even if they contradict what you believe in your analytical mind. You need to explore your spiritual side and accept your gifts as being a part of who you are and not a burden in your life. You will have great insight about yourself during this period. Meditation is an important tool for you to use to begin communicating with your Spirit guides, your Soul and to help you discover the true essence of who you really are. There will be many surprises in store for you to discover.

Blueprint Personal Experience Learning 8:

During this period, you will concentrate on your finances and keep working towards your financial freedom. You should have good executive abilities and enjoy managing other people, as long as you do not overstep your boundaries. You are prosperous and it is as if anything you touch turns to gold. The reason you have good returns in your life is because of your clear mind and ability to take wise decisions. You should have strong self-confidence that brings out your charisma, wit and charm. It is because of these characteristics that people like you and learn to trust you quickly.

Blueprint Personal Experience Learning 9:

During this period, you will learn and understand the importance of forgiveness and compassion. You always find the good in all people. You enjoy being of service to others. You dedicate your life toward helping and assisting others. You are a humanitarian and have a very compassionate personality. You will always put yourself out in order to help someone in their time of need. You believe in your cause and you will do anything in your power to bring comfort to others. The world today needs more of your qualities in order to help make it a better place.

Blueprint Personal Experience Learning 11:

During this period, you will be inspired to be and do more in your life. Something is shifting in your life that will inspire you to go after what is important to you in your life. You have a vision to be someone special, so stop living in your dreams, live your life and make that reality as real as possible now. In order to accomplish your vision, you need to stop being dependent on others and allow your creative side to surface and trust it. You need to be able to handle people more effectively. You are here on this plane with a vision of making a difference in the world and humanity. Start by making a difference in your own life first, then you can be free to go and conquer the world around you. You need to let go of your past in order to allow your vision to manifest. You need to balance your spiritual life and your material life. The world is becoming a small place for you and you feel capable of spreading yourself easily.

Blueprint Personal Experience Learning 22:

During this period, you will have very strong energies around you that you may have a hard time understanding. This can potentially bring lots of confusion in the beginning, but if you keep searching for the truth about your life, the Universe around you and role you play here, things will eventually become clear to you.

You are here to bring your own vision, or take someone else's vision and spread it worldwide. You still have a lot to accomplish in this world and many Souls are counting on you to touch their lives and are waiting to hear from you. Many ideas come and go in your head, and it can be overwhelming to you to the point that you might even begin to feel you're crazy!

If you are running into any major hurdles or issues in your life, keep in mind that suicide is not the answer or the way out. People with this master vibration can feel drawn to that type of drastic measure when they are down, but please search for other ways to solve your issues. You are capable of letting go of the past and stop it from haunting you. Remember, you can achieve the impossible because you are a Master builder.

3. Blueprint Harvest Result Interpretation

The age starts at age 58 until end of life.

During this period, you reap the rewards of what you have sown in your life until now; it is your harvest time and the time for you to pick up your dues from the Universe. If you feel you have more of the negative characteristics of this number in your life than the positive, then you need to stop immediately and re-evaluate your life. Don't you think it's time for a change and a new way of looking at yourself? You need to be living in your positive vibrations at this point.

Your harvest is the result of what you accumulated in terms of learning during your life. With more positive results in your vibration, there is nothing else to be said except you will be doing very well.

If, at age 58, you are still showing more negatives in your vibration than positives, then isn't it time for a major shuffle in your life? The old ways of living did not work for you in your life, so why hang on? It is time to let go of your past and whatever it is that you are stuck with and start improving your own ratings. Change to being more positive and you will see how your life will change according to your input. The law of attraction works nicely here. You owe it to yourself, you owe it to your family, to your friends, and to anyone in your life who is still looking up to you. It is time for you to do something, so act fast because there is still time for you to make a difference. Age should not be your obstacle but your motivator. You are older and wiser, and should use that to your advantage and stop repeating all the patterns of your past once and for all. It has not worked for you so far, and it will never work. You need to re-invent yourself, without losing hope, and start living your new life according to the standards of the new and improved you. Be the master and creator of your life, of your Blueprint Destiny and live today in this present moment.

Whatever the vibration you have written in your chart, evaluate both the positive and negative aspects to begin the process of switching your life.

Write down all of the positive aspects of your number on a piece of paper; then write all the negative aspects of that same vibration. Which one weighs more than the other in terms of your life?

Evaluate what you need to do and then ACT! When you become aware, there are no more excuses.

Blueprint Harvest Result Learning 1:

Positive Side

Executive ability; entrepreneur; always positive; always happy; determination; independent; confident; leadership; self-sufficient; self-reliant; courageous; stability; take action; full of life; assured; robust; will power; focused; mentally creative; original; dynamic; achiever; strength; happiness.

Negative Side

Feeling stuck; stubborn; impatient; addictive; arrogance; dependent on others; insecure; changeable; no self-confidence; too much pride; headstrong; egotistic; lack of vision; controlling; selfish; domineering; aggressive; bossy; impulsive; a tyrant; bluntness; being overlooked; not using talents.

Blueprint Harvest Result Learning 2:

Positive Side

Humble; collaborate; good relationships; responsive; helpful; clear sense of limits; clear sense of boundaries; adaptable; diplomatic; knowledgeable of inner gifts; supportive; considerate; sincere; aware of details; good companion; harmonious; thoughtful; gentle; balanced; good relationships; peacemaker; insightful; sensitive.

Negative Side

Rude; indecisive; careless; inconsiderate; uncaring; ashamed; uncertain; self-depreciating; unplanned change; lack of patience; overly sensitive; falling into trap; unconcerned; too emotional; a loner; resentful; dishonest; fault finding; two faced; lies; self-pity.

Blueprint Harvest Result Learning 3:

Positive Side

Energetic; self-expressive; joy of life; inspirational; magical; instinctive; uplifting; sociable; considerate; snobbish; kind; always happy; sympathetic; fun to be around; charming; loves a good time; affectionate; sensitive; charismatic; good heart; good fun.

Negative Side

Scattered all over; wasted time; self-doubt; withdrawn; depressed; unforgiving; cheerless; gossipy; unkind; snobbish; indiscreet; pessimist; biased; complains all the time; evasive; prone to exaggeration; childish; extravagant; superficial

Blueprint Harvest Result Learning 4:

Positive Side

Stability; Devoted; Practical; Organized; Stability of all elements; Calm; Highly practical; Conservative; Confident; Realistic; Concentrated; Well off financially; Determination; Traditional; Cautious; Sensible; Balanced

Negative Side

Joyless; careless; envy; jealousy; filled with doubt; opinionated; dogmatic; gloomy; limited viewpoint; rigid; intolerant; procrastination; contradictory; selfish; impatient; rude; resists change; filled with doubt; lost; disorganized; lazy.

Blueprint Harvest Result Learning 5:

Positive Side

Expansion; free-spirited; energetic; enjoy freedom; resourceful;

enjoy change; broad minded; versatile; adaptable; enjoy life; explore traveling; enjoy attention; live purpose; creative; exciting; adventurer; passion; non-conventional; motivated; magnetic; opportunistic; very persuasive; charming; gifted.

Negative Side

Impulsive; restless; purposeless; joyless; stagnant; unstable; cautious; moody; unpredictable; dependent; fear of risks; feeling stuck; nervous; childish; over-sexed; drinking all time; shallow; superficial; irresponsible; wasteful; fear of freedom; denial; passionless; purposeless.

Blueprint Harvest Result Learning 6:

Positive Side

Responsible; fair; gentlemanly; generous; healer; advisor; good listener; helpful; intuitive; family value; good health; affectionate; loyal; sacrificing; patient; protective; lovable; sympathetic; romantic; supportive; good listener.

Negative Side

Worried all the time; suspicious; secretive; confused; argumentative; unreliable; unfriendly; prejudice; greedy; perfectionist; unforgiving; over protective; victimized; fault-finding; judge self; judge others; selfish; over-responsible; secretive; impersonal; dissatisfied.

Blueprint Harvest Result learning 7:

Positive Side

Thoughtful; spiritual; loner; eccentric; specialist; clever; intuitive; very gifted; capable; analytical; resourceful; patient; strong medium; strong psychic; attentive; intellect; efficient; truth-seeker.

Negative Side

Skeptic; pessimist; fear of own gifts; uncertain; fear of failing; fear of being successful; insecure; apprehensive; aloof; insensitive; impatient; non-committal; hesitant; withdrawn; over-analyzer; insecure; fanatic; nervous; inferiority; paranoids; inflexible.

Blueprint Harvest Result Learning 8:

Positive Side

Executive; achiever; material freedom; organizer; decisiveness; courage; goal oriented; focus; inner abundance; ambitious; capable; skillful; direct; practical; respected; achieving recognition; clever; supportive.

Negative Side

Dishonest; manipulative; stressed; careless; timid; self-sabotage; unorganized; unprepared; runs into patterns; vulnerable; ashamed; fear of being recognized; demanding; controlling; domineering; abuse of power; materialistic; workaholic.

Blueprint Harvest Result Learning 9:

Positive Side

Integrity; inspired; compassionate; dedicated; caring; sympathetic; missionary; modest; emotional; supportive; humanitarian; warm; loyal; artistic; enthusiastic; broad-minded; humble; humane.

Negative Side

Doubtful; distant; joyless; unkind; uncaring; lack of compassion; submissive; dissatisfied; unsympathetic; temperamental; resentful; narrow-minded; superficial; aloof; biased; detached; unforgiving; letting go.

Blueprint Harvest Result Learning 11:

Positive Side

Awareness; communication; channelling; cooperation; creative; diplomat; energetic; enlightened; individual; enthusiasm; humanitarian; idealistic; illumination; inner-growth; inspired; intuitive; inventive; mystic; messenger; natural coach; peacemaking; religious leader; romantic; speaker; special powers; spiritual; strong medium; teacher; team-player; visionary; writer.

Negative Side

Cowardly; denial; depression; discourteous; drug abuser; egoistic; ill-mannered; impractical; inconsiderate; indecisive; indifferent; insensitive; intermingled; lack of development; living in a fantasy; negligent; nervous; only dreamer; overly-sensitive; pathetic; rude; running from own reality; self-depreciating; sluggish; spiritless; temperamental; tension; unconcerned; unexcited.

Blueprint Harvest Result Learning 22:

Positive Side

Determined; inspired; stability; organized; financial freedom; stability; devoted; charismatic; confident; faithful; financial stability; visionary; master builder; genius; practical idealist; Soul mission; responsible; philanthropic; universal transformation; spiritual; balance; diplomatic.

Negative Side

Lazy; very domineering; uncommitted; uncaring; unconventional; unfocused; substance abuse; unaccountable; cowardly; unorthodox.

Blueprint Harvest Result Learning 33:

Not applicable.

i. Blueprint Challenge

Blueprint Challenge 0:

When you have a 0 as your challenge, it means that either you have no challenges at all in the 'challenge' period, or you will be challenged with any or all of the numbers that exist from 1 to 9. In such a case, this means you are still resisting change and are having a hard time letting of whatever it is you are holding onto.

Blueprint Challenge 1:

You will be challenged in learning to be independent, and to stop counting on others so much. You need to stand on your own two feet and be true to yourself. You need be able to defend yourself and stop allowing other people to control your life.

Blueprint Challenge 2:

You need to avoid being shy and a doormat for other people. Start bringing cooperation into relationships with others and learn how to assist people with their needs without you becoming a victim and disregarding your own needs. This is a time for bringing harmony and balance into your life.

Blueprint Challenge 3:

You need to be positive, happy and less critical. Learn to express your feelings and emotions at the right time. You may dislike work and routine. You may have a lack of concentration in your life and need to begin focusing on working harder to achieve your goals.

Blueprint Challenge 4:

You need to learn about stability, hard work and discipline, although at times, this can be unpleasant for you. You might experience carelessness, laziness and a lack of patience during the period of this challenge. Handling your money and starting your own family can be part of this challenge. This will help you to become more responsible and start living life on this plane being more grounded.

Blueprint Challenge 5:

You can be very restless and impatient with this challenge. You easily become tired of things and get very bored quickly. You keep skipping from one event in your life to another, and from one career to another. You will be forced to change many aspects of your life to become more grounded. You are stuck in a rut that the Universe will try to pull you out of, but you need to take risks to make the first move.

Blueprint Challenge 6:

You set yourself up with too high standards, and this may have caused you to fail in the past. During this challenge, you will be forced to balance your life with the loved ones in your life. You need to understand that you are not the one responsible for everyone in your life and it is not necessary for you to overlook your own needs just to help others. You need to provide your unconditional love by letting others make their own decisions in life and live according to their own wishes. You will be challenged with your need for perfection.

Blueprint Challenge 7:

You need to learn more about yourself, start feeling comfortable in your own skin and express who you are, and accept it so that other people will accept the way you are, too. You are always complaining and can often be sarcastic. You will be forced to evaluate your life from a more positive perspective. You will learn to accept your gifts because they are part of who you are. Have faith in yourself and in the Universe around you and that it will bring a major change in your life. You will be challenged by your fears during this period. Resisting this challenge will only complicate your life. You need to go with the flow of life.

Blueprint Challenge 8:

You will be challenged to start valuing life more in order for you to attain your wealth and success. During this period, you will be likely to make a considerable effort toward attaining money, status and power. You need to place emphasis on your material freedom, although without trampling on other toes to get there. You will be challenged on your weaknesses during this time.

Blueprint Challenge 9, 11, 22, 33

Not applicable.

j. Blueprint Attainment

Blueprint Attainment 1:

General Characteristics - Influences Underline:
   Express your own individuality and identity.
   Show your originality and use your own ideas.
   Being fully independent.
   Being a leader and directing others.
   Using your confidence and creativity.
   Executive ability.

First Blueprint Attainment:

1 - Is in your first Blueprint Attainment. During this period, you always differentiate yourself from others and you always have bright and original ideas. You learn a lot during this period. You learn how to lead and be a leader.

You learn how to rely on yourself.
You need to avoid being stubborn, egoistic and self centered.

Second Blueprint Attainment:

1 - Is in your second Blueprint Attainment. During this period, you require to develop your talents in order to achieve the accomplishments you desire. People enjoy the liveliness in your energy and the positive attitude. You learn to become mentally creative. You always enjoy being independent but not withdrawn.

Third Blueprint Attainment:

1 - Is your third Blueprint Attainment. For some people, it is a continuation of your second blueprint and for many others, it is your first time with that vibration. You require developing your talents in order to achieve the accomplishments you desire. You are here to lead, so people are looking up at you. Your ability to associate with other people makes you attractive and trustworthy for people to work with and be with.

Fourth Blueprint Attainment:

1 - Is in your fourth Blueprint Attainment. During this period, slowing down or retiring at this point is hard. Life is always dynamic to you and you keep adjusting to the flow of energy that comes your way.

Blueprint Attainment 2:

General Characteristics - Influences Underline:
    Being diplomatic and cooperative.
    Being friendly, affectionate and modest.
    Understanding relationships.
    Working better with people than working alone.
    Explore your inner gifts and your female energy.
    Being sensitive.

First Blueprint Attainment:

2 - Is in your first Blueprint Attainment. During this period, you are feeling a victim of everyone in your life until you learn to turn your over-sensitivity down in your life and learn to balance your life and become more diplomatic. You need to learn to express your sensitivity and stop living in your own unrealistic dreams. Your father might not be available in your life during this Blueprint Attainment.

Second Blueprint Attainment:

2 - Is in your second Blueprint Attainment. During this period, you learn to enhance your responsibility and to become aware of details, and start to reflect the quality represented in you. If you haven't learned about your over-sensitivity, that might be the issue you still need to work on in your life at this point.

Third Blueprint Attainment:

2 - Is your third Blueprint Attainment. During this period, if you haven't learned about your over-sensitivity, that might be the issue you still need to work on in your life at this point. It is time to stop believing that everyone around you is here to hurt you. If that is the case, you are hurting yourself more by the way you think. The Universe wants to bring closer to balance your relationship with yourself and your relationship with other people.

Fourth Blueprint Attainment:

2 - Is in your fourth Blueprint Attainment. During this period, slowing down or retiring is attainable at this point in your life. By now, you should be happy and fulfilled in your body. Harmony and companionship bring you to a nice happy ending as long as you're not stuck in the past.

Blueprint Attainment 3:

General Characteristics - Influences Underline:
    Emphasis on social life, having fun and enjoying life.
    Being expressive and magical.
    Opportunity to express by writing, singing, dancing or any form of communication.
    Being charming and enthusiastic.
    Popular and enjoying talking.

First Blueprint Attainment:

3 - Is in your first Blueprint Attainment. During this period, it is a learning curve for you to understand many aspects of yourself and your interaction with other people. You are the comedian, but learning to express your emotion might be a little bit difficult, but you have plenty of time during this period to practice. It is an important period in your life in which you need to understand your life and simply be happy and enjoy life.

Second Blueprint Attainment:

3 - Is in your second Blueprint Attainment. During this period, you need to enjoy life and be happy, but this period you will bring your magic. Be more considerate towards other people. People enjoy your wit and charm.

Third Blueprint Attainment:

3 - Is in your third Blueprint Attainment. During this period, you learn to be more adaptable when you deal with other people's feelings. You have lots of enthusiasm and the joy of being alive. You need to express yourself better with writing, singing, dancing, public speaking or any other means to make yourself reach bigger audience, in order to bring them a smile and uplift their lives.

Fourth Blueprint Attainment:

3 - Is in your fourth Blueprint Attainment. During this period, a happy ending can be in place. You might start to be more creative.

You express better your affection and feeling. You can be very popular.

Blueprint Attainment 4:

General Characteristics - Influences Underline:
   Organized, disciplined and highly practical.
   Order, methodical and structured.
   Balance, require for hard work.
   Mental, physical, emotional and spiritual stability.

First Blueprint Attainment:

4 - Is in your first Blueprint Attainment. During this period, you started to learn about life at young age. This is a demanding period in your life where you had to be older than your actual age and pick and learn about work and responsibility at that time in your life. You might feel your childhood passed you by while you were occupied with life responsibility.

Second Blueprint Attainment:

4 - Is in your second Blueprint Attainment. During this period, you will learn about what it means to be stable and about what life's routines and your capacity for hard work will bring into your life. More focus and interest in detail will show in your behaviors and devotion.

Third Blueprint Attainment:

4 - Is in your third Blueprint Attainment. During this period, stability will be your focus at this time in your life and should bring you all the necessary knowledge about hard work and being consistent in your life. For many, it is time to focus and start your own family if you haven't done that already.

Fourth Blueprint Attainment:

4 - Is in your fourth Blueprint Attainment. During this period, hard work is always the focus for that attainment, and your ability

to slow down might be in the back of your mind because it all depends on how life has guided you until now. For some, that period can be very relaxing and fulfilling, and for others, some still struggle to keep up with life's demand for a better future.

Blueprint Attainment 5:

General Characteristics - Influences Underline:
 Sudden and unexpected change, freedom, little responsibility.
 Jumping from situation into another, from adventure into another.
 Search for independence, need more discipline.

First Blueprint Attainment:

5 - Is in your first Blueprint Attainment. During this period, you can be everywhere. You can hardly concentrate on one thing. As a growing baby, you always needed something to stimulate your curiosity about things or you got bored fast. You could have many changes and movement in the family.

Second Blueprint Attainment:

5 - Is in your second Blueprint Attainment. During this period, commitment and stability are your major focus but are sometimes hard to attain. Keep trying and never lose hope and focus.

Third Blueprint Attainment:

5 - Is in your third Blueprint Attainment. During this period, you are very adaptable to any situation, but stability and commitment are still important for mental, emotional, physical and spiritual health.

Fourth Blueprint Attainment:

5 - Is in your fourth Blueprint Attainment. During this period, it is time to grow up and you should seriously consider by this time the need to slow down and settle, and be more responsible in your life.

Blueprint Attainment 6:

General Characteristics - Influences Underline:
   Responsibility, family and balance.
   Obligation and sacrificing to help other people.
   Enjoy guiding, advising and teaching others.

First Blueprint Attainment:

6 - Is in your first Blueprint Attainment. During this period, there are pressures on you from a young age from family, culture and sometimes religion at that you have to follow. For some, an arranged marriage at young age might be possibility but not always in your interest.

Second Blueprint Attainment:

6 - Is in your second Blueprint Attainment. During this period, family is the main focus in your life and comes before anything in your life. You might have a hard time leaving home and prefer to always be living with your parents. Family will interfere with your work desire, and obligation to family business might be in your face to handle.

Third Blueprint Attainment:

6 - Is in your third Blueprint Attainment. During this period, your heart is part of your community, and helping organize events will make feel you belong to something useful. Family is important during that period in your life and you will come under pressure to settle down if you still have not done that by now.

Fourth Blueprint Attainment:

6 - Is in your fourth Blueprint Attainment. During this period, stability at home, family, and kids are big part of your life at this point. Retirement is possible for you because you enjoy your life, your home and the surroundings you created in your life.

Blueprint Attainment 7:

General Characteristics - Influences Underline:
   Curiosity to learn, study and investigate to understand yourself and life around you.
   Being withdrawn and alone. Enjoy working alone.
   Little concern about material things and more interest in spirituality, metaphysics and religion.

First Blueprint Attainment:

7 - Is in your first Blueprint Attainment. During this period, you do not have many friends at this time and have difficulty in knowing yourself, and that will make you afraid of being around other people. Pressure to study or being in school is hard for you because you may believe it is a waste of time.

Second Blueprint Attainment:

7 - Is in your second Blueprint Attainment. During this period, a need to associate with and be around people. You have a tendency to be philosophical and are interested in the occult at this time, even though you might be afraid of it at the same time. However, your curiosity to find out more deeply how the Universe functions, and the ability to communicate with the other side of life always fascinates you.

Third Blueprint Attainment:

7 - Is in your third Blueprint Attainment. During this period, your curiosity toward your spirituality opens for you to start investigating or even being involved in it as part of your life. You are gifted and the Universe will test you with your gifts and help you provide the answers you always wanted.

Fourth Blueprint Attainment:

7 - Is in your fourth Blueprint Attainment. This period can be a time where you have difficulties finding someone you can share your interest with. Some adjustment may be needed in order to

bring change in your life. If loneliness is your way of life at this point, some major shift in your thinking and way of life is needed in order to attract someone into your life at this point.

Blueprint Attainment 8:

General Characteristics - Influences Underline:
    Ambitious, success, recognition and prestige.
    Material freedom, generosity and inner abundance.
    Resourceful, skillful and consistent.
    Good management and ability to lead.

First Blueprint Attainment:

8 - Is in your first Blueprint Attainment. During this period, you will be involved in business or learning about money and the good life from an early age, and that will bring your excitement about your life and the opportunities that you will draw to yourself.

Second Blueprint Attainment:

8 - Is in your second Blueprint Attainment. During this period, your enjoyment of a good living will make it possible for you to achieve any task at hand and set an example for others to follow. Money, power and recognition are your motivation and you won't accept no as an answer. You keep on trying until you succeed.

Third Blueprint Attainment:

8 - Is in your third Blueprint Attainment. During this period, you are trying to secure your retirement and your ambition is still strong to be somebody who people talk about or recognize. Money is always your motivation. Avoid being stuck in your own pattern.

Fourth Blueprint Attainment:

8 - Is in your fourth Blueprint Attainment. During this period, retirement is big possibility for you and this becomes a matter of a choice for all the hard work you did in your life.

Blueprint Attainment 9:

General Characteristics - Influences Underline:
   Need for compassion and understanding for a wider picture.
   Clearance for emotions and letting go.
   Humanitarian, integrity and enlightenment.
   Drama and emotional completion for a major situation in order to be free.
   Unconditional love.

First Blueprint Attainment:

9 - Is in your first Blueprint Attainment. This is a hard period for you at this time. Many difficulties or trauma can be part of your life but will prove to be beneficial the moment you let go of all the emotional baggage from your system. There will be a light at the end of the tunnel so just be patient.

Second Blueprint Attainment:

9 - Is in your second Blueprint Attainment. During this period, there is likely to be some drama and emotional cleansing needed in order for you to be free and more compassionate in your life.

Third Blueprint Attainment:

9 - Is in your third Blueprint Attainment. During this period, some situation in your life can bring the light of a major breakthrough in your understanding about your life, your Soul and humanity.

Fourth Blueprint Attainment:

9 - Is in your fourth Blueprint Attainment. During this period, you dedicate your life to your cause and a lot of work towards humanity. Retirement is a possibility but being involved in helping humanity is not work to you, but fulfillment in that you are capable of helping others in their misery.

Blueprint Attainment 11:

General Characteristics - Influences Underline:
  Lack of concern with valuable and substance matters.
  Interest in metaphysics and religious matter.
  Awareness to things around you on the physical and non-physical.
  Nervous tension.
  Look also for 2 lower vibration influences.

First Blueprint Attainment:

11 - Is in your first Blueprint Attainment. During this period, some may detect a glow around you and they are not mistaken. You have enough charisma to charm people and make them listen to you. The Universe introduces you to this level of vibration in order for you to bring up from within yourself all the knowledge and wisdom that your old Soul is bringing with you into this life.

Second Blueprint Attainment:

11 - Is in your second Blueprint Attainment. During this period, your vision will become clearer on what tasks you like to be involved with. You are gifted with a high vibration energy that may be expressed through inspirational teaching, preaching, leading, acting, art and invention. You have access to predictive wisdom and your positive outlook is a transformational strength in other people's lives. The Universe will draw those types of energies around you as long as you are receptive to it.

Third Blueprint Attainment:

11 - Is in your third Blueprint Attainment. During this period, you and the Universe are in direct link, and communication allows you to inspire others to dream and to make their dreams come true. You are so well-rounded and gifted psychically that at times, you might feel like you're bursting with information and insights that allow you to assist others.

Fourth Blueprint Attainment:

11 - Is in your fourth Blueprint Attainment. During this period, the glow you possess will reflect on the way you handle yourself and other people, and how you deal directly with everyone around. This vibration at this point in your life brings the additional push that allows you to explore all over the world. Action is required from you in order to explore all the opportunities open to you.

Blueprint Attainment 22:

General Characteristics - Influences Underline:
    Full of life, very influential and large scale recognition.
    Practical idealist.
    Master builder bringing order to the world.
    Nervous tension sometime suicidal.
    Look also for 4 lower vibration influences.

First Blueprint Attainment:

22 - Is in your first Blueprint Attainment. During this period, it's hard to use the influences of this vibration at young age. Check the lower Blueprint Attainment 4.

Second Blueprint Attainment:

22 - Is in your second Blueprint Attainment. During this period, the energies around are concentrated on your vision and goals in life, and the world is your playground.

Third Blueprint Attainment:

22 - Is in your third Blueprint Attainment. During this period, it's time to put your presence into large scale businesses that will help you to retire. Your strong will and vision make you the best to reach the stars.

Fourth Blueprint Attainment:

22 - Is in your fourth Blueprint Attainment. During this period, it's time to help others achieve their best potential and you are the best source to accomplish that.

Blueprint Attainment 33:

General Characteristics - Influences Underline:
 Spiritual teacher, worldly influences and healer.
 Skill & fame and worldly success.
 Good relationship.
 Worried tension.
 Look also for 6 lower vibration influences.

First Blueprint Attainment:

33 - Is in your first Blueprint Attainment. During this period, it is hard to use the influences of this vibration at young age. Check the lower Blueprint Attainment 6.

Second Blueprint Attainment:

33 - Is in your second Blueprint Attainment. During this period, at times you feel you don't belong on this planet, yet on the other hand, you know you need to do something. The Universe is your access to the ancient wisdom that will drive your compassion, and the world is your source for all the knowledge and wisdom you might or might not be aware of yet.

Third Blueprint Attainment:

33 - Is in your third Blueprint Attainment. During this period, you are a master and teacher of all teachers, and you have access to all the wisdom of your old Soul that will assist you in reaching the level you desire. Connect with your Soul.

Fourth Blueprint Attainment:

33 - Is in your fourth Blueprint Attainment. During this period, the stronger your Soul connection is, the stronger your compassion towards people will be. You will move towards helping, assisting or doing just about anything to bring a smile, or be an example for people to follow.

k. Blueprint Subconscious

Your subconscious self is the energy that motivates you to act without having conscious awareness of how or why you are doing it. This energy is the reason behind why you keep acting the same way over and over again in your life. This vibration reveals the hidden part of your character that needs to be worked upon to strengthen and improve in your life. It also reflects the confidence you have in your own personal power and capability of dealing with sudden events and situations. This vibration will reveal to you the way in which you assess situations that you encounter in life, as well as how you respond to those situations. The Subconscious Self also reveals the areas of your character that need to be strengthened.

The Subconscious Self is derived from your Karmic Lesson chart.

Blueprint Subconscious 1 & 2:

Not applicable

Blueprint Subconscious 3:

You respond to sudden events and emergencies in your life by looking to other people for support, to help take care of you and your problems. Because of this, life will eventually be forced to make you begin tackling these incidents until your learn to use your own power. You may marry an older person for protection, safety and security. You can exaggerate things until they are way out of proportion. For some you might have a hard time growing up and will always act like a child.

You have to pay attention to your choice of friends. It is time for you to stop attracting people who support your emotional neediness, as this encourages you to avoid dealing with those emotions in the first place.

Blueprint Subconscious 4:

You react slowly to situations and can easily get lost in details. You pay attention to the 'non-sense' of situations just to justify your own way of thinking. You have to learn to trust your instincts and act quickly. You are prone to hesitation, so you must avoid uncertainty and procrastination. You need solid grounding and a strong foundation for you to be able to build some values upon in your life. You question your abilities, and this tends to make you avoid reacting quickly and with force, causing you to lose control of situations.

Blueprint Subconscious 5:

You are all over the place. You have a tendency to scatter your energies everywhere so that nothing important to you is accomplished. You always try to escape or avoid situations instead of dealing with life's challenges head-on. You have a strong urge to escape difficulties by forcing change, instead of trying to work out the problem. You do familiarize yourself to change very well, however, and may become more grounded once you're settled with career and family.

You require discipline and organization in your life. Your accomplishment in life depends on your capacity to ground yourself and accept responsibilities.

Blueprint Subconscious 6:

Family and friends are your source of encouragement whenever you need it. You enjoy helping others, often to the extent that you sacrifice yourself and forget to pay attention to your own needs. You emit Universal love and genuine interest for others. Your first and foremost concern is that of your home and your family. You are responsible and when you have a secure and happy home, you will be quite capable of overcoming many hurdles.

Blueprint Subconscious 7:

Many see you as you being cold and distant. You are grounded and well-balanced. You are a survivor and have enough patience to handle many storms that happen in your life. During stormy days, you will always be able to find your own inner retreat within yourself, and that will help you to focus and recharge yourself.

You have an analytical mind. You enjoy being by yourself and having your own space. You have hard time expressing your feelings.

Blueprint Subconscious 8:

Challenges are a big part of your life and you enjoy overcoming all obstacles that come your way. In a sense, it's as if you would feel empty and were living in a void without challenges. It's all right to enjoy life in its simplicity, so take it easy! You do not repeat the same mistake twice. You always learn from your mistakes. You are a quick learner, and are dependable and trustworthy.

You enjoy being recognized for your efforts and accomplishments when it comes to the material side of your life. You have executive capabilities and a quick mind that knows what to do and how to do it in many situations. You are a survivor and display the qualities of leadership and dependability in your life, and because of this, people trust you easily.

Blueprint Subconscious 9

You are somewhat distant and may be complicated to get to know. You may have difficulties in recognizing your own weaknesses, and will tend to exaggerate things whenever you have difficulty in handling life situations. You are often incapable of seeing the big picture of a situation. You have difficulty in expressing your affection and may appear to others as arrogant and proud, even though you bear a great sense of compassion on the inside. You do not portray to others the essence of who you really are.

You have no particular karmic lessons to learn, therefore, are not exposed to life's ups and downs as others may be. You might feel bored at times because of this.

1. Blueprint Family Name

Blueprint Family 1:

The Blueprint Family 1 came together in this lifetime to learn about emphasis on traits such as originality, independence, individualism, self-reliance, determination, masculine energy, change, executive ability and creative and unique leadership. There is competition between the members of family 1 and that can bring a lot of pressure to measure up compared to other members in the family. They always look to be the best in everything they do and touch. Always, someone will brag about someone else's success. Someone is always boasting to another family member over their achievements, and that can bring envy, pressure and even jealousy between family members.

Leadership is good in the home of family 1, as support for success is always available. Family 1 members are always very proud of their accomplishments and many times, they deserve it for the big effort and perseverance they put into achieving their goals. Entrepreneurship runs in the blood of this family. Owning your own business or working for yourself, being a doctor, inventor, artistic or any other area in life, makes you exceed your boundaries. Generations in a family 1 follow the footstep of their parents or grandparents. For example, if the grandfather is a doctor, the father is a doctor and then the son or daughter wants to be a doctor to follow family traditions. They live and cherish their own circle and the world they build around them to live in. A Blueprint Family 1 is a masculine family, as they are driven through their achievements, but they hardly express their emotions, which can pile up and bring strain in the relationships between them. They regard talking about emotions as a weakness that can be shown especially outside the circle of the family.

A lot of superficiality and sometimes snobbishness can exist in the Blueprint Family 1. Emphasis on the achievement may never end in their family gatherings. Some talk loud and express their self-centeredness and arrogance.

Problems always occur when you are trying to impress or imitate another member of a Blueprint Family 1, as there is never good enough to match them, so originality and independence in this Blueprint Family are emphasized here. With this vibration in your Blueprint Family, emotional talk is not a strong asset because it is portrayed as a weakness.

The major lesson to learn within the boundaries of Blueprint Family 1 is to express the emotion between each other, to enhance the relationships between them.

Competitiveness between Blueprint Family 1 members is always so obvious that you need to step out of it to avoid falling into insecurity and low self-confidence.

Blueprint Family 2:

The Blueprint Family 2 is here to learn about cooperation, diplomacy, connections with each other businesses, affairs and emotions, intuition, patience, nurturing, peace within themselves and self-worth. They are dominated by a strong feminine influence and you can see it in the way they express the details of any situation in their life. This Blueprint Family depends on a lot of intuition and members keep inspiring each other to achieve it. This is a very gifted family and they enjoy talking about their gifts. They do have a tendency to exaggerate the events to boost the self-worth they always look for and like to have in their life. They enjoy sharing to hear about each other, regardless of how small or big their achievements.

They are very open with each other and there are no secrets between each other. They enjoy each other's company and they usually stick with each other. They are sensitive and tend to express themselves by crying. That is not weakness but a way of release, even though it's a temporary measure. It is rare to have a single family member, since they always like to be with someone else. Starting a family at an early age is a way of life. They enjoy long hours of talk in the kitchen or any comfortable setting where you find the joy of being with others. This 2 Blueprint Family's stress comes from over-sensitivity that can lead to certain abuse and being a victim or a doormat for other people.

Blueprint Family 3:

The Blueprint Family 3 is here to learn about the joy of life, being happy in each other's company, humor, appearances, illusions, creativity, beauty, talents, communication, and the power of words and expressiveness. This family comes together to learn how to communicate constructively and honestly. The talk between each other might have lots of surface talk with no essence of expressing their true emotions and inner feelings, but there is always joy, kindness and consideration. They need to learn to express their feelings and emotions freely and avoid all gossip, arguments and superficiality.

There is something different about this family. They are gifted and all sorts of communication is part of their daily life. For example, many in this family are very sensitive and are able to be strong mediums who can develop their psychic capability very easily, which is also a sort of communication, too. Others in that family are good at art, or dancing, singing, writing or any form of creativity that allows them to express their feeling and emotions. The Blueprint Family 3 can never miss fun between each other. They enjoy partying, good times and big gatherings. People have a hard time figuring out their true intentions, because they seem to anyone on the outside, to confuse how serious or non-series their true motives are. Being serious or joking for a Blueprint Family 3 can be a challenge at times.

They are very sociable and can exceed any expectations when it comes to sales as a career because they enjoy talking, and part of their charm is the way they express when they want to sell. The Blueprint Family 3 can give the appearance of happiness and friendliness, as long as they don't have a hard time expressing their own emotions which they have to deal with at some point in their life. In this family, there are many secrets between members, and sometimes jealousy. They have a habit of abruptly changing the subject, which often confuses those who really would like to take these people more seriously! That can happen specially when they have a hard time expressing their emotions. Usually it takes two seconds for a 3 family member to change the subject when they do not want to talk about it.

This family can be very loud because first they enjoy talking and usually they talk on top of each other to be heard which can give them a sense of being important and knowledgeable. It's fun to be around this family because they are lots of fun, spontaneous and know how to entertain themselves and others at the same time.

Blueprint Family 4:

The Blueprint Family 4 comes together to learn about success. They are here to bring success through organization, structure, effort, hard work, tolerance, love, detail and order in their life, and to overcome limitation. But the most important factor for a Blueprint Family 4 is the enjoyment in their life on this planet. As much as it seems this family vibration to be dull or boring from the outside, it would be hard for anyone to understand them until they become part of the family circle.

Hard work is the essence of this family. This family has tendencies that can seem weird, dull and unusual, yet they tend to be very serious and structured in the way they approach life. They are here on this plane to enjoy life on Earth and enjoy every detail in their lives, such as the things they enjoy collecting and the gadgets they like to use or play with. It is the seriousness concerning work-related matters and the way they pay attention to details that is most noticeable. No matter how laid-back or eccentric they try to be, there is always a sense of caution, and devotion to anything is part of their life family, work, and the surrounding of the cocoon they build around them. Family is important to them. They enjoy lots of hobbies and interests, and you get to know them the moment you try to adopt to their way of looking at life and people in general. This family has inherited a down-to-earth approach, with hard work put into achieving the goals they set themselves to bring comfort and stability to life.

In this family, inheritance can be passed from one generation to the next, and family value is solid with each other. They believe there is a proper way to do things, and their way is the proper way and sometimes the only way. The way they see life is the only way for them to succeed in life, and many people find them dull and boring, but they are very successful due to their consistency, perseverance and dedication.

Loneliness is felt by most Blueprint Family 4 members at times and they have the tendency to judge others according to the way they see life, without giving any concern to alternative ways of understanding life and other people's experiences. They think and even believe they are always right. In general, this family is good in management, guiding other people, discipline and routine, while never complaining. Managing their money, their career and their personal stability in life are important to them, but most often, they forget to have fun at the same time. They are seen as workaholics, and they need to watch for contradictions in their life that can often be their worst enemy.

Blueprint Family 5:

The Blueprint Family 5 is learning about freedom, expansion, adventure, variety, discipline, sexuality, life indulgence and the physical body. They possess a strong charismatic presence. Their way of looking at things, or attitudes, beliefs, temperaments, and occupations can be diverse, making it difficult to see any kind of common thread between them. This family reflects 'Jack of all trade but good at none.'

They are very resourceful and have a hard time sticking to one thing at a time. They can be skilled when it comes to careers that involve the use of the hands, such as giving massages, being a physiotherapist, a reflexologist or anything that puts them in contact with another human Soul's vibration.

They get bored very easily and find earthly responsibility a drag. Nature is good and important for them as their mind/body/Soul expands beyond just the physical to bring a higher fulfillment in their life. They have their own unique view of the world and their own definition of success and happiness. Although this is true of most families, 5s are the most diverse, broad-minded and free-spirited of all families. Earthly rules do not apply to them. Traveling and adventures are big parts of their life experiences, so being away from home and from each other is fact of life, yet a strong bond remains with each other.

They have a tendency to deal with sudden and sometimes traumatic situations more easily than others, and they bring acceptance to any situation in their life. They need constant excitement in their lives, so Blueprint Family 5 members can be prone to substance abuse, gambling, sex addiction, drinking and taking careless chances. They are sensitive to each others' feelings, but tensions arise when differing opinions arise and when feelings are held inside. They thrive on openness, curiosity and creativity. Sometimes, they have a hard time learning from their mistakes and keep repeating the same situations over and over. Growing up and stability are major lessons to learn in this life.

Blueprint Family 6:

The Blueprint Family 6 is about family, responsibility, domestic matters, love, education, healing, judgment, sacrifice and balance. The main focus of the Blueprint Family 6 is respect to each other and loyalty. Their sense of duty and responsibility is enormous. They are considered good listeners and are usually very generous in nature and emotional. Being individuals in a Blueprint Family 6 can be very hard as you are part of the family and everyone is in everyone else's business. They all want the best out of life, but decisions are often based for the best for the family.

Food is a form of expression between each other and towards others. The kitchen is the most comfortable room at home, where they enjoy meeting family and friends. They are a lot of fun and laugh among themselves, bringing up old memories of things in their life to remind them of their roots. The Blueprint Family 6 is a warm and wonderful place to be because it thrives on entertaining, healing and teaching.

Unconditional love within this family is very noticeable but anyone from outside their belief system is judged accordingly. They must learn to apply the principle of unconditional love to those whose experience of life is different from their own. Problems always occur when they judge themselves or others according to their own particular set of beliefs. They have a tendency sometimes to be prejudicial and suspicious, so they need to work at bringing Universal love into their life. They often sacrifice of themselves in order to help each other and keep things within the family.

Blueprint Family 7:

The Blueprint Family 7 comes together to focus on their spiritual awareness and its relationship to their life. The importance of this environment of a Blueprint Family 7 is to learn about trust in themselves and each other, and to enhance their belief system in a higher Universe. Spirituality, the inner self, reflection, privacy, intellect and inner wisdom are big parts of the Blueprint Family 7. There are usually secrets in the Blueprint Family 7, many of which need not be secrets at all, especially from a family vibration that practices spiritual belief.

Blueprint Family 7 members want to retain their dignity at all costs and often feel that it would be undignified to let certain truths about themselves be known. They are usually withdrawn and they enjoy solitude and time to themselves, unless it is becoming loneliness, so they need to socialize and be around other people. As a whole, people find them weird, withdrawn and detached, but the problem is not that they are that way because they want to be, but most often they do not know how to express anything about themselves that they have not understood themselves first. They have a tendency to always look to perfect things in their life by over-analyzing things around them, in themselves and in the Universe, until they completely disregard what they were trying to do in the first place.

They are considered very lucky and things fall in their lap. Also, they can turn anything to their favor unless they over-analyze it. They keep a low profile, and can go to great lengths to maintain their privacy. They hate being criticized and being in front of things because of having a hard time expressing what they believe in and trust the most. But that is a phase they go through in their life. They sometimes show a tendency of feeling paranoid, and analyzing and criticizing others. However, when they become comfortable with the spiritual and intellectual path they chose to travel together, the 7 family becomes interested in the sciences, religion, spirituality, philosophy, and/or technology, and there are probably a lot of books in the family home.

They need quiet and peace. They must learn, on the other hand, that thinking or being alone achieves very little. They express their feelings with as much passion as their thoughts with only the people who allow them to be themselves without any judgment. They convince themselves that they are better off alone, but on the contrary, they enjoy being with someone else in their life as most often they learn about loneliness.

They have many fears in their life. The fear of their own gifts, the fear of failure and the fear of success are very obvious in their life, and they need to emphasize overcoming all their analyzing of their fears in order to attain what they came here to do in the first place. Blueprint Family 7 are here for themselves first but then, with their knowledge and awareness, they can be very helpful to humanity. They can be very gifted psychics and mediums.

The Blueprint Family 8

The Blueprint Family 8 comes together to learn about power, money and achieving recognition, wealth, tolerance, self-acceptance, love, sharing and material freedom. They assist each other to achieve their goals but they do run into a pattern of defocusing from the ultimate goal they are trying to reach.

Often focused on success and status, they are willing to work hard and be a workaholic as they want to achieve a goal they have in mind. Life is a competition for them to be the best they can be, and everything is about the image or status they portray about themselves. They succeed in their own business or in high-level positions in major companies. They love to control other people, and playing with other people's money will drive them to success. They tend to be ambitious, resourceful and skillful, but also they tend to control, being authoritarian and demanding. They need to balance that with joy and happiness. Sometimes their concentration on material freedom makes them forget about their needs towards their personal life. They often do things to bring the best of things in the family but many times, they can disregard their own needs.

Other people find them always in their faces and very demanding and too direct, but most often they themselves do not mean any harm, and it's just their way of expressing themselves. They need to avoid being workaholics and abusing their power, especially when they self-sabotage themselves.

You feel abundance in their presence and they pump up anyone to follow their example. They are very persuasive, consistent and respected at the same time. At an early stage in their life, they tended to be greedy but later on when they reached their goals, they tend to become more sharing of their blessings generously, and they can be very good assets to organizations that need to raise money for their cause. Many tend be involved in humanitarian causes because they understand there is abundance in the Universe and that it's okay to share it with others.

Blueprint Family 9:

The Blueprint Family 9 comes together in this lifetime to learn about compassion, service, love, assistance, peace, humanity, global awareness, freedom, completion and letting go. This family needs to learn about flexibility and to understand their emotions, which they tend to express well. This family often appears to be all over the place, with no organization, but when put to the test, they deliver what is needed from them. The 9 family in general is the family vibration that brings the end of patterns, beliefs and ideas that do not support their growth, in order for them to jump into higher awareness and express their emotions through their humanitarian work.

Many sudden events can come up in their life, in order to deal with it, learn to let it go and move on in their life. The biggest learning for them is letting go, and sometimes, it might take a while to do so, but their concern with humanity and human issues can sometimes overcome the need to look after themselves and help them to see that their problem has no significance compare to other people's misery.

They are usually outgoing people who will fight for what they believe in. The Blueprint Family 9 is the end of the experience they have, having lived all the first 8 levels of Blueprint Family, and they are here for a closure for their Soul to move to a different level of understanding and awareness.

They are very humanitarian and missionary in nature, and support any cause and care a lot about animals and nature in general. They can lead any cause they believe in … and they believe in such a wide variety of things. The common thread running through this family is compassion, the desire to understand and the willingness to help others. They love each other deeply and have strong feelings, expressing their emotions clearly.

This is the end of a Soul journey to be in a 9 family, as every Soul will go through all the Blueprint Family learning and understanding. Following this comes the Master number Blueprint Families 11, 22, 33 and a rare 44. With those vibrations, a Soul brings with it to this plane a higher Universal awareness and higher Universal understanding in order to uplift humanity.

Blueprint Family 11:

The Blueprint Family 11 came together in this lifetime to learn about being leaders, artists, celebrities, dreamers, visionaries and inspirational to others. This family often appears to be driven to be leaders with a new hope to others.

This Blueprint Family 11 members are here at this point to bring awareness, higher communication and illumination. They have a glimpse into the higher understanding of the universe, and are here to uplift humanity through their individual work. Usually they are very intuitive, mystic and messengers, trying to uplift humanity one more notch.

Many times in a Blueprint Family 11, they run into their inner problem, which can be drug problems, depression, ego, pride or stubbornness. They can live in a fantasy only being a dreamer, as if running from their own reality.

In order for a Blueprint Family 11 to succeed, they need to understand Blueprint Family 1, and Blueprint Family 2 as 2 is the lower vibration of 11.

Holding a master number vibration 11 means a lot of knowledge, awareness and vision, but also with this vibration, once you are down, you can go down even greater than a normal family would because deep inside of you, the member of this family knows they should be doing greater things than they are currently doing, so it becomes a big pressure to perform. However, such stress is not needed here because their Soul is bringing with it lots of wisdom of many lifetimes. Whatever distracted that family from pursuing their Blueprint Destiny's calling, they need to snap out of it, refocus their energy, and start seeing the bigger picture instead of dwelling on their daily routine. They need to be 100% of whatever they are preaching about ... and live it in their daily life. The vision of the Blueprint Family 11 is greater than life. Having much vision, you should be an inspiration to others. You can open doors and help others to greater achievements.

Blueprint Family 22:

The Blueprint Family 22 came together in this lifetime to learn about being dedicated, true to themselves with a firm future vision and a strong devotion to help others.

Blueprint Family 22 members often appear to be trustworthy, straightforward and practical idealists. They need to be well prepared in order to deliver and live their Soul mission. They are very dependable, faithful and have the financial stability that allows them to go after their vision or the vision of others to pursue that world recognition. They are visionary and should bring with them at this time a Universal transformation that uplifts humanity to bring order and change.

In order for Blueprint Family 22 succeed, they need to understand Blueprint Family 2 and 4, as 4 is the lower vibration of 22 (2 +2 = 4 and 22 contain two 2s).

This Blueprint Family 22 possesses the qualities of imagination, loyalty, secrecy, optimism, and heightened perception. Holding a master number vibration 22 has a lot of essence of knowledge, awareness and vision as this master number brings in this life. However, once you are down, you can go down even deeper than with normal family vibrations because deep inside of you, the members of this family know they should be doing greater than what they are doing at the moment, so it puts pressure to perform. However, such stress is not needed here because their Soul is bringing with it lots of wisdom from the many lifetimes their Soul has lived. Whatever distracted that family from their Blueprint Destiny's calling, they need to snap out of it to refocus their energy and start seeing the bigger picture instead of dwelling in their daily routine. This Blueprint Family 22 does even greater things than Blueprint Family 11. They need to be 100% of whatever they are preaching about, and live it in their daily life.

Blueprint Family 33

The Blueprint Family 33 came together in this lifetime to learn about compassion, their emotions, affection and devotion. These Blueprint Family members hold enormous wisdom as they all come from very old Souls who have had lots of lifetimes of experiences and awareness, and understanding much about humanity and the human issues. Their caring, passionate side helps and services humanity even if they need to sacrifice themselves. They are also resourceful, soft-hearted and unselfish.

This Blueprint Family 33 often appears to be into worldly success. They are here to fulfill their Soul mission on a large scale in order to promote humanity. In order for Blueprint Family 33 to succeed, they need to understand Blueprint Family 3 and 6, as 6 is the lower vibration of 33 (3 +3 = 6 and 33 contain two 3s).

As with 11 and 22 families, once you are down, you can go down even more than normal families they know they should be doing more than they are doing. They need to be doing 100% of whatever they are preaching about and live it in their daily life. The Blueprint Family 33 are teachers to all teachers and should be very down to earth type of people. You would be a master teacher who could guide the inquiring student into all areas of the known and unknown fields of knowledge and human experience. The fully developed Blueprint Family 33 would be enchanting an audience while teaching them whatever that family chooses to impart.

Note: Regardless of where your master number is in your chart, that master number is worth nothing unless you get up and start doing something in your life, otherwise you are operating on your lower vibration of your master number.

When an old Soul decides to come back into this plane, they come with the task to fulfill a life mission and make the most of their time here after so many lives on other planes in the Universe.

Don't let a master number in your chart go to your head, or you will go nowhere. Master number people should put the needs of others before their own needs, for they are here to make a difference.

The same way a master number person is here to do great things, but master numbers can have, as with any other vibration, a negative and positive vibration. You can be the saviour of humanity yet at the same time, you can be the most destructive, too. Think about it!

m. Blueprint Intensity Table

Blueprint Intensity:

In my personal opinion, it is important to use your name and stick with it. Every time you change your name, you will have a positive or a negative effect on your Blueprint Intensity table.

A normal blueprint intensity table should have the following quantities. A name can have normal quantities. But not all names will have the normal quantities; if that is the case, we can have either a blueprint karmic or weak vibration.

Number	Letters	Normal Average in a Name
1	A J S	3
2	B K T	1
3	C L U	1, 2
4	D M V	1
5	E N W	3, 4, 5
6	F O X	1, 2
7	G P Y	0, 1
8	H Q Z	1
9	I R	3

That table will help you determine if you are below or above Blueprint Intensity which means how weak or strong you are in a particular vibration. So you can have the vibration in you but it can be weak or strong. That can bring a few lessons to learn from those vibrations.

The number that is outstanding in your name is considered as your major blueprint intensity vibration.

Looking at your normal average in your name from the above chart:
- If it is below average, that will bring some weakness in that vibration so some part of the negative aspect of that vibration needs to be watched at times.
- If it is above the average, that can bring a negative impact where you might be abusing the power of your particular vibration so you need to watch for that at times.

If you have a weak vibration, just read the negative aspect of that vibration from my section 'Meaning of Numbers.'

If you have a missing number and you have a 0 as vibration, then here are the interpretations for the missing numbers.

Read the interpretation for Blueprint Karmic lesson in case you do not have that number in your name and also in your chart.

If you do not have the number in your name but still have it in your chart, then it will become a Modified Blueprint Karmic lesson, so read the negative aspect of that number to find what lesson you might need to learn.

1. Blueprint Karmic Lesson

Blueprint Karmic Lesson 1:

Your best way to bring good karma in your life today is to concentrate less on your own aims, and show others the way to their success. You might find getting your needs met difficult in this life. You feel such a lack of confidence in your own ability that you find it hard to promote yourself. You find yourself going along with others despite feeling that you won't get anywhere with what you are doing at the moment. It is part of your lesson for you to figure this out and get out of the pattern. You have a hard time being independent. You lack confidence to follow through on your ambition and dreams. This karma is extremely rare, so those who have this karma find themselves having little faith in their own powers and always looking to others for direction, and you have a hard time making decisions and standing on your own two feet.

Blueprint Karmic Lesson 2:

Loving yourself and taking care of yourself will enable you to love and take care of others in this life without sacrificing your dignity and self-esteem. You find yourself extremely considerate, and helpful towards others but sometimes you find yourself a part of other people's problems. With this karma in your life, some people find you lacking in sensitivity and not being considerate enough for others in your life. Your lesson is to practice letting go of such toxic emotional habits as possessiveness, jealousy and obsession.

Blueprint Karmic Lesson 3:

You have the tendency to scatter your energy all over the place. You have a hard time expressing yourself and have little joy of life. You tend to be withdrawn or uncomfortable in social situations and promoting yourself.

Build your confidence in order to do the creative things you love to do just for the sheer joy of doing them ... and the money will come to you. If you start feeling that the world owes you a living, immediately go out and practice an act of random kindness or work for a charity to humble yourself. You are running in your own circles and having a hard time finding yourself. It is important to learn what makes you happy in order to find confidence in yourself.

Blueprint Karmic Lesson 4:

You need to find peace and harmony inside. As you are such a caretaker of others, you are advised to take time out from your focus on others and regularly reconnect with your higher self by practicing yoga or meditation. You lack awareness of practicality, organization, hard work and concern with detail. You need to bring some discipline to your life and stop looking at hard work as a limitation. You feel stagnation and procrastination in your life, and need to bring stability in your mental, emotional, physical and spiritual aspects of your life to find peace.

Blueprint Karmic Lesson 5:

You lack awareness in your freedom, and need to define your freedom – freedom of religion, freedom of culture, freedom from negative people around you, freedom of your own way of thinking and of your own thoughts that do not support you. You have hard time with change, and need to learn to adapt and deal with situations with versatility. You have little understanding of tolerance. You have a hard time learning from your experiences, and keep repeating your pattern over and over again. This karma is extremely rare. Dispensing with pride and learning to be humble are often corrective to your karma.

Blueprint Karmic Lesson 6:

You lack awareness of duties and responsibilities. You judge yourself and others in every move you make. You lack responsibilities in your life. Responsibility is a very important part of your karma. You have much responsibility to carry and you feel the pressure of caring for others who cannot or will not care for themselves. Instead of helping with responsibility, family and friends are apt to be the primary burdens in your life. You need to learn to take care of your own needs before caring for others. You need to learn to balance your needs and caring for others.

Blueprint Karmic Lesson 7:

You lack awareness of the inner life, refusing to understand the deeper spiritual values. You need to appreciate the non-material world. Although faith in spiritual values may be key to your growth, it may have little interest to you. 7s can also create good karma by learning to master their greatest fears, such as fear of abandonment or fear of 'letting go.' You must bypass your fears of your own gift, your fear of being successful and your fear of failing.

Blueprint Karmic Lesson 8:

You show lack of awareness of the practical necessities of life, including the need to earn and use money. Your attitude towards money shows in your life. You need to learn to handle your own material affairs and make reasonable and practical judgments. You run into patterns when it comes with your value to money, achieving recognition in your life and your authority towards others in your life. 8s reap the greatest karmic rewards by having faith and working diligently to accomplish their goals no matter what others say. 8 is a karmic symbol when it is put on its side as an infinity sign that you keep turning and always come back to the same results in your life. You need to get out of your patterns.

Blueprint Karmic Lesson 9:

You show little concern for others. You are likely to be self-centered and unaware of, or repressing, your own feelings. You are subject to emotional upsets, disappointments and separations in your life until you learn to be concerned with others and show compassion and love as a clear expression of your feelings. 9s can correct their karma by displaying more faith in the concept that the universe is a benevolent, rather than a cruel place. Detaching from your emotions and consistently displaying an upbeat and positive attitude usually brings you great rewards.

Blueprint Karmic Lesson 11:

There is no karma 11 but if you have the Master number 11 in your chart and you have any karma with 1 and 2 in your chart, you need to work on opening up Master numbers in your life, because your karma with 1 or 2 can slow you down in opening your Master number 11.

Blueprint Karmic Lesson 22:

There is no karma 22 but if you have a Master number 22 in your chart and you have any karma with 2 and 4 in your chart, handle those karmas in order to help you open up Master number in your life, because your karma with 2 or 4 can slow you down in opening your Master number 22.

Blueprint Karmic Lesson 33:

There is no karma 33 but if you have a Master number 33 in your chart, plus you have karma with 3 and 6 in your chart, handle those karmas in order to open up Master numbers in your life because your karma with 3 or 6 can slow you down in opening your Master number 33.

2. Modified Blueprint Karmic Lesson

Modified Blueprint Karmic Lesson 1 has less pressure and depth of the lesson for you to learn than just the Blueprint Karmic Lesson. The intensity of the lesson here is much easier to deal with but, for some, it is still hard to learn. Review the negative aspect of this number and see what one word or two you can relate to in your life from vibration 1.

Modified Blueprint Karmic Lesson 2 has less pressure and depth of the lesson for you to learn than just the Blueprint Karmic Lesson. The intensity of the lesson here is much easier to deal with but, for some, it is still hard to learn. Review the negative aspect of this number and see what one word or two you can relate to in your life from vibration 2.

Modified Blueprint Karmic Lesson 3 has less pressure and depth of the lesson for you to learn than the Blueprint Karmic Lesson. The intensity of the lesson here is much easier to deal with but, for some, it is still hard to learn. Review the negative aspect of this number and see what one word or two you can relate to in your life from vibration 3.

Modified Blueprint Karmic Lesson 4 has less pressure and depth of the lesson for you to learn than the Blueprint Karmic Lesson. The intensity of the lesson here is much easier to deal with but, for some, it is still hard to learn. Review the negative aspect of this number and see what one word or two you can relate to in your life from vibration 4.

Modified Blueprint Karmic Lesson 5 has less pressure and depth of the lesson for you to learn than the Blueprint Karmic Lesson. The intensity of the lesson here is much easier to deal with but, for some, it is still hard to learn. Review the negative aspect of this number and see what one word or two you can relate to in your life from vibration 5.

Modified Blueprint Karmic Lesson 6 has less pressure and depth of the lesson for you to learn than the Blueprint Karmic Lesson. The intensity of the lesson here is much easier to deal with but, for some, it is still hard to learn. Review the negative aspect of this number and see what one word or two you can relate to in your life from vibration 6.

Modified Blueprint Karmic Lesson 7 has less pressure and depth of the lesson for you to learn than the Blueprint Karmic Lesson. The intensity of the lesson here is much easier to deal with but, for some, it is still hard to learn. Review the negative aspect of this number and see what one word or two you can relate to in your life from vibration 7.

Modified Blueprint Karmic Lesson 8 has less pressure and depth of the lesson for you to learn than the Blueprint Karmic

Lesson. The intensity of the lesson here is much easier to deal with but, for some, it is still hard to learn. Review the negative aspect of this number and see what one word or two you can relate to in your life from vibration 8.

Modified Blueprint Karmic Lesson 9 has less pressure and depth of the lesson for you to learn than the Blueprint Karmic Lesson. The intensity of the lesson here is much easier to deal with but, for some, it is still hard to learn. Review the negative aspect of this number and see what one word or two you can relate to in your life from vibration 9.

n. Blueprint 9-Year Cycle

Year 1 - New Beginning:

This is a very good time to start new projects. These projects can be on the emotional level, material, business, or conscious awareness level, or on the level of your Soul's journey of evolution. This year is a very good vibration for you, especially if you made a proper assessment and are ready and prepared to go after, what it is you want out of life. Embark on your journey! This is a time to begin making totally new plans or to initiate a complete change in your life direction. Be independent and original. Work to activate your plans, your ideals, and all the many changes you want to go after. Your power level is high this year and it is time to ACT. Hard work may be necessary to get a venture up and running.

I remember personally that, in 2002, when I entered my first year of the cycle, I started 3 new projects:
1. I started a new relationship.
2. I started my journey with writing.
3. I opened 'The Free Spirit Centre' web site.

It is not required for you to start 3 things at once, only one thing will do – we all work according to our own speed and life alignment. However, do not let your 1st Year go by unnoticed without bringing something new into your life.

A proper study of your own situation and an ability to focus is needed to make your start a more productive one.

Your beginning can be on any level and, in order to properly start a new beginning, you need to ask yourself a simple question regarding what it is you want to start: "If it's a relationship, a business, or something related to emotional or mental concerns, am I ready to let go of the past issues related to what it is I would like to start?"

Negative aspects of the 'Year 1 Cycle' of a '9-Year Cycle':
1. You have a big ego.
2. You have too much pride and lack of humility in your life.
3. You need to work on your self-confidence.
4. You are dependent on other people.
5. You are very stubborn.
6. You are very spoiled.
7. You are self-centered. Me - Me - Me.
8. You are only a dreamer with no focus.
9. You must avoid your addiction (drugs, gambling, drinking, etc. ...).
10. You need to control your temper.

Solution for this year: it is time to grow up and face your life's reality. Stop repeating these patterns.

Year 2 - Foundation:

This year is the best time to take what you started with in Year 1 and build the foundation around it. If your new beginnings were business-related, then your second year's mission will be to build your foundation and make your business more secure. If you started a new relationship, this is the year to make it solid by investing in yourself, your partner, discovering Yourself and your Blueprint Destiny 227 and assessing your relationship. It is important in this case to let go of your old experiences or patterns. Letting go is necessary in order to make your new relationship work. Whatever your new project was in that first year, you will need more cooperation, patience and understanding, especially with regard to your past circumstances.

Learn to listen and avoid being sarcastic with others when it comes to dealing with events and situations you encounter in your life.

Whatever venture you began in your first year, know that it will develop slowly. Time is vital for plans to fully mature. Do not take action at this time, because it is likely to force conditions in less than constructive directions. Any wrong move is often followed by problems. Be patient and accept delays, detours and blockages. Pay attention to even the smallest of details.

Negative aspects of the 'Year 2 Cycle' of your '9-Year Cycle':
1. You are too sensitive.
2. You hate to be criticized.
3. You are very impatient and are suspicious that disharmony is provoked intentionally.
4. You have a problem with self-control.
5. You are jealous of others.
6. You feel self-pity.
7. You feel high levels of tension.
8. You have trouble learning to listen.
9. You are still a doormat for others.
10. You have an uncontrollable need to gossip.

Solution for this year: focus on what you started during Year 1. Be patient, and stop allowing other people to control your life.

Year 3 - Joy of Living:

This is a year for you to enjoy life and meet new friends. Self-expression is important at the moment. New people and friends will be in your surroundings, as long as you allow yourself to let loose and have some fun. Entertaining, or being entertained, is the theme of this year. Take a break from your old routine and start bringing lighter energies of fun and relaxation to your mood. There is time for you this year to look after what matters most to you. Hobbies, massages, short trips and anything fun and relaxing are always recommended. This is a year of flirtation, talking, and expressing yourself in whatever form, as it is a way of showing your creativity. It is a pleasant year for social affairs, especially after the last 2 years of hard work. Traveling and entertainment are always on your agenda. People are drawn to you because of your wit and charm. Networking is essential in Year 3, and a good opening for the years to follow. Stay optimistic and cheerful. You should start to see some results on the goals you set in Year 1. Hold on to them while you are still having fun. When you are around people, you take over with your cheerful attitude and magnetism.

It's not a good year to start a relationship. It is hard to choose, or decide what you want when you are having so much fun!

Negative aspects of the 'Year 3 Cycle' of your '9-Year Cycle':
1. You can lack the ability to express your deepest emotions.
2. You waste your energy.
3. You gossip or divulge too much in all the wrong places.
4. You are always pessimistic.
5. You are self-centered.
6. You are moody and full of scattered energy.
7. You always complain at the slightest of things.
8. You are always depressed.
9. You lack of direction in your life.
10. You are full of self-doubt.

Solution for this year: Take time out to pamper and enjoy yourself. Hard work with no fun becomes a drag. If you stay like this, you will lose concentration and direction. Enjoy yourself this year!

Year 4 – Construction Time:

Time for fun decreases this year, as you need to devote more serious attention to whatever you are working on at the moment. It is time to start getting back to life's obligations. This is a hard-working year. It is required that you begin to add the walls to the foundation you built during your Year 2 cycle. This year is for stabilizing your venture, and establishing a solid base for the future development of your project(s) started in the Year 1 cycle.

You must concentrate on adding a solid base to your foundation. Hard work, either mental or physical, is required of you this year. You must strengthen all of the weak areas in your projects or relationships. Take care of all of the details, put everything in order and be ready for potential growth. Good management is required of you at this time and your work will need your full attention and concentration. Year 4 is a time to be practical in regards to your health, particularly when you have a lot of work to deal with. Keep all legal papers in order, documents, insurance, etc. Keep things in order when it comes to business and property.

Remember, if you started your Year 1 on an emotional level and you survived your relationship so far, it may become necessary to make your relationship more solid and invest further. Do NOT take it for granted.

Negative aspects of the 'Year 4 Cycle' of your '9-Year Cycle':
1. You need to accept routine work.
2. You need to avoid becoming impractical and careless.
3. You need to avoid becoming rigid, dogmatic, stubborn, too fixed an approach or closed-minded.
4. You need to avoid becoming bossy, dominant or an excessive disciplinarian.
5. You can be envious of the progress of others.
6. You are lazy.
7. You try to skip steps in your personal growth or life journey.
8. You are very narrow-minded.

9. You are impatient.
10. You are confused.

Solution for this year: This year is a hard year and requires an investment to make whatever project you started in your Year 1 Cycle more solid. This year requires your full concentration and dedication to make it worth while to you.

Year 5 - Another New Beginning:

This year is a lighter year than the previous one. You still have to face some discipline in this cycle; however, it is less intense than the previous year. This year's lesson is about handling discipline and freedom, and the Universe is offering you a chance to go traveling and experience adventures. This year is a year for change or expansion in a new direction, perhaps in the business you started in Year 1. Invest more in your relationships, change your home, move in together, or take a trip together somewhere exotic and adventurous. This year will provide you with new opportunities and provide chances for growth on different levels. You should concentrate on feeling free. You should move away from old routines and patterns, but do so constructively. If you feel bogged down, this is a good time to seek out new directions and options. It is time to drop your seriousness and bring some fun into your life.

In some cases, couples can separate with the vibration of this year cycle, especially if one partner becomes too demanding, egoistic, or selfish while disregarding the other person. Remember, this year is about freedom. Keep your goal in mind and plan how you would like to advance with it.

Negative aspects of the 'Year 5 Cycle' of your '9-Year Cycle':
1. You need to be less impatient.
2. You are restless and scattered in all directions.
3. You need to avoid being stuck in a rut.
4. You need to avoid feeling stuck.

5. You need to avoid being moody.
6. You need to let go of feeling discontented.
7. You need to stop being 'Jack of all trades, master of none.'
8. You need to avoid too much access to drugs and alcohol.
9. You need to avoid being bored and constantly changing the course of your life.
10. You need to stop pretending you are happy.

Solution for this year: Change is the name of the game for you this year. You need to let go of negativity from your life, especially other people's negativity. You need to focus on your own energy.

Year 6 – Responsibility:

You will have more responsibilities on your shoulders this year as family and community work become your obligation. You are more involved with your family, either in a positive or negative way; it all depends on your situation with them. It is a year of service to others and you will feel more driven to help. Your heart is more affected by what goes on around you. It is a good time to be involved in a relationship or even consider getting married.

You will feel more compassionate towards other people and be more affectionate than ever before. This year is meant for you to concentrate on your home life. Sacrifice will play a big part in your life at this time. You will find universal love, friends, warmth and contentment in your life. Love energy is all around you, and lots of rewards will fall into your lap this year. Blessings from the sky will make this year a success. Keep your energies balanced.

Negative aspects of the 'Year 6 Cycle' of your '9-Year Cycle':
1. You need to avoid doing things for personal gain.
2. You need to let people handle their responsibilities their way.
3. You need to stop being responsible for everybody.
4. You need to pass up being hypercritical.

5. You need to stop judging others.
6. You need to stay away from being a perfectionist.
7. You need to withdraw from situations to avoid becoming confused.
8. You need to stop judging yourself.
9. You need to stay away from being irresponsible.
10. You need to avoid getting lost in petty details.

Solution for this year: Compassion and Universal love are in your surroundings this year. Enjoy them and surround yourself in them. The key for you this year is balance in your life. Make things happen.

Year 7 - Inner Reflection:

Personally, I believe this year 7 is the most important year in the 9-Year Cycle. This year is our God-given year for us to cleanse our system completely. This is the year to clean your thoughts and emotions, and to ground yourself and reflect on life. It is a year for inner reflection, to find out who you really are? What do you want out of your life? Where are you going with your life? It is a year to build trust in yourself again, and in your own capabilities. It is a year of conscious awareness of the Universe around you. This year might pique your curiosity to investigate and for you to expand your mind. Start digging into your deeper being, and touch your essence, your very Soul. It is good year to start meditation or Yoga.

The Universe will force you to go within, whether you like it or not. It is not going against your free will, of course, but if you are stuck in patterns, habits, and circumstances that require your deepest and most inner attention, you will have no choice but to be driven into getting to know yourself, and discovering what it is you really want out of life. Why are you always repeating the same patterns in your relationships? Why are you having problems when it comes to your career? Have a good look at the question marks that exist. Discover Yourself and Your Blueprint Destiny 233. Try to discover what it is you weren't capable of finding before. Now is the time to search for the answers. Look back at your previous year's cycle and see what occurred at this period. Were you laid off from your job in your last Year 7? Did you break up with your partner in your Year 7? This year can be a dreadful year to start something new in your life because you will not be sure about what you really want at this point.

Many people will find themselves forced to leave their work during this year. You can easily change jobs. I do not recommend you take on any heavy work, or even start a new relationship. These things can distract you from learning about yourself and the changes you need to happen. Your concentration this year should be on you, and only you. You need a lot of quality time for yourself. I recommend meditation, yoga or any activity that makes you happy and relaxed. You might feel like you need to be alone or stay by yourself. If you are in a relationship, try to have some quality time for yourself. You might have the desire to study the world of consciousness and spirituality, or investigate life more deeply. It is a good time to start writing in your journal. It is a year to relax and pay attention to yourself. You have many questions hanging over your head that need to be attended to and answered this year.

Negative aspects of the 'Year 7 Cycle' of your '9-Year Cycle':
1. You appear cold or detached.
2. You are skeptical.
3. You have an air of sarcasm around you.
4. You have an air of ignorance.
5. You fear failure.
6. You have a problem trusting yourself.
7. You are paranoid.
8. You experience bitterness.
9. You believe you have been betrayed.
10. You are pessimistic.

Solution for this year: Luck can be on your side this year. Isolation is the key to delving within yourself. Understand yourself, know yourself and be yourself. The discoveries you make this year will save yourself from going through many unnecessary and unwanted experiences in the future.

Year 8 - Rewards:

This is the year to pick up all of your rewards, recognition, power and money, as long as you have done what was necessary for your growth during the previous years. If not then, the beginning of the Year-8 Cycle might turn into a karmic year. This is to give you the chance to deal with all the loose ends and whatever else you have been avoiding all of these years. You might have to deal with everything you did not deal with before, and that will be a lot of work. If you have had any unfinished business from previous years, it will now become more intense for you to really face it and deal with it once and for all. Eight is also a karmic number, one of which I personally enjoy. I say 'karmic' because it forces us to face our own reality, and make us work harder in order to understand its lessons. Of course, you can choose to resist all of this and pass up the work, but you will have to repeat it all over again in your next 9-Year Cycle. This is how we end up stagnating in life and waste time repeating the same experiences over again and again. As you will see, 8 is like the sign of infinity right-side up.

This indicates that the energies will continue circulating to their original starting point. We all have patterns we need to let go of, so it is time to stop running through the same things in the 9-Year Cycle time after time. We need to focus on learning whatever it is we need to understand and move on with our lives. If this year is very rewarding, it is in appreciation of your hard work. You should know better by now, and not take things and your life for granted. Achievement vibrates for you this year. Opportunities for advancement will come your way if you have planned, organized, efficiently managed, and worked hard in the past to reach your goals. This is a year of abundance.

Negative aspects of the 'Year 8 Cycle' of your '9-Year Cycle':
1. You need to stop hanging onto material things that have outlived their usefulness.
2. You need to steer clear of being dominant in your love life.
3. You need to avoid trying to control or overpower other people.
4. You need to stay away from being greedy.
5. You need to deal with your patterns.
6. You need to deal with your life.
7. You need to live your present moment and stop dwelling in the past.
8. You need to avoid abusing your power.
9. You need to stop being greedy.
10. You need to be careful of self-sabotage.

Solution for this year: This is an energetic year that will get right to the heart of things in your life that you need to face and deal with. It is cut-and-dried sometimes, but it's all for the best. This is a good year to look into your financial and job situations.

Year 9 - Completion:

This is the end of your 9-Year Cycle. Whether you counted your year beginning in January, or the way I do starting from your birthday, the first six months of this year will require you to look back over the last 8 years and evaluate them. Writing in your journal is highly recommended. You need to look at the past years in an objective way, in order for you to realize and understand what does or does not work for you in your life. It is time for you to let go of your habits and patterns, and allow new things to surface in your life. In the remaining six months, start projecting what you would like to see happening for yourself in the next 9-Year Cycle. Initiate your plan and study it; after all, it is about your life and you should start taking action to improve it. This year is about completion and is the perfect time to tie up any loose ends in your life. Remember it is the most crucial year for you because anything you did not let go of or resisted changing will stay with you and will replay itself in your next 9-Year Cycle. Avoiding repeating experiences is your responsibility and will be determined by the way you make decisions this year. Letting go of events, situations and even people in your life is important this year. Take charge of your life!

Negative aspects of the 'Year 9 cycle' of your '9-Year Cycle':

1. You need to discard the old and worthless things in both your business and personal life.
2. You have lost sight of your higher purpose.
3. You feel lonely.
4. You are locked in your mind.
5. You are out of touch with heart and intuitive guidance.
6. You are impractical.
7. You feel bitterness.
8. You are indecisive.
9. You are superficial.
10. You are all over the place and withdrawn.

Solution for this year: This year is a year of change. Make the decisions that bring change and new vital energy into your life. Clear away all things that no longer serve you.

o. Blueprint Temperamental Behavior

(1 and 8) If you have many number ones and eights, you are a mental person and represent mind qualities.

One is an independent thinker, originator, and a leader. However you may have strong likes and dislikes. You could be opinionated and bored. You don't like to be told what to do.

Eight is run by logic and reason. You have executive ability, and are striving for power. You like to make a good performance, as you have much pride. You are always striving for the betterment of yourself and sometimes you push others around you to be the same. You like to be the boss, and do not follow orders readily. You like to control other people.

(4 and 5) If you have many number fours and fives, you are a physical type of person. Practicality, common sense and free spirited is your model in life.

Four is practical, efficient, hard working, and can be depended upon for responsibility. You are not creative, for you have very little imagination. You may be argumentative since you are not open to new ideas.

Five is adventurous and inquisitive, but you are not as practical as the four. You like change, the unusual, new things, and original ideas. You are restless when forced to do routine work. As active individual, you are a promoter and a natural salesman.

(2,3,6) If you have many twos, threes, and sixes, you are an emotional person, and allow your emotions to dictate your decisions.

Twos represent feeling and imagination, for you are very sensitive. You like detail, collecting facts, and all forms of beauty. Since you lack self-confidence, you should be in partnership with another and not own your own business. You are subject to worry, fear, and have a feeling of inadequacy. You are musical and spiritual. You always take pleasure in being with someone in your life.

Threes are very artistic, and you have considerable talent for using words in writing or speaking. Many threes have a tendency to be disorderly and unsystematic. You do not like to be tied down to pure facts, as your imagination is strong. You are very creative, but you act impulsively at times. Being versatile, you are apt to scatter your talents. Threes are not at their best doing manual labor. You can make others happy, for you are entertainers.

Sixes can carry much responsibility. You can be depended upon to follow through with plans. You are artistic but practical. You need a home and family, and are a good disciplinarian. You are also interested in community and welfare work. Negative aspects of a six are that you can be demanding and domineering. Because you try to insist that others live up to their ideals, you often fail to gain the affection you strongly desire. Sixes may experience many difficulties through their children. Pay attention to not being taken for granted.

(7, and 9) If you have many sevens and nines, you are an intuitive or spiritual person. You are very gifted even if you don't admit it.

Sevens are psychic, and analytical. You have a hidden sixth sense in you or intuition for guidance. You are excellent in scientific affairs. Sevens are reserved, refined and venerable. You are not very friendly or socially inclined. You demand perfection for yourself and from others. Sevens can be critical, sarcastic, and show considerable temper. Sevens investigate the hidden forces of nature.

Nines are very deep thinkers. You can work with all people. You are dramatically inclined. While they are impersonal, you can become distressed if you fail to get love and approval, for you like to appeal to the crowd and be admired. Nines are usually tolerant, sympathetic, and generous. You need guidance, for you are often a dreamer. You tend to be humanitarian in nature and in your heart. You do enjoy a generous type of personality.

p. Universal Blueprint

In 2009, the Universal Blueprint is $2 + 0 + 0 + 9 = 11 = 2$, so here with the new beginning you started in 2008, you need to set up the foundation of what you started to make your start solid. It is a hard-working year between nations as well as every one of us in one way or another but your 9-Year Cycle will have an effect on many circumstances in your life during that cycle.

In 2010, the Universal Blueprint is $2 + 0 + 1 + 0 = 3$, and year 3 in a Universal Blueprint can bring lots of new talks between nations as they become friendlier, and we have less tension in the world. It is a more relaxing year. The same goes for every one of us. It is a relaxing year, but relaxing in coordination with where you are in your 9-Year Cycle. Overall, it should be a softer year for everyone.

Section V

A. Blueprint Karma

I 'Googled' the word 'karma' to find out how others define it, and I picked up the first two results I found to use in this chapter. The first is from Wikipedia, the free encyclopedia, which reads as follows:

"The philosophical explanation of karma can differ slightly between traditions, but the general concept is basically the same. Through the law of karma, the effects of all deeds actively create past, present, and future experiences, thus making you responsible for your own life, and the pain and joy it brings to you and others. The results or 'fruits' of your actions are called karma-phala. In religions that incorporate reincarnation, karma extends through your present life and all past and future lives as well."

In Buddhist teachings, the law of karma is defined like this:

"For every event that occurs, there will follow another event whose existence was caused by the first, and this second event will be pleasant or unpleasant according as its cause was skilful or unskillful. A skilful event is one that is not accompanied by craving, resistance or delusions; an unskillful event is one that is accompanied by any one of those things. Events are not skilful in themselves, but are so called only in virtue of the mental events that occur with them."

Most of us have heard about karma, and even though we are familiar with the term, many of us are still trying to figure out our karma. Many people blame all their life's issues on their karma and use it as an excuse for not dealing with it, as if it's a given. So what is right or wrong when it comes to karma and how we handle it? Do we really have karma, and what can we do to understand, evaluate and deal with our karma if we do? There seems to be so many questions, yet so little answers out there when it comes to the subject of karma.

Karma does exist whether you believe in it or not. Karma deals with the law of cause and effect, where every thought, word or action you produce is a 'cause,' like an intention, which in return creates an 'effect' that becomes a situation which you will experience in our life. Karma is also connected with reincarnation, where we believe that Souls reincarnate into numerous lifetimes to fulfill unresolved karmic deeds from previous lifetimes until all learning has been fulfilled and the need to reincarnate no longer exists.

I like to refer to 'karma' as 'Blueprint Karma,' so this is how you will see me refer to it here. Your Blueprint Karma contains the blueprint of your Soul, and all the information related to your Soul and what it came here into this life to accomplish. As I said before, your journey in this lifetime is a part of your Soul's evolution, and is a continuation of the many experiences your Soul encountered in previous lifetimes either here on this plane, or in other planes. Some of those experiences go as the Soul expected, and others play out in a completely different direction. Other experiences create karma between Souls.

When a Soul decides to return again into physical life, it takes a great deal of preparation in order to plan the appropriate experiences that will obtain the lessons the Soul needs and to fulfill its karma as a result. Your Soul is aware of all the experiences it needs to go through to complete its current cycle of karmic evolution.

Blueprint Karma is the aspect of your life that exists to help you heal your past experiences. It consists of the lessons we are here to learn, to understand and to deal with in life. The more we resist handling those experiences, the more complicated and stagnant life will be. So, as the Universal Law of Karma, or 'cause and effect' states, every thought, word and action carries energy into the world and affects our present and future reality, so how you choose to handle your experiences today sets the stage for your life tomorrow. That is one reason why predicting a future for someone can be useless and inaccurate as your experiences will shape the direction of your Blueprint Destiny.

The word 'karma' can also refer to the 'work' you have ahead of you in your life that you have to handle. This work also includes lessons from both your past and your present lifetime.

I have divided Blueprint Karma into two categories, Blueprint Karma and Blueprint Karma Awareness.

Blueprint Karma is when the Soul has brought its baggage from a past life, in order to be re-experienced in this life so the lesson can be understood and finalized in order to close and move forward from the cycle of that specific karmic lesson. This type of karma is usually difficult in principle because for a Soul to come back and repeat experiences from past lives means the lesson is very important for its karmic growth and evolution. Although the lessons may seem difficult to handle, in essence they can be simplified depending on how you choose to approach the situations. It is important to try to understand what you are dealing with from a wider perspective, looking at the bigger picture of your life, and it will be helpful to you if you are able to separate yourself somewhat from the experiences in order to view them clearly for what they really are, from a more emotionally detached perspective. This way, you will see things for what they really are from more of a Soul level.

Blueprint Karma Awareness is your daily actions and reactions to everything that occurs on a moment to moment basis in your daily life. This is an important type of Karma as it really involves the use of your free will, whether you are aware of it or not. With this type of karma, you have the power to create your experiences at any given minute of your life, and the more consciously aware you become of your actions and reactions, the more you will be able to create your life exactly the way you would like it to be. Again, I will mention that it is important to pay attention to your thoughts, words and actions and the way you express yourself, whether negatively or positively, because these things create the basis of your present, and your future reality. When it comes to this type of karma, it is required of you to become fully responsible for all of your actions and reactions, knowing that you are using your free will in every moment as you choose the words, thoughts and actions you send out into life. The law of karma recreates every moment of your experiences with these boundaries in mind.

So where do we find the karma in your chart?

Firstly, the way I see it, your Blueprint Challenges are a huge part of your Soul's learning, and are a significant part of the obstacles you face and learn from on a daily basis.

Secondly, your Blueprint Karma is located in your Blueprint Intensity table, and is found when there is a vibration missing from your name. That missing vibration becomes your Blueprint Karma and constitutes the major lessons and experiences you are here to encounter in your life.

I believe that Blueprint Karma is great for our psyche because it provides us with the means to evolve and improve our life. It also guides us in the right direction toward fulfilling our Blueprint Destiny because the more we deal with our challenges and learn from them, the closer we become to growing and achieving all the accomplishments our Soul intended for us in this lifetime.

Many people dwell over their experiences and challenges, and therefore dwell over their karma. As a result, they become stagnant and tend to lose focus of their direction in life and become lost as a result. People in a situation such as this one and who are aware of karma and what it means tend to blame their misfortune on their Blueprint Karma. Technically, it is unfair to blame anything on karma when we are fully responsible for choosing how we handle our experiences. We are all able to change our life and our attitude at any given moment. Having free will, combined with the law of karma, means we have the power to change our life as long as we are ready and willing to do so.

You are not here, alive today for a picnic. You are here to gain wisdom and awareness through experiences that will help your Soul evolve and progress in its Universal journey of becoming closer to our Creator, God. Although we are all here for the same purpose, our journeys through this life and all others are unique and are expertly designed by our Soul to help us gain knowledge and experience that we will understand in our own special way, and which no one else can ever understand because we all view life from our own personal perspective.

Please keep in mind that your Blueprint Destiny is not about all about your work, career or status in life. Those things are a part of it, of course, but Blueprint Destiny is more about your inner experience and the growth and satisfaction you can achieve from fulfilling your inner desires that connect you with your Soul. Being accomplished is less about being arrogant, snobbish or even superficial and self-centered when it comes to your accomplishment. It is more about having so much inner fulfillment that you want to reach out to others, share in the wisdom you have gained in your life and help others to achieve the same level of inner and outer success that you already have, whether it is in the area of financial freedom, understanding love and forgiveness, or just a simple appreciation for life and all the many lessons and experiences it brings to us. The outer circumstances are not important; it's the inner circumstances that arise as a result of what is going on in our environment that contributes to our Soul growth.

Our goal in life is to understand the dynamics of the Universe and how Universal Laws such as free will and karma operate. Understanding these laws will enable us to deal with our karma, evolve beyond our karma and as a result grow to the fullest potential we possibly can in our lifetime, without creating more karma that will tie us to the obligation of reincarnating over and over again to repeat the same old lessons. When you function according to the Universe's way of functioning, you will begin to attract the type of experiences that are pleasing to you and are in alignment with your true inner goals and desires. This is the way life was intended to be; however, we have become lost along the way and caught up in so many karmic ties that keep us locked into cycles of repeated lifetimes over and over again. Let's now strive for awareness that will take us out beyond our karma and share that with others to help them improve their life, too. And if we all worked individually to evolve consciously to a new level of looking at life, then we will help raise the collective consciousness of our planet and live life as it was initially intended to be ... by design.

Blueprint Karma is definitely something that people should embrace instead of despise, because this is the basis of what they are here to experience in life. The Law of Attraction can help you greatly when it comes to understanding the Law of Karma, because when you understand that your Blueprint Karma is attracted to you as a result of your choice of words, thoughts and actions, you can then begin to become consciously aware of what you are attracting in your life and begin choosing what it is you wish to experience, or not experience in your life. Isn't that an empowering thought? You are the master of your own Blueprint Destiny, and it is time now to reclaim your power to take charge of your own life circumstance instead of circumstances taking charge over you. It is your choice, and the Law of Free Will states that the Universe will support your choice either way ... and even if you choose not to choose, you are still making a choice. Think about it.

B. Blueprint Karmic Debt

Any time those numbers – 13/4, 14/5, 16/7 and 19/1 – appear in your chart, then that vibration is a karmic debt in whichever core of your chart. This karmic debt is to emphasize the importance of that vibration lesson in your life at that time.

13/4 Blueprint Karmic Debt

Blueprint Expression 13/4 and Blueprint Birthday 13/4 means:

You will find your opportunities considerably limited. No matter your abilities or motivation, you will seem to keep running into walls and get boxed in with few acceptable options. The opportunities may be as restrictive as they appear to you. More likely, the limitations are produced or reinforced by your unbending views coupled with your lack of constructive adaptability.

You pursue your ability persistently in a rigid, one-minded direction. You hardly listen to others' opinions as you are always right. The power of your drive may work to your advantage, but the effect of this drive is likely to be negated by the limitations of your vision and resistance to making a change in your life. You drive your life with lots of procrastination while you envy and are jealous of others for reaching their goals

Blueprint Soul Urge or Blueprint Inner-self 13/4 or Blueprint Family means:

You are dissatisfied with the limitations imposed by your significant workload. You always try to skip steps of growth and see yourself further behind than you started in the first place. You are hard worker and you often accomplish the work at hand but receive little satisfaction from the achievement. The reason for that is the lack of appreciation of yourself and any accomplishment you have achieved so far, regardless how small or big it is. You need to start learning to recognize that you are highly practical, consistent and confident in the things you do and start believing in them, too. You feel loneliness and contradiction in the way you conduct your life.

Your Blueprint Attainment 13/4 means:

With this karma in your attainment, you need to watch being rigid, lazy and dogmatic. You have a hard time stabilizing your life, either in your home situation, your work situation or your emotional situation, such as fear over committing to anyone for fear of losing them or fear of responsibility. Watch procrastination and loneliness.

Your Blueprint Maturity or Blueprint Growth 13/4 means:

Many events will make you feel powerless in your experiences and some of those experiences were part of your early experiences in life when you lacked stability, commitment, focus and concentration on your goal. You will find your opportunities considerably limited. No matter your abilities or motivation, the opportunities may be as restrictive as they appear to you. More likely, the limitations are produced or reinforced by your unbending views coupled with your lack of constructive adaptability. Focus, centering and being grounded are the keys for you to get out of your restlessness.

14/5 Blueprint Karmic Debt

Blueprint Destiny 14/5 and Blueprint Birthday 14/5 means:

You must learn the lesson of change – to begin and nurture an interest or relation, to experience it in full bloom, and to detach from it when it is completed. This will tend to be a difficult lesson. Instead of appreciating the beauties that enter and leave your life, you may be beset with disappointment at losses, which are either beyond your control or caused by your lack of awareness.

Your Blueprint Expression 14/5 means:

You are confused at first with your identity and you are always undecided and confused of your direction. You seek attention in the wrong places. You have an unrealistic or unclear view of the use and limitations of your talents. You are apt to meet disappointment in your work and must constantly regroup your energies to move ahead. Changing is part of your everyday experience but no fulfillment is achieved in your life. The indistinguishable, vague or unreasonable nature of your career commitment adds to your difficulties in your life. You thrive on multifaceted talents but your energies are all over the place.

Blueprint Soul Urge or Blueprint Inner-self 14/5 or Blueprint Family means:

You feel the urges of self-indulgence, where you value nothing and no one at times in your life. Your personal relationships can be marked by delays and interruptions. Your impatience, discipline and light view of responsibility add to the problems. You act in many ways as irresponsible and inconsistent. You can find yourself caught in events in your life where you find it hard to free yourself of the situation.

Your Blueprint Attainment 14/5 means:

This karma in your attainment is bringing to you many choices and opportunities where you might find yourself ending up with no opportunity or choice to make to the lack of a solid decision you need to make. Stop repeating same mistakes over and over, and start learning from your past missed opportunities. You need to watch your indulgence in physical activities such as gambling, food, sex, alcohol and drugs.

Your Blueprint Maturity or Blueprint Growth 14/5 means:

You've probably heard too often that it's now time to grow up and settle down. You need to get it in your head that with some discipline in your life, you're not going to miss out on anything in life as long as you do things in moderation, because you can end your life as 'Jack of all trade and master of none.' You must learn the lesson of change – to nurture an interest or relation, to experience it in full bloom, and to detach from it when it is completed. This will tend to be a difficult lesson. Instead of appreciating the beauties that enter and leave your life, you may be beset with disappointment at losses, which are either beyond your control or caused by your lack of awareness. You are very clever and need to use your cleverness to your advantage.

16/7 Blueprint Karmic Debt

Your Blueprint Destiny 16/7 or Blueprint Birthday 16/7 means:

Life is likely to provide you with many examples of the transient nature of reality. This impermanence is apt to be expressed in the meaningful areas in which you would like to exhibit positive growth. Your status, wealth or power may change for the worse. Your living relations may shift abruptly. Other matters may end in sudden or unusual ways. You may be the cause of your own undoing, or you may be the seeming recipient of some curious quirk of fate. Acceptance of impermanence will ease the burden.

Your Blueprint Expression 16/7 means:

You are overly philosophical and can argue just for the sake of arguing. You are bored because you see no results in what you are trying to convince yourself to be. You may lose what you have gained due to some sudden or unusual circumstances. You should not lean too heavily on your material attributes. Your wealth, position and influence may prove short-lived. You isolate yourself from everyone in your life, then you complain that no one really understand you. Do you really know what you want? Figure that out and things will change drastically.

Your Blueprint Soul Urge or Blueprint Inner-self 16/7 or Blueprint Family means:

You have a very rigid way of looking at life and at yourself being part of it, and that can be in the way you select your friends and associates. You are apt to be severely tested. People on whom you rely may prove unreliable. People you trust may act against your interest in a manner difficult for you to understand. Close friends may cease being close because of some sudden or unusual circumstances. Luck is actually on your side but can also bring unsatisfactory feeling of insecurity in you.

Your Blueprint Attainment 16/7 means:

Karma is in your attainment at this point, and you can very opinionated and hard to work with. You have difficulties expressing yourself and/or associating with others. You convince yourself that you don't need anyone in your life and that you are happy but, at the same time, you yearn to be with someone. However, maintaining any type of relationship is difficult for you at this point. Follow your own life lesson and try to understand ... and stop being in the same situation at all time.

Your Blueprint Maturity or Blueprint Growth 16/7 means:

At this point in your life, you might need a major shake-up in order for you to start seeing that things are not the way you have been convincing yourself they are. Switch off your analyzing for a moment and start looking for alternatives, because you are gifted and hopefully, by now, you've realized that. You have something very special and unique that you need to tap into, but mostly you need to build a stronger trust in yourself and the fact you can share your experiences, knowledge and wisdom. Going within is your best solution to understand yourself, but don't take too long to do so because time is passing you by. At a younger age, you probably had a hard time expressing what you didn't have an answer for but now in the age of Blueprint Maturity or your Blueprint Growth, you should have an idea, but you can start with what you know and things will fall on your lap because you always have luck on your side.

19/1 Blueprint Karmic Debt

Your Blueprint Destiny 19/1 and Blueprint Birthday 19/1 means:

You can see the opportunities, but the path is overwhelmed with obstacles, many of your own making. If you confuse independence and selfishness, you find your egotistical approach limiting your understanding of the experience or situation you're involved in. Your actions initiated with positive ends in sight will often undo the very things you anticipated realizing, leaving more behind than when you started. You will always find yourself trapped by your own misapplied energies, often exposed as the dominating selfish person you are.

By overwhelmed by being dependent, you will find yourself constantly held back with strong anxiety keeping you from breaking free. You probably waste much time and energy because of your inability to understand the realities of the situation or experiences and use them to your advantage.

Your Blueprint Expression 19/1 means:

You have some difficulties expressing your abilities to your advantage. Your controlling aggressiveness and self-centered approach may turn others off so that your potential is downgraded. People see your dependent side which will make it hard for others to see and appreciate your gifts. You have an executive ability but have to be always reliant as people like to see your full charismatic leadership.

Your Blueprint Soul Urge or Blueprint Inner-self 19/1 or Blueprint Family means:

The strong determined force of your inner desires will be difficult to handle. Others will read your self-centered ways, your pride and ego, no matter how you attempt to hide them. Your innermost secrets may be exposed to your disadvantage. Also, the leadership in you will be questioned for your lack of confidence and arrogance.

Your Blueprint Attainment 19/1 means:

With this 19/1 in your chart, you need to rise above these weaknesses in your life. Watch your ego, laziness, insecurity, being domineering and controlling. Also you need to watch your stubbornness, your confidence, your pride and always feeling vulnerable.

Your Blueprint Maturity or Blueprint Growth 19/1 means:

Your stubbornness can lead to you being sad, empty and lonely. You are meant to lead but, on the contrary, you always look to others for the attention that will fill the void in your life, which you strive to avoid at any cost. At times, your confidence might be shaky but that is a good thing sometimes, with the way you look at your circumstances. You can see the opportunities, but you always find an excuse to bring out the worth of every situation. You need to have a grip on your ego, especially your pride, and show others your leadership to attract them to your charisma instead of allowing people to see only your pride and ego.

C. Time to Heal and Move Beyond Your Karma

Many of us are looking for answers to our life's issues. Some of us, as a last resort, go from one medium or psychic to another, to see if they can provide the answers we are looking for to change our life, yet life still seems to be either standing still, or even going backwards! Nothing is changing and many 9-Year Cycles have passed in your life, yet you are still at the same place. Many people claim that they have dealt with their old experiences and issues, yet complain that their life is still the same. They are bored and lost in life's direction. Does that sound familiar?

You pay attention more in your life by what makes you feel better on the outside, such as decoration of your house as you fill every corner, fearing any empty space as a reflection of the emptiness in your life. When your house is so full of stuff that there is no more space, then we start considering other things such as a facelift, Botox, boob job, and other cosmetic operations as if it will fill that inner emptiness you are experiencing. However, with all you've accomplished in your life, you discover nothing has changed and your life is still filled with that emptiness that goes so deep in you that it has you thinking of covering up everything about yourself in which you might feel shame, worry, sadness, superficiality or stubbornness. So we just need to be honest with ourselves for a change.

There is no one in this world, including psychics, who knows you better than yourself. In the end, you can ask for all the help and guidance you like from the outside, or you can even cover up yourself with all the makeup, hoping to feel better for a moment, doing your exercises, or following new trends in life. However, it's all about you taking responsibility for your own life and for you to figure out what has happened in your own experiences. Events from your past won't change, but it is your responsibility for you to change. The past has a meaning for you, so just understand it.

That's the bottom line but no one wants to do that or even admit they have a problem. We live our lives in contradiction of what is happening in our life today and what it is we're trying to convince ourselves of who we are, but in the end, you are the one who knows your own reality and you are living with it.

You believe you dealt with your experience but:
- If I asked you what you learnt and understood about your experiences, what would you say?
- If I asked you why you jump or react every time your father, mother or a member of your family in general is mentioned in front of you, what would you say?
- If I asked you why you still get angry every time someone mentions your experiences, what would you say?
- If I asked why you have shut down completely in your relationship because of a past experience, what would you say?
- If I asked you whether your present day experiences have some similarity to what happened in your past experiences, would you agree that they compare to a previous event that happened in your life? What would you say?
- If I ask you if you're gay or lesbian because of an experience from your past, or is being gay or lesbian your way of life and has nothing to do with your past, what would you say?

So you seek help from other people and by doing so, you put the power behind your ability to heal in the hand of others, while you refuse to listen to your own inner voice, the inner guidance that is always trying to be heard. There is nothing wrong with seeking help from others for guidance, but in the end, the best guidance you will ever receive is the guidance that directs you toward going within and searching out the answers you need from inside yourself. You are the best and only healer of your life.

You are the only one who can make change happen for you, however, my question is: Do you really want to make change happen in your life? What will it take for you to have the courage and strength you need to decide to change and to act on it? In the end, you will still have to deal with your life and all your experiences, regardless of how much resistance, anger or hurt you have? It is time to grow up and start acting, instead of dwelling over your experiences and allowing them to rule your life today.

Your Soul chose to reincarnate back into this plane in order to work toward healing and balancing the energy of unfinished business left over from the experiences of a previous life, or lives. The unfinished business requires you to understand the experience from a different perspective, keeping in mind that no matter how rough or tough those experiences may seem to you, on a higher level of your understanding and being, you chose and accepted the challenge of those experiences. It is now time for you to understand your experiences and stop stagnating.

We are born to go through those experiences at an early stage in life in most cases; however some people's experiences may come later. Regardless of when those experiences happened for you, you here to learn and understand your life and for that, there is no shortcut. It is cut and dried; you learn either from your experiences and move on, or you hold on to them, resisting change and remain living in your past. As a result, you allow diseases to take over your life, so you die without finishing your task in the first place, just because you were stuck, too stubborn to change and were incapable of controlling your ego and pride. If that is your choice, then you should not complain about the state of your life, because you made your choice, and with choices come consequences, and those consequences become the circumstances of your life experience as a result.

Regardless of how terrible the life situation you are in may seem, you still have the chance to bring order into your life and make a difference for yourself and the other people you affect around you. Do not make your age today as a way for you to give up. At any age, we can change as long as there is a will and with a strong intention. Then the Universe will work with you. Why on earth you want the Universe, your guides, even God, to help get over your past when you yourself do not have the initiative to do so. Think about it!

Also, it is important to note that you cannot substitute working on healing and understanding your experiences by filling your inner void by buying stuff! You can have all the money in the world, but if you have not discovered the essence of who you really are or if what you came here to do in this life has not yet been fulfilled, you will never be truly happy. You go through the phases in your life, but how often do you go back in your memory to revisit all those old, stored memories that were shoved away to be ignored and denied? Even if you do travel back in your mind and remember your past and the things that haunt you well, what are you doing to stop them from hurting you? Remembering is worth nothing without the action to heal and transform those thoughts from being something that caused you great pain to becoming a teacher of the heart.

Your numerology chart is the guideline that can help you identify with and work through those experiences that need to be dealt with; however, even that cannot help you if you are not ready to move forward in your life. As I mentioned earlier in a previous section of this book, we commonly become stuck in the first two vibrations before our final Blueprint Destiny Number, and those numbers are a very crucial part of the path toward fulfilling what we came here to do. Those numbers need to be well understood if you wish to move forward in your chart.

If you are confused and feel out of place in your life today, it is very important to watch the name you are currently using today and find out how it affects you and the karma it creates for you. Any name we use has its own ups and downs, and the karma that a name brings to us changes, of course, according to the name you use because each name has its own energy vibration. So if you are using more than one name in your life today, then it is probable that you are feeling confused and out of place. Keep in mind that if you have karma to deal with based on your original name you are already having a hard time dealing with, how can you possibly be able to handle the all the different karma that comes from using multiple names? A big part of your own healing is to be able to settle down and accept one name that you enjoy using, and have a chart drawn up based upon that name and your date of birth to find out what it means now to you, and how it affects you. If your parents are alive today, ask them how they picked your name? In most cases, they have no idea but sometimes a simple flash, dream, a person with similar name dropped by from nowhere or even all of the sudden they decided to name you after a star. You are so powerful with the different energies that your name can hold that, most of the time, we have no idea what we are made of.

Your name is as powerful as the strength of your Soul. You were meant to use your name but most of the time we use different names or a nickname. Doing this is very bad as long as you are aware what name you changed to, because you might trigger some additional experiences and lessons for you learn. I do believe from my own Soul and the lifetimes I feel I have been doing numerology that your blueprint was well drawn, so why are you trying to mess it up by making the changes. It's time for people to stop using a middle name or nickname for their children that they know they will not use just to fulfill a life obligation. You are just confusing the child. Just trust your heart and that the first name that comes to you in whichever way should be used without using any additional names.

In summary, in order to start healing yourself and your past using numerology and before you start to understand your full chart, you have to be aware and understand five things about yourself and your experiences from your chart:

1. Understand the first two vibrations that add up to bring you to your Blueprint Destiny. This is calculated from your date of birth.

2. Decide upon one name you would like to use and learn the strengths and weaknesses that come with it. What is your Blueprint Karmic lesson?
3. Pay attention and learn about your first two Blueprint attainments and your challenges in life in your chart.
4. Learn about your influential learning vibration, which usually runs in the first 27 years of your life.
5. Know what cycle you are in your 9-Year Cycle and try to see the pattern from your past cycles.

The moment you pin down those five factors of yourself, you will be able to solve 85% of the problems you are facing in your life today and all the rest will become mechanics.

As a result of giving numerology consultations during the last 17 years, my life has taught me how to understand the human psyche. Unfortunately we live in a world that is driven by results, striving to achieve them in the fastest way possible. As I said before, this does not work when it comes to your life; your life requires your attention and long-term commitment. From what I have seen over the years, people do not want to do any work to achieve anything, but they all want things to change. Everyone wants answers, but instead of searching for answers within, they prefer to go after predictions, yet that is not the way life works I am afraid. You are supposed to be an active participant in your life, not a passive observer, and that means you have to work to find your own answers to your problems without expecting another person to be able to provide them for you. Really, what is the point of a prediction when you have not been able to handle your life until now. Will that prediction suddenly make you able to? Do you think for a moment that your prediction will be realized without you actually creating the changes that are necessary before you can actually make the Blueprint Destiny you are dreaming of a reality?

Unfortunately, psychics, mediums, astrologers and numerologists and the like can never ever really help their clients unless those clients are willing to work toward making the necessary changes happen in their life. People offering these forms of guidance need to remind their clients that in order for things to happen in their life, there are some things that need to be worked upon, so that clients put themselves into alignment with the Universe so things can manifest. Your thoughts, your habits and patterns, your way of speaking and your way of expressing yourself are the exact and precise result of what happened in your past experiences and how you are related to them. Any experiences that you never dealt with until now are exactly what you are manifesting today on an unconscious level. Just listen carefully to yourself when you speak and pay attention to your thoughts and the nature of your thinking. Does it remind you of anything from your past? I will give you an example here:

How many people today feel that they hate their mother for whatever reason, and are having a hard time of letting that experience go, and then, one day, realize that they act exactly like their mother?

On the one hand, you hate your mother for the way she treated you, yet at the same you act exactly like her. Don't you see your contradiction there? So you are living in denial and still have a hard time accepting and forgiving your past, because if you did, you would identify with yourself and see that your life today and how you act is a direct reflection of that past. You want things to change, yet the way you see the base of your life never changed and you are living it all over again, so how can you possibly change?

Healing begins with forgiving your past, regardless of how tough it was. Your resistance toward your past will cause you to stagnate unless you deal with it. It is time for you to move on and heal your past, and then you will advance in your life and begin to realize the Blueprint Destiny that was meant for you in the first place.

Neither I nor anyone else can really predict your Blueprint Destiny because your course can change on a daily basis, depending on how you make your decisions using your free will. Think about it! Your Blueprint Destiny is for you to discover, and no one is really meant to be able to tell you what it is all about except you.

Remember, maybe the missing numbers in your chart are giving you more intense energies to pay attention to and deal with once and for all, and you must deal with it because, unfortunately, the negative sides of those numbers will never leave your vibration until you do.

Evaluate again your past experiences and have your chart drawn up to help guide you and provide you with the insight you need to help you discover your Blueprint Destiny through understanding your past.

In the end, go see a numerologist or an astrologer, or a medium or even a psychic for confirmation of the work you have been working on in your life, but never go for answers or predictions about your life. You will never get an answer that way.

D. Conclusion

Your life is a series of events that your Soul has chosen to experience for the purpose of growth and evolution. Many people go through their life with no real value, or understanding of life, existence and the evolution of humanity and what it really stands for. Many of us think and assume the value of life is judged according to the amount of material belongings we amass, but that on its own means nothing without awareness.

Many walk through life feeling purposeless ... and that is a waste of life! You will progress in life anytime you start investigating what is going on in your own reality and then acting to promote change for the better. All of us are responsible for being aware of the purpose of our existence here because otherwise, our lifetime will be wasted.

Humanity as a whole is going nowhere, and I am sure many will agree with that. Unfortunately, many people are not moving forward in their evolution when it comes to understanding the dynamics of the Universe and its laws. On the other hand, humanity is moving forward from a technological standpoint; however, unfortunately it is our technology that might destroy us one day, taking us farther away from fulfilling our purpose and Blueprint Destiny in this life collectively.

Your existence today is one link in the chain of a lifetime of experiences. Those experiences have given you the knowledge and understanding that has led you to where you are today. You are not where you are today by coincidence. Coincidence only exists in the mind and part of our worldly illusion. We have a Blueprint Destiny that carries us toward a specific goal that our Soul wishes to accomplish based on a set of events designed to lead us toward that goal.

We are guided toward our Soul's goal until the moment we use our free will and make a choice that leads us away from our goal. As a result of our choice, life unfolds accordingly, taking us from one event to another until we realize we are going nowhere and have a feeling of emptiness and purposelessness inside because our inner urge always tries to get us back in the direction of our Soul's true Blueprint Destiny.

All is not lost, however, regardless of how lost you feel after taking your detour; you always have the power to change your life at any moment. Your free will may have allowed you to move away from your Blueprint Destiny, but it can also give you the power to move back in alignment with it.

I am sure many will respond to that by saying, "Changing your life is easier said than done." Perhaps it is, but what have you really done to try to change your life. We are all capable, we are all gifted and we all have the same potential. We are all born with the wisdom of our Soul and its lifetimes of knowledge and experience within, so why not go within and seek some guidance from your Soul. Draw upon that inner wisdom you have because isn't your Soul the main reason behind your existence after all? We are all different with unique personalities and characteristics, but we are all striving for the same goals – to live happy, rich, satisfying and fulfilling lives.

Here is a list of some of the possible personality types that exist in our world today, as you can see there are many different types of people that make up our world. An individual could have one, or many of the following characteristics in his or her character, and this shows you how unique we all really are:

You could be a simple person, or wise, or deep, or skeptical, or religious, or a humanitarian, or a prejudiced, angry, hateful, fearful, weak, jealous or a happy person

Those are some of the things that could make up the sum of who you are in this life, and of course there are many other possibilities. Who you have become as a result of your experiences is significant when it comes to understanding what your Soul wanted you to learn for your growth in this lifetime. Your experiences are also important when it comes to having an awareness of what life on this planet is really like. The issues you encounter during your lifetime can help you identify with what it's like to be jealous, weak, fearful, hateful, angry, prejudiced, a humanitarian, religious, skeptical, deep and wise. Over and above all of those life characteristics, what your Soul really wants despite all the challenges you experience is for you to learn how to accept humility, to be able to forgive yourself and others, to feel compassion and to bring Universal love and value to yourself for all your strengths and weaknesses.

To live fully and with purpose, it's really important to become conscious of your Soul, because it is your Soul that holds the key to all the insight, wisdom and understandings we are searching for in our life. If we are not close to our Soul, then how can we ever be close to God? There are many on this plane who are very religious and spend their lives being devoted to God, yet how devoted are they to their own Soul when they spend so much time worshipping something they believe exists outside of themselves? Our God is a God of compassion, Universal love and is the infinite energy that exists in each and every one of us, no matter who we are or what we have done without any judgments. Judgment is a human characteristic, and is an element of fear often used and abused in an attempt to keep masses of people living in fear so strong that it will bind them to a specific faith, belief system or religion in the hope that it will one day save them. These judgments and fears are created by human beings for the control of other human beings; they are not a characteristic of God.

Our experiences serve us and our Soul to help us learn and to understand the nature of human beings and to see and experience just how low we can become toward ourselves and each other. Many might ask the question, "Why is it necessary to suffer through so much pain during our life? Why do we need to feel the experience of being raped, being angry, being hateful, sabotage ourselves, being afraid and all the many other possible agonizing pains that the majority of us have went though in this life? What is it all for? Why do we have to suffer for the sake of our Soul's evolution?" Many people might even say they do not care about their Soul.

Your experiences can be good or bad depending on how you choose to look at them. I am not saying that it is easy to always approach life with a positive attitude, but by looking at your experiences as learning opportunities as opposed to them being like a punishment, you will definitely see the value in what is happening in your life. How you choose to think is very empowering and you can turn your experiences around from being a victim of your circumstances, to becoming a wise and aware person who always looks for the lesson and opportunity for growth and awareness in every event that takes place.

Your task in life is to evolve out of the suffering, the fear, the anger and the jealousy, and turn your life into a positive existence by having an understanding and awareness of your experiences, what they stand for and how you can make them work for you instead of against you. This is the ultimate achievement of any human in their life because by looking at life in this way means you have the power and ability to transform any situation into one that works for you to propel you forward in your growth and evolution, instead of keeping you stuck and feeling helpless and victimized by experiences you think you are not able to handle.

Many of us believe we have no purpose in life because we are too occupied with problems and issues. If you are having problems accepting your current situation, it means you are experiencing resistance when it comes to change. In such a case, you need to ask yourself why you are resistant to change and consider the fact that perhaps it's your own pride, ego, and stubbornness getting the best of you, preventing you from accepting a bit of humility and convincing you that you always need to be right when it comes to your life. Your life experiences, especially those of your early childhood are the purpose of your life and why you are here. Whether or not you will reach the Blueprint Destiny your Soul planned for you before you were born depends on how much you understand, accept and learn from those experiences. They are here to help you in the end, not to hurt you.

How many of us are limited in our way of thinking?
How many of us are afraid of the unknown?
How many of us are confused?
How many of us feel stuck?
How many of us feel blocked?
How many of us are stubborn?
How many of us are a doormat for other people?
How many of us complain?
How many of us are arrogant?
How many of us are self-centered?
How many of us are naïve?
How many of us are shy?
How many of us are gossips?
How many of are jealous of others?
How many of us are ashamed?
How many of us are withdrawn?
How many of us have self-doubt?
How many of us have problems expressing their emotions?
How many of us always criticize others?
How many of us having problem to forgive?
How many of us are spoiled?
How many of us have problems with responsibility?
How many of us judge ourselves and others?
How many of us are perfectionist?
How many of us are skeptic?
How many of us are paranoid?
How many of us have trust issues?
How many of us have fear?
How many of us are impatient?
How many of us are unhappy?

With all of those questions above, and considering the many other possibilities we could be, how many of us complain we have no direction in life? How many of us complain that we are stagnating in this life? Have you ever stopped to ask yourself why you might be stagnant and lacking in direction? If this situation sounds familiar to you, then perhaps it's time to shift the focus off the feelings, and instead start taking responsibility for why you feel that way in the first place.

Begin now by looking at which of the 'How many of us' questions above relate to you and try to identify with the experiences related to your feelings and what you can learn from them instead of feeling victimized. Doing this will help you to begin seeing things from a fresh perspective, and will give you the ability to handle experiences in a new and more empowering way. Looking at all of your experiences from the outside and from a more detached perspective gives you the opportunity to clear your mind of any emotional or mental clutter, helping you to envision your life purpose clearly.

We are all here for a reason and have many gifts up our sleeves to help us fulfill our reason for being here. Our life is meant to be joyous; happiness is our birthright and is attainable no matter how rough our life has been. The outcome of our life depends on how we choose to look at those experiences, and how much growth and wisdom we achieve from them as a result. At the end of the day, we are all striving for that happy ending, and we can reach it as long as we are willing to understand and deal with all of our issues.

If you try to envision your Blueprint Destiny from the perspective of being caught up in your unresolved issues, then you are unlikely to go far. On the other hand, by looking toward your Blueprint Destiny from perspective of understanding your life experiences, and the lessons attached to them, you will have the insight and awareness required to get you moving forward on the path of your Blueprint Destiny.

Have you ever stopped to wonder just what it is you are meant to be doing on this planet? Do you think you are just here for a picnic? Unfortunately no, your life is very important and is divided into two parts. The first part is that you are here to learn and grow from the lessons and experiences that you have had, or are still going through in your life. The second part of your life will be realized only after you have dealt with and understood the first part, your life purpose and Blueprint Destiny in this lifetime will then begin to unfold and make sense to you. You will never experience the second part of your life as it was meant to be by your Soul if you have never dealt with the first part because that sets the stage for the rest of your life that will follow. I mentioned before if you failed to graduate from high school how could you possibly ever expect to succeed in university. It would not be possible. The same goes for your life.

Your experiences and lessons, the way you are, the way you look, or how famous you become are not by coincidence. They meant to be that way.

Some people have things easier than others. We call them lucky but they are meant to be the way you and me are meant to be in the first place. We each choose to be part of an experience in order to help us deliver the purpose we need to do to uplift humanity.

For example, famous people are famous but we need to look beyond the surface, their fame and see beneath the person for what they become, the difference they are making in people's lives and the influence for change they are bringing with them into this life. It is a hard burden but many of us bring envy, jealousy and sometimes hate.

Many famous people are here with Master Numbers to make changes. Some people are destined to be famous and they have a mission beyond their message.

For example, do we look at Angelina Jolie's looks and we judge her according to that while ignoring the humanitarian work she is doing. Or do we look at Bill Gates as the genius who turned a company into a world player in the software world or we look at him from the way he helps other people through the humanitarian work he does with his wife, Melinda.

In the end, you have a choice and you are the only Master of your own Universe. That is, only you and you alone can make a change, a difference to your own environment that will spread to your own friends and family then to your community, your state or province and keep spreading to your country and then the world. That is possible because you made a choice, and whatever the choice you made, you will attract according to your intention to manifest your full potential for you to have a full productive and fulfilling life.

I will leave you with that and say, "Just think about it! Make a first step and start walking, and the Universe will support your move and you will start to attract what you need to bring to humanity.

Namaste.

About the Author

Joseph Ghabi, B.Msc., has always been intrigued by spiritual phenomena and this has been a major influence on him since early life. At the age of eight, he discovered his clairvoyance. A natural medium, he shares his gifts with others through meditation classes, numerology and spiritual healing.

Since developing his healing gift, Joseph has worked actively to help other people by offering private healing consultations and specifically 'Healing Childhood Experience through Numerology.'

Joseph has a Bachelor of Metaphysical Science and a practitioner diploma from the University of Metaphysics/University of Sedona, and is currently working toward his Doctorate of Metaphysical Counselling.

He has worked over the last fifteen years in understanding the relationship between our life experiences, our growth and development of our human consciousness. He believes that understanding this relationship is the key to healing childhood experiences and living a healthy life, understanding our Blueprint Destiny, and working through the issues and patterns keeping us stagnant and stuck.

http://theblueprintofyoursoul.com
http://www.freespiritcentre.info
http://www.numerology4life.com